THE
CONSTITUTION
STUDY

THE
CONSTITUTION
STUDY

Returning the Constitution
to We the People

PAUL ENGEL

Paul Engel
The Constitution Study
344 Virgil Crowell Road
Unionville, TN 37180

http://constitutionstudy.com

Contents

Every member of the State ought diligently to read and to study the constitution of his country, and teach the rising generation to be free. By knowing their rights, they will sooner perceive when they are violated, and be the better prepared to defend and assert them.

John Jay, First Chief Justice of the supreme Court of the United States

Preface

John Jay, America's first Chief Justice of the Supreme Court, said, "Every member of the state ought diligently to read and to study the constitution of his country and teach the rising generation to be free." As a nation we are guilty of not doing so, and rarely consider the consequences. Millions do not understand their rights and responsibilities as citizens, yet every couple of years we ask them to choose people to represent them in Washington, D.C. Most Americans know very little about what the Constitution says, much less what it means, or how the government it created is supposed to work. We can change that, but where do we start?

The goal of *The Constitution Study* is to help everyday Americans read and study the Constitution for themselves, and this book is designed to help you along that journey. Many people have read the Constitution, and that is a good start, but John Jay said read and study it. So how does someone go about studying the Constitution?

Whether small group or Internet forum, this book will help equip you to not only understand what the Constitution says, but to discuss it with confidence. Rather than another scholarly work targeted at the towers of academia, this book is written in everyday language for ordinary people. And don't forget what John Jay said, "and teach the rising generation to be free." If we want our children and grandchildren to live in the land of the free, it is up to us to teach them. This book is written so everyone from student to seasoned citizen can study and learn for themselves about the rights and responsibilities of being an American.

You will learn about the government our states created, and how the Constitution was designed to help us keep it in check.

So whether you are looking to improve your knowledge or share it with others, this book is designed to help you.

Acknowledgements

While my name is on this book, a project like this cannot be done alone. So I want to take the space to acknowledge those who have helped this book become a reality.

My wife has been a tremendous help. She not only had to listen to me as I worked through different parts of this book, but was kind enough to edit and correct both it and all of my web articles. My daughter, who has sat through more discussions about the Constitution than she probably wanted to. My father and step-mother have been a fount of advice, helping me work through the editing and publishing process. And all those on social media who have encouraged me to complete this work. All of you have helped turn this from a simple idea into the book you have in your hands.

To all of you, I say thank you.

Introduction

Every member of the State ought diligently to read and
to study the constitution of his country, and teach the
rising generation to be free. By knowing their rights,
they will sooner perceive when they are violated, and
be the better prepared to defend and assert them.[1]

Like many of you, I am a product of the public schools, in my case
mostly through the 1970s. It speaks poorly of our education system,
but I learned more about our Constitution from School House Rock
than I did in all the social studies classes in 12 years of government-run
schooling. Little did I realize how far we had drifted from the supreme
law of the land! I didn't know because I didn't care. Like many of you, I
thought the Constitution was for lawyers and judges. Then I stumbled
across a gentleman by the name of David Barton and his organization
WallBuilders.

We often hear 'what you don't know won't hurt you', but experience
tells me that it's what you know which isn't true that gets you in real
trouble. It was through David Barton and the WallBuilders podcast
that I started to learn how much I didn't know about how our form of
government is supposed to work. More importantly, I began to learn
how much of what I had been taught just wasn't true. And it wasn't just
their opinion: WallBuilders has one of the largest private collections

---

[1] John Jay's Charge to the Grand Jury of Ulster County (1777) and Charge to
the Grand Juries (1790).

of original documents from the early years of our nation. Using these original documents David Barton and WallBuilders showed what our Founding Fathers had set up, why they did it the way they did, and how our country operated for the first century and a half of its existence.

The more I learned the more frustrated I got, not only with how our government operates, but what we expect from our legislators. The John Jay quote beginning this Introduction encouraged me to read and study more. I read the Declaration of Independence, the Constitution, and the Federalist and Anti-Federalist papers. I sought out other teachers and podcasters, always comparing them to the original documents to see if what they were saying was true. During this time, I not only learned how much I didn't know, but how much most people didn't care.

Then one day I was at a family cook-out at my cousin's place. It had become routine during these cook-outs that I would sit down with my cousin's two oldest boys and discuss politics, the Constitution, and current events. Occasionally, one or two people would sit in for a while, but it was mostly just the three of us. This cook-out would turn out to be different.

As I got up from the picnic table where I had been sitting with my two cousins, a couple of family friends asked if they could discuss something with me. Always ready for a good discussion, I said "sure" and sat back down. The topic at hand happened to be capital punishment, but what is more important to this story is what happened during the discussion. As we discussed the topic from a Constitutional, Biblical, and moral point of view, I eventually noticed several people had stopped their conversations and either joined us at our table or turned their chairs to listen. Within 15 minutes I was "holding court" with about a dozen people listening to my point of view on the topic and the methods and reasons I had for that point of view. When we had finished, the family friends thanked me for helping them understand a complex and contentious topic using language they could easily understand.

This made me think: Could part of the problem with a lack of understanding of our Constitution be how it was taught? Could it be that a focus on names and dates was less effective than the stories and reasons behind the document? Could a practical application of Constitutional ideas engage people better than a "history lesson"? More to the point, if I could keep a dozen friends and family engaged in a discussion on how to apply our understanding of the Constitution to a topic, could I engage more people as well?

If the family cook-out kindled the idea of teaching others about the Constitution, a friend's Bible study really got the fire going. I was driving home from said Bible study one night listening to a WallBuilder's podcast. In this episode, David Barton brought up the report "The State of the First Amendment: 2013" from the First Amendment Center. The report summarizes the findings from their 2013 survey of the attitudes of Americans about the First Amendment. In this report, they found that 36% of those surveyed could not name a single freedom protected by the First Amendment.

If this survey was representative of the nation as a whole, more than one-third of Americans had no idea what freedoms are protected by the First Amendment! I must admit, I didn't hear much more of the episode as I fumed over the ignorance of my fellow Americans, the carelessness we use to teach our children, and the utter failure of the education system to teach the young. No wonder we see college students who don't know when the Revolutionary War was fought or against whom. Even worse, this would explain why we see people clamor for government to do something when they have no clue what the federal government was designed to do in the first place.

Then a radical thought hit me. Why can't we study the Constitution the same way I had just studied the Bible? Not with high-school teachers or college professors spouting dates and names from books that don't even reference the historical documents they claim to be reviewing, and certainly not with long-winded dissertations how a passage means the exact opposite if what it plainly says. Could we go back and read the documents themselves, discuss them in small groups, express our opinions, and then compare them to the actual words on paper? If I could learn about the Constitution on my own, would others be interested in doing it themselves as well?

I discussed the idea with friends and family and many agreed it would be a good idea. One friend took the initiative and reached out to the local public library to see if we could have the studies there. We set a date and time, I put together an outline for our first meeting, and the Constitution Study was born.

I remember sitting in the library's meeting room with my daughter, wondering if anyone would come. Was this just a fool's errand? Would other people take time out of their busy days to discuss the Constitution? First one friend arrived, then another. Then a couple of people I didn't know but had heard of our study by word of mouth, then another who saw the sign we had put in front of the library. All totaled, 15 people came and looked to me to see what this Constitution Study was all about. I asked them to name the five freedoms listed in the First Amendment and got answers similar to the 2013 First Amendment report mentioned above. I then described how important it was for the people to understand how our government was designed to work and how this Constitution Study would work.

Studying the Constitution is not as hard as you may think. Over the years we have delegated the privilege of reading and understanding the Constitution to a high priesthood of nine people in black robes: The supreme Court of the United States and their acolytes: The judges, lawyers, and clerks of our legal system. However, this is not how the Constitution was written. (You may have noticed that I do not capitalize "supreme" when referring to the court. That is because in the Constitution supreme is an adjective describing the court, not a part of a proper noun.)

We sometimes act like reading the Constitution is some grand accomplishment. The U.S. Constitution is only approximately 8,000 words long, including all the amendments, and the Declaration of Independence only adds about 1,500 more. Compared to the King James Bible (approx. 780,000 words), War and Peace (approx. 585,000 words), or the first Harry Potter book (approx. 76,000 words), it's just not that large. In fact, the average reader should be able to get through the Constitution in about 20 minutes and the Declaration in another 5. I try to read it through 2-3 times a year; it doesn't take much time and it reminds me how things are supposed to be.

Some people say only lawyers can understand it. In one word I say: HOGWASH! The Constitution was sent around the country for everyone to read before the states voted to ratify it. Newspapers carried essays for and against certain provisions of the Constitution. These essays were the Federalist Papers and Anti-Federalist Papers. They were also written so that the average 18th century farmer could read and understand them. Sure, some of the words are unfamiliar to us and some of the clauses may require us to think about them to understand, but are 21st century Americans not as literate as an 18th century farmer? Or have we been taught that it's too difficult, so just leave it to the professionals? Our Founding Fathers didn't think so. Remember John Jay's quote? "Every member of the State ought diligently to read and to study the constitution of his country ..."[2] Not "every lawyer and politician should read it" (though I wish they would) and not only the "trained should read it," but everyone should read it. This is our heritage and was created to guarantee our freedom! Don't you think it's worth 30 minutes to read? Don't you think it's worth some time to study with others?

> *Now more than ever the people are responsible for the*
> *character of their Congress. If that body be ignorant,*
> *reckless, and corrupt, it is because the people tolerate*
> *ignorance, recklessness, and corruption. If it be*
> *intelligent, brave, and pure, it is because the people*
> *demand these high qualities to represent them in the*
> *national legislature. . . . [I]f the next centennial does not*
> *find us a great nation . . . it will be because those who*

---

[2]   John Jay's Charge to the Grand Jury of Ulster County (1777) and Charge to the Grand Juries (1790).

> *represent the enterprise, the culture, and the morality of*
> *the nation do not aid in controlling the political forces.*[3]

I'm sure you've all heard the joke: "How can you tell when a politician is lying?" The answer, of course, is "When their lips are moving!" While this is a sad commentary on the state of politics in the 21st century, it's an even sadder commentary on the state of our society. What does it say about us that we hire people to represent us who we know are lying to us? What does it say about Americans that those who lie the best keep their jobs the longest? If these people represent us, what does their character say about us as a nation? It seems to be a universal truth that, more often than not, our government represents the worst of our natures, not the best. It is ultimately our fault if there is a problem in Washington. If that is the bad news, the good news is that we can fix it, but it will take a long time and is probably not the path you expected.

In Colonial times, people would get together in taverns to discuss news, politics, and whatever was of interest at the time. In colleges and universities now, it is common for students to form study groups to help each other. I picture a Constitution Study as a merger of these two concepts. I want to see local and Internet communities get together to discuss the Constitution and the news of the day. Like a group of students, they should be there to read and study the material at hand, i.e., the Constitution. Someone should coordinate the meetings and plan a schedule, but it should be a free and open discussion of the document and how it applies to events of the day. The standard must be what the Constitution actually says and the original intent of those who wrote it and those who ratified it. The states ratified the Constitution and its amendments based on the words on the page and their common meaning at that time, not what some 21st century judge can twist the words to mean. Remember, the Declaration, the Constitution, and the Federalist

---

[3]   James A. Garfield, The Works of James Abram Garfield, Burke Hinsdale, editor (Boston: James R. Osgood and Company, 1883), Vol. II, pp. 486, 489, "A Century of Congress," July, 1877.

and Anti-Federalist Papers were all written for, read, and discussed by 18th century farmers.

If we want to change Washington, we must first take responsibility for the state that it is in and for our lack of knowledge about how it should work. One look at the recent debate about the repeal and replacement of Obamacare should show that, once people get to Washington, they are probably already too far gone to make meaningful change. No, we need to look at this a different way. How do you eat an elephant? One bite at a time. We only need to do three things to restore some semblance of sanity in Washington.

First, we must educate ourselves and those around us on how our government was designed to work. So much of what Washington does is blatantly unconstitutional, yet millions of people ignore this fact and, in many cases, asked the government to do it in the first place. Until we know and understand the different roles and responsibilities of the different governments that make up this nation, we will be sailing the open ocean with neither star nor compass to guide us.

Second, we must look for candidates in local and state elections who will uphold their oaths to support the constitutions of both the United States and their individual states. While it is extremely difficult to get a meeting with a U.S. Congressman or Senator, I've found sitting down with my state representatives quite easy. In fact, most of them seem to like getting information directly from their constituents.

Shortly after I moved to Tennessee, I reached out to my state senator and representative and asked for a meeting. I told them I was new to the area and wanted to learn what were the big issues that should have my attention. Not only did we have an excellent meeting and discussed many issues, but I found I was able later to email them about a variety of subjects and get responses. I now make it a habit to reach out and talk, if not meet, with both representatives after every session. I congratulate them on legislative actions I thought were good and ask their reasoning on those with which I disagree. I learn about issues and concerns they see coming and try to reply with positions and research that may help or at least reinforce my suggestions. While I cannot claim I've made a change at the state level, I have at least influenced the people who represent my neighbors and myself at the state capital. Maybe one day they will run for federal office, and hopefully I have made an impression they will take with them.

Third, we must hold our elected representatives accountable for their actions. Voting is important, but even more it is a solemn duty, one which too many of us shrug off, like getting out of jury duty. We need to be looking for men and woman who have demonstrated they will support the Constitution with their deeds and not just their words. Too often we wait until the second Tuesday in November and choose the lesser of two evils. Do you know what you get when you choose the lesser of two evils? You still get evil! Don't wait until the week before the election to decide who to vote for, and please do not vote that party line. Start learning about the candidates during the primaries, or even better, before then. Meet them, talk to them, ask them hard questions, and ask them to show you what they have done to support the Constitution. After all, that is what they are going to swear to do if they take office.

When my congressman voted for something that was plainly unconstitutional, I wrote and told him that he had violated his oath of office (which includes supporting the Constitution) and it was therefore my patriotic duty not only to vote against him, but to do all I could to find someone better to replace him.

> *Freedom is never more than one generation away*
> *from extinction. We didn't pass it to our children*
> *in the bloodstream. It must be fought for, protected,*
> *and handed on for them to do the same, or one day*
> *we will spend our sunset years telling our children*
> *and our children's children what it was once like*
> *in the United States where men were free.*[4]

---

[4]   Ronald Reagan Speech to the Phoenix Chamber of Commerce March 30, 1961.

Will you join me? Will you take the first step and begin learning what the Constitution really says and how our government was designed to work? Will you help me return our nation's liberty town by town?

To help you, I have compiled the notes from my original study along with some narration to help you apply it to your life today. I am also working on other resources to help you whether you plan to run a Constitution Study of your own or simply for your own family education. Either way, I hope you join me on this journey to diligently read and study our Constitution. Together we will learn what it means to "plead the fifth", where you can actually find the much vaunted "Separation of Church and State" (which is NOT in the Constitution), and we'll discuss the infamous case of yelling "FIRE" in a crowded theater. We'll look at why we have both a House of Representative and a Senate and why the Constitution gives them the roles they have. We'll even explore why we haven't had a constitutional presidential election in the last 70 years, why the Electoral College is necessary to the republic (it may not be what you've heard in the past), and how the 16th and 17th Amendments helped destroy the republic. Oh, and you'll also learn why I consistently refer to the "republic" rather than our "democracy."

> *I must study politics and war, that our sons may*
> *have liberty to study mathematics and philosophy.*[5]

I hope to find you as another patriot fighting to restore our nation to its proper order. John Adams said he studied politics and war so his children could study mathematics and philosophy. Let us study the Constitution so our children may study mathematics, philosophy, or whatever they want, in a country where men and women are still free!

---

[5]   John Adams, Letters of John Adams, Addressed to His Wife.

Constitution Study Principles

The guiding principles for our Constitution Study

When studying any document, it is important to have a set of guiding principles so the document is telling you what it means and not you twisting the words to get the meaning you want. In this study we shall use six guiding principles.

1) The Constitution means what it says

The Constitution means what it says on parchment. It's popular today to refer to a "living Constitution," but is there such a thing? Any document that is called "living" means nothing, because if a document only means what the current reader thinks it means, then no document can mean anything. Imagine a contract where you agree with a builder to build you a house based on included blueprints and documented features. As your house is being built, you notice the floor plan in the contract doesn't match the building being constructed. You contact the builder who informs you that, according to his interpretation of the contract, all is going well. You take the builder to court. Imagine your reaction if the judge says it's a "living" contract and can mean whatever you or the builder thinks it means. Even though they might be different things? What then? Wouldn't you want to enforce the original written words?

Likewise, the Constitution is a compact, the legal term for a contract between sovereigns, in this case the states. If this contract is a living document and can mean whatever someone says, then the question is:

Who decides what this amorphous document means? Judges of course, and especially the justices who sit on the supreme Court. That is how courts have taken it upon themselves to be the arbiters of the law and Constitution.

The concept of judicial or Constitutional review, while not entirely new, first appears in U.S. legal doctrine in the 1801 supreme Court decision in Marbury v. Madison. In the unanimous decision, Chief Justice Marshall said "it is emphatically the province and duty of the judicial department to say what the law is."[6] Nowhere in the Constitution does it give the judicial branch the authority to say what the law is, only to judge between parties based on the law. Chief Justice Marshall also said, "Those who apply the rule to particular cases must, of necessity, expound and interpret that rule. If two laws conflict with each other, the Courts must decide on the operation of each."[7] Today law school students are taught that Chief Justice Marshall took upon the court the authority not only to determine what the law is, but ultimately whether it is Constitutional. But when we look at the actual writing of the Chief Justice, we see a limited power to review the laws pertaining to a particular case and apply them properly.

Jefferson disagreed with Marshall's decision, saying "You seem to consider the judges as the ultimate arbiters of all constitutional questions; a very dangerous doctrine indeed, and one which would place us under the despotism of an oligarchy."

Jefferson's prediction has come true. Today, judges routinely determine what is and isn't Constitutional regardless of the plain reading of the law or the Constitution they have sworn to uphold. Furthermore, these opinions, often erroneously called rulings, are now called the "law of the land." Only Congress can make laws, but the meaning of the Constitution has become putty in the hands of judges and justices in black robes and others in the legal system across this nation.

---

[6] Marbury v. Madison 5 U.S. 137.

[7] IBID.

For any agreement to be workable, it must mean what it says. Judicial opinions are just that: Their opinion. They have no force of law and it is only the will of the political class that keeps this fiction alive. In this study, we will focus on the precise meaning of the words in Constitution.

2) The writers established meaning

The words of the Constitution mean what the writers understood them to mean. Remember our mythical building contract? Imagine it stated you would have granite counter tops, but the builder used a solid surface composite. You thought granite meant granite, but the builder thought it meant any solid counter top.

Words have meanings. Today we hear people use words and we wonder if they really know what they mean. Common use of words does change over time. When I was a child the word "gay" meant happy, not homosexual. Does that mean when people refer to the 1890s as the "gay 90s" it was full of open homosexuality? No, in the 1890s gay meant happy. The fact that the word is used differently today doesn't change the meaning of the phrase.

When we study the Constitution, we need to use the definitions the authors used. Politicians today think "shall not be infringed" means they can put limitations on them, but is that what our founders thought? When the Constitution says "All legislative Powers herein granted shall be vested in a Congress of the United States," it means "All legislative Powers" not all legislative powers except for administrative law or bureaucratic regulations.

How can we know how our founders defined the words they used? One way is the 1828 Webster's dictionary. Yes, Founding Father Noah Webster wanted an "American English" to distinguish us from Great Britain, so he wrote an American dictionary in 1828. (It's one of the reasons we spell color without a "u.") If you want to know what the people who wrote and ratified the Constitution meant when they used a word, best look it up in the dictionary closest to what they would have used. The other is to read what our Founding Fathers said. Most were inveterate writers, keeping journals and correspondence which we have access to today. If we want to know what they were thinking when they wrote the Constitution, all we have to do is read their comments.

3) Original documents or bust

All analysis MUST refer to original documents. Let's go back to our building contract. If you take your builder to court claiming breach of contract, what is the first thing you're going to show the judge? The original contract, because that is the standard by which the dispute should be judged. For some reason, it seems most history books today don't refer to the original contract: The Constitution. Instead, we are expected to accept what an expert believes the document says rather than the document itself. That's like the builder telling the judge, "Don't read the contract, trust me. I'm an expert." Don't think that would happen today? Check the headlines.

> *The right of the people to be secure in their persons,*
> *houses, papers, and effects, against unreasonable*
> *searches and seizures, shall not be violated, and*
> *no Warrants shall issue, but upon probable*
> *cause, supported by Oath or affirmation, and*
> *particularly describing the place to be searched,*
> *and the persons or things to be seized.*[8]

The Fourth Amendment seems clear cut, and we've all seen crime dramas where the police must get a warrant before entering a residence or arresting someone. Yet, today, we have FISA courts that issue warrants without probable cause that a crime is imminent[9], and civil asset forfeiture laws that allow police departments to confiscate private property without even charging an individual, much less convicting them.

---

[8]   United States Constitution, Amendment IV.

[9]   The Foreign Intelligence Surveillance Act of 1978 - https://it.ojp.gov/ PrivacyLiberty/authorities/statutes/1286.

Does that sound like people being secure in their persons, houses, papers, and effects? What about agencies like the EPA that declare private property is federally protected by fiat, or IRS audits where they claim the right to rifle through your papers looking to see if you did anything wrong? These and other abuses only survive because we let those who judge get away with not using the letter of the law and the Constitution.

In this study, we'll refer to the original documents, readily available online for all to see. While we may use other commentaries for example or assistance, ultimately it is the original words, on the original documents, with their original meaning that will guide us here.

4) Understanding ambiguity

When a firm understanding of the intent of the writing is not attainable, personal opinion is allowed, but it must be in harmony with overall established intent. A good example would be the term "the people", used five times in the Bill of Rights. Any argument about what the term "the people" means must be consistent with all other uses of the phrase. For example, if someone were to argue that "the people" means individuals in one place and a people group in another, that would be inconsistent and the argument must be either modified or dismissed.

Another way to deal with an ambiguous term or statement is to consult the writings of the authors. Not only are the debates around the Constitution and its ratification available online, but during the ratification debates essays were published which we now call the Federalist and Anti-Federalist Papers. These and other writings of the time can help us put the Constitution in context. Context can be very helpful in understanding what the Constitution means, if the opinion we form is in harmony with the document itself.

5) Opinions do not trump fact

Whenever possible, we will be charitable with the opinions of others, but not to the detriment of the plain reading of the Constitution. There are areas where we can honestly disagree. Believe it or not, this is not a bad thing. It's good to open up, question our positions, and let the facts win out. The only way our assumptions can be tried is if we allow them to be examined in the light of other people's opinions.

I had a discussion with someone a while back about the Constitution. It was quite obvious to me that this person's opinion did not match up with the facts in the document. We discussed it and debated it, but when I offered to show him the Constitution to support my position, he refused; he did not want the facts to get in the way of his opinion. I will not always be right. I will make mistakes, uncover new information, or simply come to a new understanding through the study of the documents. I encourage discussion and debate as long as it is civil and with the agreed upon goal of finding the truth, not proving the debater's point of view.

6) Time to think

It's easy to read or hear something and jump to a conclusion. Instead we need to think through a position, examine it from every possible angle, and then decide where we stand in light of all that the Constitution says. Only by calm, reasoned examination can we come to the correct conclusion. Otherwise, we're just another pundit putting forth our opinion while thinking it to be fact. I encourage all of you, when you read or hear something (especially something that challenges what you currently believe), to take the time to examine it well. You may find you were correct, you may find you were wrong, or you may find that the truth is actually somewhere between the two. I believe it's this level of examination that will distinguish those in this group when we discuss the Constitution with others.

With these six principles in mind, let us being our journey in earnest.

The Declaration of Independence

How 13 colonies became free and independent states

Wait, I thought this was a Constitution Study. Why are we starting with the Declaration of Independence?

In short, if we want to understand the Constitution, we need to understand the Declaration. If you have ever incorporated a church or business, you are familiar with two documents: The articles of incorporation and the by-laws. The articles of incorporation describe the church or business and its goals, and describe the reasons the entity is being born. The by-laws are the rules by which the corporation will operate. Our Founding Fathers wanted to start a new country. Specifically, they wanted to start 13 new countries, but more on that later. Like articles of incorporation, they needed a way to tell Great Britain and the world what they were doing and why. This document became known as the Declaration of Independence.

The Lee Resolution

Our Declaration of Independence didn't spring up out of thin air. Our Founding Fathers didn't wake up one morning and decide to declare independence from Great Britain. After years of injustices and infringement on their rights as British citizens, the colonists, through their representatives, sent messages to King George III and Parliament asking for a redress of their grievances. These requests were either ignored or led to even more egregious infringement on the colonists' rights. After years of discussion and debate in Continental Congresses, on June 7th, 1776, Richard Henry Lee of Virginia introduced a resolution:

> *Resolved, That these United Colonies are, and of right*
> *ought to be, free and independent States, that they are*
> *absolved from all allegiance to the British Crown, and*
> *that all political connection between them and the State*
> *of Great Britain is, and ought to be, totally dissolved.*
>
> *That it is expedient forthwith to take the most*
> *effectual measures for forming foreign Alliances.*
>
> *That a plan of confederation be prepared and*
> *transmitted to the respective Colonies for*
> *their consideration and approbation.*[10]

As you can imagine, many members of the Second Continental Congress were concerned about such a resolution. This was not another request to the king to respect their rights, but a declaration that each of the colonies should be their own free and independent state. So on June 11th the Congress formed three committees, one to draft a declaration of independence (called "The Committee of Five"), a second to draw up plans for forming foreign alliances, and a third to look at how to form a confederation. The work of these committees gave delegates time to get instructions from their colonies. Finally, on July 2nd, the Second Continental Congress unanimously adopted the first part of the Lee Resolution (declaring independence), with the New York delegation abstaining.

Congress immediately began debating the document the Committee of Five had submitted and, on July 4th, officially adopted it. Interestingly, only two men signed the Declaration on July 4th. Those men were Thomas Jefferson and Charles Thomson.[11] It wasn't until July 9th that

---

[10]   Lee Resolution of 1776.

[11]   The Declaration of Independence.

the last colony (New York) officially approved the Declaration. At that point it was considered "fairly engrossed" and signed by the remaining members of Congress. Another intriguing point is the original title of this document: "The unanimous declaration of the thirteen united States of America".[12] The "u" in "united" is not capitalized because it was not one country that declared independence, but 13 individual States. These states were united together in their goal of independence, not in a single nation.

---

[12]   IBID.

The unanimous Declaration of the thirteen United States of America

In Congress, July 4, 1776.

The unanimous Declaration of the thirteen united States of America, When in the Course of human events, it becomes necessary for one people to dissolve the political bands which have connected them with another, and to assume among the powers of the earth, the separate and equal station to which the Laws of Nature and of Nature's God entitle them, a decent respect to the opinions of mankind requires that they should declare the causes which impel them to the separation.

The Declaration starts where a document of such monumental import and magnitude should: With why they were doing it.

Necessary to dissolve the political bands

The colonists had suffered injustice after injustice and injury upon injury. Their rights as British citizens had been infringed and all reasonable and prudent efforts had been made to resolve the dispute within the rules and laws of Great Britain. In the minds of our Founding Fathers there were no other cards to play, no other courts to hear their case. There was only one remedy to their situation, which was to dissolve the political band with Great Britain. The states would secure their own rights if the British government refused. They were British by heritage and tradition, but they would no longer be British by polity. Our Founding Fathers viewed this as necessary; this was neither a whim nor a rash decision.

Assume the power

These states were assuming the powers and station that was entitled to them. Just as Great Britain, France, and Spain had power and responsibility over their subjects, these united States would have power and responsibility over their citizens. These united States were entitled to this and this document was going to explain why.

The thirteen united States

Notice that the first sentence is "The unanimous Declaration of the thirteen united States of America"[13] with 'States' capitalized and 'united' not. No, this is not a typo. This document was not the declaration of a single nation's independence but 13 independent nation states.

Today we think of states as a political subdivision under the federal government, but that is not what was created in 1776. Massachusetts, New York, and Virginia were each an independent country, with all the rights and station of any other nation. That is why the Lee resolution included the need to plan how they could form a confederation. The "united" in this declaration is an adjective describing these 13 states, not the title we think of today.

Laws of Nature and Nature's God

Our Founding Fathers did not appeal to reason or human rights, they declared that the Laws of Nature and Nature's God entitled these states to position and power. Looking upon the world and its condition, our founders saw how states had been created in the past, what

---

[13]   IBID.

distinguished one state from another, and the station they held among other states. The Laws of Nature, what today we call "Natural Law", and of its creator "Nature's God", entitled these 13 colonies the right to call themselves states and to assume the same station any other state in the world was entitled to.

Declare the causes which impel them to separation

These men were not spoiled children stamping their feet and throwing a tantrum because they didn't get what they wanted. No, since they had a decent respect for mankind, it was therefore incumbent on them to explain themselves and why they would take such bold and forceful action. While I doubt they believed that King George and the British Parliament would agree, they believed other nations would recognize the legitimacy of their cause. They wanted a chance to explain themselves to the king, to Parliament, and to the world, and to show that their actions were right and just. This was not a just rebellion against their government, but a war to restore the freedoms they were due as British citizens.

We hold these truths to be self-evident

We hold these truths to be self-evident, that all men are created equal, that they are endowed by their Creator with certain unalienable Rights, that among these are Life, Liberty and the pursuit of Happiness.

Our Founding Fathers thought these truths were so obvious they were simply assumed to be true. They did not need to be written down or debated to be recognized; they were staring everyone in the face. What was so evident that anyone could see it? "(T)hat all men are created equal." These were 18th century British colonies. Slavery was not only allowed; it was required by British law. So, how could these men look at the world and declare that all men are created equal?

It is important to remember that slavery neither started in the colonies, nor was it created by our Founding Fathers. Slavery was an evil brought to these shores by the laws and practices of Great Britain. Many of our Founding Fathers detested slavery and spoke out against it. As President of Congress Henry Laurens said,

I abhor slavery. I was born in a country where slavery had been established by British Kings and Parliaments as well as by the laws of the country ages before my existence. . . . In former days there was no combating the prejudices of men supported by interest; the day, I hope, is approaching when, from principles of gratitude as well as justice, every man

will strive to be foremost in showing his readiness to
comply with the Golden Rule ["do unto others as you
would have them do unto you" Matthew 7:12].[14]

Thomas Jefferson said,

He [King George III] has waged cruel war against
human nature itself, violating its most sacred rights
of life and liberty in the persons of a distant people
who never offended him, captivating and carrying
them into slavery in another hemisphere or to incur
miserable death in their transportation thither. . . .[15]

Some colonies passed laws to end slavery, but they were overturned by the king. This was one of the "long train of abuses" that Jefferson quoted in the list of reasons why the colonies should separate themselves from Great Britain.

We'll see later in the study that while neither this Declaration nor the Constitution ended slavery, they put in place the mechanism to first minimize and eventually end slavery in America.

Endowed by their Creator

We'll discuss rights below, but first we will consider the origin of those rights. Whether you believe in the God of the Bible, Allah, Buddha, astrology, or evolution, the concept that our rights come from our creator is extremely important to our republic.

Why would the idea of a creator be so important to our nation? The answer is simple: Is there anything or anyone bigger than government? If our rights come from the government, they can be taken away by the government. The idea that there is something above that, something

---

[14] Frank Moore, Materials for History Printed From Original Manuscripts, the Correspondence of Henry Laurens of South Carolina.

[15] Thomas Jefferson, The Writings of Thomas Jefferson, Albert Ellery Bergh, editor.

the government is ultimately responsible to, means the government is limited and can be controlled. If government isn't the big dog, then there is an authority above them you can apply to, a standard to which you can hold them accountable.

This concept that the federal government ISN'T the supreme authority has been lost by most citizens of this great nation and those elected to represent them. When we want something done we too often ask the federal government to do it, and I rarely hear anyone ask if it has the Constitutional authorization to do so. When the supreme Court "rules" on anything, it's called "the law of the land" even though the Court cannot make law or permit the federal government to do something it isn't Constitutionally allowed to do. Without the concept of a creator giving us our rights, the federal government has the authority to do whatever it wants. At that point the federal government becomes a kingdom and we become its subjects.

What are Unalienable Rights?

Today I hear a lot of talk about rights. Gay rights, native rights, transgender rights, the right to not be offended, ad infinitum. Then you've got the right to housing, the right to healthcare, and the right to a living wage. In short, it seems like any time somebody wants something, it suddenly becomes a right. Worst of all, claiming a right seems to be used most often when someone wants to infringe on the rights of another. Every time I hear this, all I can think of is the quote of Inigo Montoya from the movie *The Princess Bride*.

"You keep using that word. I do not think it means what you think it means" [16]

---

[16] Inigo Montoya in the 1987 romantic comedy The Princess Bride.

Rights

First, we need to define what a right is. Rights can be categorized based on two criteria: 1) Are they alienable and 2) Are they positive or negative. An alienable right is one that was given to you and therefore can be taken away, while an unalienable (or inalienable) right is one you have just because you exist. Whether you believe you were created by the God of the Bible, Allah, Buddha, or chance, as a human being you are endowed with certain unalienable rights. These rights cannot be taken away from you. Sure, they can be infringed, restricted, or declared illegal, but you still have those rights.

The question of positive versus negative rights is a little more complicated. A positive right is something someone must do for you, like the right to vote or to a jury trial. A negative right is one where someone cannot prevent you from doing something, like the right to worship, speak, or publish your ideas without government interference. ("Congress shall make no law ..."[17])

For a right to be legitimate, it must be something you can exercise without infringing on the rights of others. Where is this in the Declaration? you ask. "(A)ll men are created equal." Therefore, if you can exercise your rights by restricting mine, then your rights are more important than mine and we are not equal.

Let's look at a few examples. The freedom of speech and the press are in the Bill of Rights. That means I can express myself however I see fit. In order for me to exercise that right legitimately, I have to do so without infringing on the rights of others. That means I have every right to go into a public theater and cry "Fire!" If, however, there is no fire, then I've infringed on the rights of others. That would be an illegitimate use of my right to free speech and all those in the theater and the owner would have cause to sue me for damages.

Some of you may be saying, "Wait, didn't the supreme Court say that yelling fire in a crowded theater was not covered under the First Amendment?" While this is common lore, the answer is: Not exactly.

---

17   United States Constitution, Amendment I.

The case most people are referring to, Schenck v. United States, had nothing to do with fire or theaters, but whether Congress, through the Espionage act, had the right to punish Schenck for encouraging men called for military service to dodge the draft. Writing the opinion, Justice Oliver Wendell Holmes used this as an example: "The most stringent protection of free speech would not protect a man in falsely shouting fire in a theatre and causing a panic."[18]

In fact, this opinion does not show that I cannot exercise the right to yell fire, but that I cannot use my right to free speech to protect myself from the consequences of doing so falsely. Justice Holmes didn't say someone couldn't yell fire, only that they couldn't use the First Amendment as protection against the consequences of that act.

Then, in 1969, in the supreme Court opinion in the case of Brandenburg v. Ohio, the court said: "Accordingly, we are here confronted with a statute which, by its own words and as applied, purports to punish mere advocacy and to forbid, on pain of criminal punishment, assembly with others merely to advocate the described type of action. Such a statute falls within the condemnation of the First and Fourteenth Amendments. The contrary teaching of Whitney v. California, supra, cannot be supported, and that decision is therefore overruled."[19]

In other words, a law which punished someone for advocacy or assembly with the purpose to advocate for or against an action, was contrary to the First and Fourteenth Amendments. Together, these two opinions confirm that I can exercise my rights, but I may be held accountable if doing so directly harms others.

There is also a right to control what I own. We think of property rights as the ability to obtain and keep property, but it is so much more. What good is a right to own a thing if I cannot control what happens to that thing? Property rights are negative, so someone cannot legitimately tell me what to do with what I own. For example, I own my home and the land it sits on. Therefore, I am well within my rights to decide whether

---

[18]   249 U.S. 47 *Schenck v. United States.*

[19] 395 U.S. 444 *Brandenburg v. Ohio* (No. 492).

I want others to hunt, fish, or bring firearms onto my property or into the business that I own. Some will say their "Second Amendment right" to keep and bear arms trumps my private property rights, but as we've seen, that is not a legitimate use of their rights. Anyone is free to keep and bear arms if they do not violate others' rights, such as those of life, liberty, or property.

Today we often hear people claim the right not to be offended, but nothing could be further from the truth. The only way someone could exercise such a right, if it existed, would be to infringe on the right of others' self-expression, thereby making it illegitimate. In fact, the First Amendment to the Constitution says I have the right to offend someone because I have the right to say or write whatever I want.

What about the so-called right to education or healthcare? The only way I could exercise either of those supposed rights is to force educators or healthcare workers to work for free. And don't forget the people that build schools and hospitals, or those that work to provide oil, gas, and electric power. How about the people who write textbooks or make medical equipment? Do you expect all these people to work for free? To buy the resources to make the books and medical equipment for no charge? Are we going to force people to do these jobs because it's our "right"?

Do you know what we call people who work for free and have no choice about where they work? We call them slaves. To that you respond, "They don't have to work for free, we'll just tax people to pay for it." But what right do you have to take other people's stuff? Tax revenues don't materialize out of thin air, they are taken under threat of punishment backed up by arms.

Do you know what we call people who take stuff from others that they haven't earned? We call them thieves. Therefore, if you don't have the right individually to come take my stuff, you don't have the right to do so collectively either. Because you know what we call groups of people who take what they want by force or intimidation? We call them gangs or mobs.

Most of what we see and hear today about rights is little more than trying to justify greed and gangland behavior.

Needs

We all have needs. We need water, food, shelter, etc. However, just because we need something, does that make it a right? No. If I have to force others to work to provide my need, then it cannot be a legitimate right since I have to infringe on others' rights to get it.

But, you ask, "If it's not a right, how do we make sure people have their needs met?" The American people, as opposed to our government, are extremely generous. I believe we all have a moral, but not legal requirement to assist others truly in need. However, our generosity does not mean you have a right to take others' money, either directly or collectively.

It is not generous to give other peoples' money away; it is theft. (Contrary to popular belief, Robin Hood did not steal from the rich to give to the poor, he stole ill-gotten gains and returned it to the people it had been taken from.)

It is not generous to force others to pay for your charitable deeds; that is greed and racketeering. (As it works today, if the government were a business it would be charged under the "Racketeer Influenced and Corrupt Organizations act," better known as the RICO act.)

In today's political discourse, it is almost exclusively when, why, and how much the government will take from you to give to others. In other words, how much those in government will steal from their people to pay for their greedy desire to get credit for helping others. I've heard it said that if the federal government only spent money on what it was Constitutionally authorized to do, the deficit would be gone and the debt paid off in ten years.

> *The American Republic will endure until*
> *the day Congress discovers that it can bribe*
> *the public with the public's money.*
>
> *– Alexis de Tocqueville*

While I have a moral obligation to help those who are truly in need, that need does not give them a right to my property, my freedoms, or my labor. If people cannot legally break into my house to steal what they need, can they authorize someone else to do it for them, whether it is a person or a government?

Wants

The other problem with treating needs as rights is that people start treating wants as rights as well. Yes, you need shelter, but you do not need to own your own home. Yet by looking at the housing market over the last 30 years, we see an ever increasing number of people talking about their right to programs that help them buy a house whether they are financially qualified or not. Even the 2008 housing bubble crash hasn't taught many in our nation that just because you want that big new house you don't have a right to it, and there are consequences for acting like you do.

Endowed Rights

We have been endowed with these unalienable rights, but what are they? The Declaration lists three types of rights as an example.

Life

Nobody has the right to take your life. Whether you are an unborn baby, an elderly invalid, or anywhere in between, nobody has the right to take your life. I can hear multiple groups yelling at me now: What about a women's right to choose? What about capital punishment? Or self-defense? I know these are hot button topics and many people hold different positions for different reasons. Our purpose here is to look at these from a Constitutional point of view rather than an emotional or agenda-driven angle.

Let's take the "easy" ones first. In the case of self-defense, the situation is where you can use lethal force to defend yourself or other innocents. You, or another innocent party, must be in imminent threat of death or serious injury. In that case, you are not violating someone else's rights but protecting your own. Basically, if someone is threatening your life without cause they are violating your rights, and by doing so have abandoned their rights for the duration of the threat. It's important to recognize that the attacker has initiated aggression against an innocent party and therefore has voluntarily waived his or her rights. Once the attack stops, so does that waiver.

This understanding helps us deal with the emotional aftermath of a lethal defense, especially from family members of the attacker. News stories and interviews often show family members describing the attacker as a good person who didn't deserve to die. I know this sounds harsh, but if a court finds that the person was the aggressor and threatened the right to life of the victim, his or her death or injury was a quite predictable consequence of their decision.

Capital punishment is in a similar vein, but under different circumstances. Some people say that, if you're for capital punishment, then you don't value life, but I think it is quite the opposite. If we have an unalienable right to life, what is a suitable punishment for taking someone's life? There is no way for someone to make restitution for taking the life of another, but there are certain crimes that involve the death of innocents and especially those with unusual cruelty and disregard for others. We can debate the details and situations, but in voluntarily taking the life of another without cause, the criminal has forfeited their own rights and therefore does not make capital punishment a prima facie violation of a person's right to life.

The last topic is abortion. Put simply, a woman's right, like any other right, ends when it infringes on the rights of another. The question then is: When does life begin in the womb?

> *On the basis of elements such as these, appellant and some amici argue that the woman's right is absolute and that she is entitled to terminate her pregnancy at whatever time, in whatever way, and for whatever reason she alone chooses. With this we do not agree …*

As noted above, a State may properly assert important interests in safeguarding health, in maintaining medical standards, and in protecting potential life. At some point in pregnancy, these respective interests become sufficiently compelling to sustain regulation of the factors that govern the abortion decision. The privacy right involved, therefore, cannot be said to be absolute. In fact, it is not clear to us that the claim asserted by some amici that one has an unlimited right to do with one's body as one pleases bears a close relationship to the right of privacy previously articulated in the Court's decisions. The Court has refused to recognize an unlimited right of this kind in the past. Jacobson v. Massachusetts, 197 U.S. 11 (1905) (vaccination); Buck v. Bell, 274 U.S. 200 (1927) (sterilization).

We, therefore, conclude that the right of personal privacy includes the abortion decision, but that this right is not unqualified and must be considered against important state interests in regulation.[20]

Even the supreme Court, in the infamous Roe v. Wade decision, recognized that the state has an interest (I would say a duty) in protecting life, even potential life. In my opinion, when in doubt life should be preserved, whether in the womb, before the bench, or on the street.

Liberty

"When government fears the people, there is liberty. When the people fear the government, there is tyranny."[21]

---

[20] *Roe. v. Wade* Decision http://caselaw.findlaw.com/us-supreme-court/410/113. html.

[21] Thomas Jefferson Encyclopedia https://www.monticello.org/site/jefferson/ when-government-fears-people-there-liberty-spurious-quotation.

Though I have found little evidence that our third president, Thomas Jefferson, actually made this statement, it does summarize the definition of liberty quite concisely. It has been my experience that while there is a lot of talk about liberty, and its cousin freedom, there is very little understanding of the terms or their proper application. Liberty, as defined in the 1828 Webster's dictionary, lists three spheres.

> *Liberty (In General): Freedom from restraint, in a general sense, and applicable to the body, or to the will or mind. The body is at liberty when not confined; the will or mind is at liberty when not checked or controlled. A man enjoys liberty when no physical force operates to restrain his actions or volitions.*[22]

I frequently heard our elected representatives make statements like, "You don't necessarily need a choice of 23 underarm spray deodorants"[23] or, "Does someone really need that much money?" I am frequently asked, "Why does someone need an AR-15 or a 30-round magazine?" For years, I didn't have any answer until I actually started studying liberty, but now I think I've come up with a very good one. "I thought we lived in a free country? If so, then I can own anything I want because I want it, and without having to justify myself to anyone unless I use it to harm others!"

The first sphere of liberty then, is the freedom from restraint. Whether related to what I do, say, or think, liberty means I am free to do it without restraint. Like other unalienable rights, my right to liberty stops when I use it to infringe on the rights of others. If I want to make 23 types of deodorant and sell them on the open market, I should be free to do so as long as I don't use force, either directly or through others, to stop my competition.

---

[22]   Webster's 1828 Dictionary http://webstersdictionary1828.com.

[23]   Quote of Bernie Sanders in CNBC Interview https://www.cnbc.com/2015/05/26/10-questions-with-bernie-sanders.html.

Liberty means I can make as much money as I want as long as I am willing to do the work and carry the risk that is necessary to do so. Being at liberty means I can own whatever arms I want (remember the Second Amendment?) until I use them to harm or intimidate others.

We in America seem to have lost this concept of liberty. Rather than "live and let live," we believe we have the "right" to tell others how to live their lives. Don't like capitalism? Use the government to restrict trade through dictatorial laws and regulations. Envious of how someone uses his or her wealth? Then let's get the government to tax it away from them and spend it on what you want. Don't like guns? Then let's pass laws that tell law abiding citizens what weapons they can own and make them go to the government to get permission whenever they want to buy them.

Look at the laws and regulations put out every year by the State and Federal governments. Rather than punishing those who hurt or infringe on the rights of others, the vast majority tell law-abiding people how to live their lives. If you want to exercise your right to liberty, ask yourself: Does the government fear you or do you fear the government?

> *Natural Liberty: Natural liberty consists in the power of acting as one thinks fit, without any restraint or control, except from the laws of nature. It is a state of exemption from the control of others, and from positive laws and the institutions of social life. This liberty is abridged by the establishment of government.*[24]

Natural liberty is the ability to act as one chooses, with natural law as the only restraint or control. This idea is frequently used by those who simply don't want to be told what to do. They look at anything that denies their ability to do what they want as an infringement on their liberty, but they often ignore the rest of the sentence, "except from the laws of nature."

---

[24] Webster's 1828 Dictionary http://webstersdictionary1828.com.

> *Natural Law: The unwritten body of universal*
> *moral principles that underlie the ethical*
> *and legal norms by which human conduct*
> *is sometimes evaluated and governed.*[25]

The laws of nature are those moral principles so basic, so universally accepted, that they don't need to be written down. For example, the laws against the illegitimate taking of human life or depriving someone of his or her property are so much a part of the human spirit that (with rare exception) everyone knows them instinctively.

Natural law is the only restraint on natural liberty.

Notice that natural liberty is exempted not only from the control of others, but from "positive laws". So what is a positive law?

> *[S]tatutory man-made law, as compared to*
> *"natural law" which is purportedly based on*
> *universally accepted moral principles*[26]

Natural law is the unwritten code by which mankind lives, while positive law is man-made. The universally accepted law that someone may not take your life unless you threaten them is a natural law, and your state law against murder is a positive law. Therefore, natural liberty is the state where the only restraints on how you live your life are those natural, universally accepted laws which all civilized people know instinctively.

> *Civil Liberty: Civil liberty is the liberty of men in a*
> *state of society, or natural liberty so far only abridged*
> *and restrained, as is necessary and expedient for the*
> *safety and interest of the society, state or nation. A*
> *restraint of natural liberty not necessary or expedient*
> *for the public, is tyranny or oppression. Civil liberty is*

---

[25]   The Free Legal Dictionary https://legal-dictionary.thefreedictionary.com.

[26] The Free Legal Dictionary https://legal-dictionary.thefreedictionary.com.

> *an exemption from the arbitrary will of others, which*
> *exemption is secured by established laws, which restrain*
> *every man from injuring or controlling another. Hence*
> *the restraints of law are essential to civil liberty.*[27]

If natural liberty is the restraint on your actions based only in natural law, then civil liberty is the same restraint for the "safety and interest of the society, state or nation." Notice the logical progression from no restraint, to laws so obvious they do not even need to be written down, to those needed for the safety of society. There is no natural law regarding speed limits, but to safely allow people to exist with traffic nearby, we need a positive law. What comes after civil liberty? What happens when a governing body starts creating laws not based on necessity for society, but to control others? "A restraint of natural liberty, not necessary or expedient for the public, is tyranny or oppression."[28] Who gets to decide what is necessary or expedient for the public?

This is what our Founding Fathers were fighting for and why they created this document. Their right to liberty, general, natural, and civil, had been taken away by King George III and Parliament. Laws were passed or overruled, not based on the needs of society as a whole, but on the needs of the government creating them. This is the second unalienable right our founders used as a basis for their separation from Great Britain.

Pursuit of Happiness

Today we think of happiness as a good feeling and a smile on our face. Think about the "American Dream", which most people consider owning their own home. What else makes us happy? A good job with a good income, the toys we like to play with, and the chance to have what we want. Maybe even the chance to leave something to our children. If

---

[27]   Webster's 1828 Dictionary http://webstersdictionary1828.com.

[28]   IBID.

Jefferson were to look at what we pursue to gain happiness, would it not be the things in our life that help us get to that state?

Money cannot buy you love, but it can give you the opportunity to do what you want. If I cannot own property, I've lost a huge opportunity to be happy. My farm, and the opportunities it gives me, brings great happiness and security to me and my family. The fact that I can use the fruits of my labor as I wish also brings me great happiness.

Notice that it says "pursuit" of happiness. Nowhere is anyone guaranteed happiness or the things we enjoy, only the chance to pursue them. That means the rules have to allow us the chance to find our happiness, but they do not ensure we get it. It also means that whatever comes of your pursuit should be protected from theft, even by the government. This idea that I own myself and the fruits of my labor, is frequently referred to as "property rights." By property rights, I do not mean the owning and controlling of property (land), but the fact that I have a right to myself and the goods and properties I create. Are property rights that important? If we look at the laws being passed today in Washington and our state houses, we find a lot of them have to do with telling us how we live our lives. In other words, they do not just tell us what we can do with our property, but dictate what we own and who we are.

Look at the recent debate about marijuana and other drug laws. In effect, they all boil down to what drugs we should be allowed to use in our bodies and under what conditions we can use them. Whether you think someone should use marijuana, opioids, cancer drugs, or alcohol, the Constitutional question is: Does someone have the right to do what he or she wants with his or her own body? The same is true of "sin taxes", zoning laws, building codes, and tax laws in general. They all boil down to the government telling us what things we should do, what must be and not be in our properties, and generally how we should live our lives.

Don't get me wrong, I think recreational drug use is dangerous and I certainly wouldn't recommend it. But how can we honestly tell a person with a terminal disease he or she cannot have a certain drug because it may harm or kill them is beyond me. Why do those in government think they have a right to tell me how I should build my house, what structures I can build where, and whether I can occupy a location? Civil liberty means I should be able to pursue my happiness as I see fit, and if I make a mistake I should suffer the consequences. If you build your house out of shoddy materials, don't complain when it falls down. If your structure collapses and injures or kills someone, I hope you have good insurance. And if you find out you built your house on a sink-hole, I guess you'll have to start again.

Happiness is to be pursued, not guaranteed. If there is no chance of failure there is no opportunity for success. In our effort not to take responsibility for our actions, we have handed over to the government the authority to protect us from ourselves, and in so doing voluntarily handed over our right to pursue happiness.

Consent of the governed

--That to secure these rights, Governments
are instituted among Men, deriving their just
powers from the consent of the governed,

What is the purpose of government? According to our Founding Fathers it is to secure our rights; nothing more and nothing less. Think about how many laws, rules, and regulations are created telling us how we should exercise our rights and how we should live, rather than protecting our rights? Laws about how we should teach our children, how we should pay for healthcare, even what should be in our pillows and rugs, and on and on and on. While I do not know the number, my guess is that only a small percentage of federal laws, much less state and local laws, actually exist to secure our rights. Yet that is why governments are created. So, what do you call a creation that does not do what it was created to do? A failure.

Notice where these governments get some (but not all) of their powers. If a government's just powers come from the consent of the governed, what about the powers they assume without the consent of the governed? Those would be unjust powers, wouldn't they? Think about all the federal laws that, instead of protecting our rights, infringe on them. Laws that dictate how we are to live our lives and punish innocent people for daring to exercise their unalienable rights, especially those specifically protected by the U.S. Constitution. If they do not protect our rights, are they legitimate? I guess that depends on what the words "consent of the governed" means.

> CONSENT: *Agreement of the mind to what is proposed or state by another; accord; hence, a yielding of the mind or will to that which is proposed; as, a parent gives his consent to the marriage of his daughter.*[29]

I have met a lot of people who would argue that most federal laws are not just powers, since they were passed without the consent of the governed. Let us think about this for a minute. If consent means an agreement of the mind to what is proposed, then do we not consent when those we've elected to represent us pass a law infringing on our rights and as a whole we do little, if anything, about it? How many visited or wrote their congressman when unconstitutional laws were passed?

As you read this book and see how often our Constitution is ignored, trampled, and virtually spit upon, ask yourself what you did to stop it. If you yield your mind to what has been proposed, then you have given your consent. You give your consent when you do not hold your elected officials accountable for the bills they vote on or their lack of action to control unconstitutional acts. Our political figures act the way they do because we have taught them over the years that this is what they must to do keep their jobs. We consent to their conduct every time we vote for them. Think about that the next time you are yelling at your TV because of something done in Washington. Look in the mirror and yell at yourself. You have elected them, and even if you didn't vote for them, we have the government we deserve.

Speaking of voting, how often have you heard someone say they don't vote, so what happens is not their fault? To be blunt, they are wrong. Not voting is simply consenting to the decision of others. If you did not vote you said, "I give my consent for others to decide for me." If not deciding is a decision, then not voting is a vote to give others your right to choose.

---

[29]   Webster's 1828 Dictionary http://webstersdictionary1828.com.

Right of the people to alter or to abolish it

--That whenever any Form of Government becomes destructive of these ends, it is the Right of the People to alter or to abolish it, and to institute new Government, laying its foundation on such principles and organizing its powers in such form, as to them shall seem most likely to effect their Safety and Happiness.

The United States has existed longer under a single constitution than any other nation on earth. (The Massachusetts Constitution has been around longer, but the U.S. Constitution is the oldest one to govern a nation.) That's an impressive achievement, but when our Founding Fathers declared independence from Great Britain, they not only recognized their parent nation had become destructive to their rights, but that any nation, including the ones they were forming, could as well. They recognized that any government that failed in its duty to secure the rights of its citizens needed to be changed. If it could not be changed, the nation needed to be abolished and started anew.

We have had 13 states independent 11 years. There has been one rebellion. That comes to one rebellion in a century & a half for each state. What country before ever existed a century & half without a rebellion? & what country can preserve its liberties if their rulers are not warned from time to time that their people

preserve the spirit of resistance? Let them take arms.
The remedy is to set them right as to facts, pardon &
pacify them. What signify a few lives lost in a century
or two? The tree of liberty must be refreshed from
time to time with the blood of patriots & tyrants.[30]

God forbid we should ever be 20 years
without such a rebellion.[31]

Jefferson, in his letter to William Smith, was not suggesting a war every 20 years; rebellion can happen at the ballot box just as easily as on the battle field. Instead, he wanted those who serve in leadership to be reminded that they hold office at the peoples' sufferance. If we are to live in liberty, we must be willing to water that tree with our blood if necessary. Part of the reason I am writing this book is to warn my fellow Americans that, if we do not take up the mantle passed to us by our Founding Fathers and dropped by previous generations, then the only way we will remain free is through our blood. I would much rather abolish the failed government in Washington by the ballot box than on the battlefield.

---

[30]   Thomas Jefferson letter to William S. Smith, Nov. 13, 1787.

[31]   IBID.

Prudence ... not be changed for light and transient causes

Prudence, indeed, will dictate that Governments long established should not be changed for light and transient causes; and accordingly all experience hath shewn, that mankind are more disposed to suffer, while evils are sufferable, than to right themselves by abolishing the forms to which they are accustomed

Changing a government is not a trivial matter. We should not throw people out because we don't like what they're doing. We should not impeach someone because our candidate didn't win. A change in government is a tremendous upheaval and should not be taken lightly. Thankfully, our Founding Fathers put mechanisms in our Constitution to help control the wickedness which shows itself to be ever present in man and his history. As we approach the day when our government has become so oppressive that we can no longer live with it, remember we have had many tools and even more opportunities to use them to keep this ship of state on the course of liberty, protecting our rights. The failure is not Washington's or the politicians', but ours.

But when a long train of abuses and usurpations, pursuing invariably the same Object evinces a design to reduce them under absolute Despotism, it is their right, it is their duty, to throw off such Government, and to provide new Guards for their future security

The colonists had suffered many infringements on their rights as British citizens. Unfortunately, the repeated response to their pleas for justice was further infringement and despotic rule. It was for these reasons the colonies declared their independence. They saw it not only as their right but their duty, not only to themselves, but as we will read later, to their posterity, to deal with these injustices now rather than later. I wish we had half their backbone to take on our government and deal with its injustices ourselves so our children and their children won't have to.

> --*Such has been the patient sufferance of these Colonies;*
> *and such is now the necessity which constrains*
> *them to alter their former Systems of Government.*
> *The history of the present King of Great Britain*
> *is a history of repeated injuries and usurpations,*
> *all having in direct object the establishment of*
> *an absolute Tyranny over these States. To prove*
> *this, let Facts be submitted to a candid world.*

Not for light or trivial reasons, but because of the long suffering of the colonies, and the establishment of a tyrannical government from London, the colonies determined it was time to alter their system of government. The colonists of what became the United States of America suffered long and hard. They tried seeking a redress of their grievances from their government and it didn't work. Finally, they could take it no more. If King George and Parliament would not protect their rights as British citizens, then it was time to remove that government and establish one that would. To prove the rightness of their decision, the Continental Congress gave 27 specific abuses which led them to this decision.

Evidences of Britain's Tyranny

He has refused his Assent to Laws, the most
wholesome and necessary for the public good.

The colonies passed routine laws they considered wholesome and necessary. The King of England, however, often vetoed them either because they freed the colonies from British control or because he didn't like them. Therefore, Britain ruled the colonies without their consent.

He has forbidden his Governors to pass Laws
of immediate and pressing importance, unless
suspended in their operation till his Assent
should be obtained; and when so suspended,
he has utterly neglected to attend to them.

The king appointed the colonial governors. He then told them they could not pass laws without his consent. Either the law had to be approved by him, or it could not go into effect until he did approve it, something he often failed to do. Again, the colonists were not being governed by their own consent.

He has refused to pass other Laws for the
accommodation of large districts of people,
unless those people would relinquish the right of
Representation in the Legislature, a right inestimable
to them and formidable to tyrants only.

Sure, you can have that law, and all you have to do is relinquish your rights. To me, that sounds like an offer from the Godfather. If government's purpose is to protect our rights, what does it say when that government extorts your right of representation for your right to be represented? Sadly, I hear echoes of this today. Sure, you can have that law you want, if you just give all the power to interpret and regulate it to the unelected bureaucrats in the executive branch.

He has called together legislative bodies at places unusual, uncomfortable, and distant from the depository of their public Records, for the sole purpose of fatiguing them into compliance with his measures.

The king let the colony's representatives meet, but he did whatever he could to make their life difficult. He moved the meeting locations to remote places, where they didn't have access to their public records. Remember, this is the 18th century. Moving the meeting place from say Philadelphia to New York is not a mere inconvenience, imagine moving it to Boston or Charleston. And now that you're at your meeting, what if you need to refer to something stored in your archives, which could be days away by horseback?

He has dissolved Representative Houses repeatedly, for opposing with manly firmness his invasions on the rights of the people.

When the colonies' representatives stood up to the king, he simply disbanded the group and started a new one. Today, when a state stands up to federal overreach, the troops don't come in and disband the legislature; they threaten to stop keeping their funding promises or keep things tied up in court until the state cries "Uncle!"

He has refused for a long time, after such dissolutions, to cause others to be elected; whereby the Legislative

> *powers, incapable of Annihilation, have returned*
> *to the People at large for their exercise; the State*
> *remaining in the mean time exposed to all the dangers*
> *of invasion from without, and convulsions within.*

Of course, the king did not immediately start a new legislature; he left the people without representation and without protection for as long as he wanted. Whether that was a purposeful punishment or not, it showed a complete disregard for the protection of the colonists and their rights. Today the federal government uses the federal courts to overrule laws that are legitimately within the state's purview to pass. Rather than disband the legislatures, they neuter them with lawsuits. After a few decades of such abuse, we understand why so many state legislatures feel the need to go begging to the federal government for permission to do what is their Constitutional duty.

> *He has endeavoured to prevent the population of*
> *these States; for that purpose obstructing the Laws for*
> *Naturalization of Foreigners; refusing to pass others*
> *to encourage their migrations hither, and raising*
> *the conditions of new Appropriations of Lands.*

The king prevented the passing of laws allowing for immigration and for states acquiring new lands. These rules were not created by the colonies' representatives, but at the whim of a monarch. Contrary to public opinion, the federal government today does not have the Constitutional authority to set immigration policy, only to establish a unified standard for naturalization.

> *To establish an uniform Rule of Naturalization,*
> *and uniform Laws on the subject of Bankruptcies*
> *throughout the United States;*[32]

---

[32] United States Constitution, Article I, Section 8, Paragraph 4.

> *NATURALIZATION, The act of investing an alien with*
> *the rights and privileges of a native subject or citizen.*[33]

The British King obstructed the colonies from bringing in new citizens. The federal government can legally set the standard by which someone becomes a citizen, but illegally extends that to who can enter a state from another nation.

Next, rather than preventing states from acquiring lands, the federal government simply takes land from them.

> *To exercise exclusive Legislation in all Cases*
> *whatsoever, over such District (not exceeding ten*
> *Miles square) as may, by Cession of particular States,*
> *and the Acceptance of Congress, become the Seat of*
> *the Government of the United States, and to exercise*
> *like Authority over all Places purchased by the*
> *Consent of the Legislature of the State in which the*
> *Same shall be, for the Erection of Forts, Magazines,*
> *Arsenals, dock-Yards, and other needful Buildings;*[34]

The Constitution gives the federal government legislative authority over the seat of government (Washington, D.C.) and to purchase, through the consent of the state legislature, land from the states to "erect forts, magazines, arsenals, dock-yards, and other needful buildings."

This does not give them the authority to create national parks, and it certainly does not give them the authority to do so without the consent of the state in which the land exists. You may love visiting national parks and you may think it's the government's responsibility to protect land for the public good. What is blatantly obvious is that such parks and preserves are legitimate only when they are created by the states, not the federal government. The federal government doesn't even bother with passing legislation to steal land from the states now; the president

---

[33]   Webster's 1828 Dictionary http://webstersdictionary1828.com.

[34]   United States Constitution, Article I, Section 8, Paragraph 17.

simply "declares" an area a "national monument" and it's suddenly under federal control.

While the federal government is taking over state land, they are also laying claim to land owned by us individually. Imagine some federal agency, say the EPA, decides without legislation or method of redress, that the pond and stream on your property are part of the "waters of the United States." You have effectively had your land taken by the federal government with no way of stopping them. You can take them to court, but by federal law it's an "administrative court." What does that mean? It means the judge who decides the case and all the lawyers, including the one who is supposed to be representing you, all work for the federal government. What chance do you have to get justice with the deck stacked against you?

Where in the Constitution is the federal government given authority to take lands from the states? Nowhere, but it happens. Do you know why? Because nobody does anything about it. The state's governor may complain in some press conference that gets little if any coverage, and a few activists may protest or put a petition together, but meanwhile the people of this nation do nothing. We don't barrage our legislators, state and federal, with demands they do their duty to protect our rights. (Yes, state sovereignty protects our rights by providing a powerful check and balance to federal overreach.) Yet we re-elect the president who exercises dictatorial powers and the legislators who refuse to check that power.

Where has all this federal land grabbing brought us? The federal government owns almost half of Arizona, half of California, Oregon, and Wyoming, two-thirds of Alaska, Idaho, and Utah, and almost all of Nevada. In short, the federal government takes what land they want and we let them do it.

He has obstructed the Administration
of Justice, by refusing his Assent to Laws
for establishing Judiciary powers.

We talk about the importance of having judges. Imagine if we passed laws appointing and confirming judges only to have the king veto them with no method of recourse. Not only was the king overturning laws, but he was making it harder and harder for the citizens of the colonies to have their cases reviewed. Whether you are a land owner waiting on a suit against you or a criminal looking for a verdict, justice delayed is justice denied.

> *He has made Judges dependent on his Will*
> *alone, for the tenure of their offices, and the*
> *amount and payment of their salaries.*

What judges the colonies did have were dependent on the king for their office and salary, and we well know he who pays the piper calls the tune. What type of decision do you think you would get if the party on the other side had their finger on the scales of justice?

Are things really any different today? It seems almost any case can be brought to the federal court system, a system where the judges are chosen by the president, confirmed by the Senate, paid by the Federal Treasury, and can only be removed by federal impeachment. Most people think federal judges have lifetime appointments, but the Constitution says they serve for the duration of their good behavior.[35] If those who represent us will not fulfill their duty to hold judges accountable to the standard set in the Constitution, are judges now any more independent than in colonial times?

> *He has erected a multitude of New Offices,*
> *and sent hither swarms of Officers to harass*
> *our people, and eat out their substance.*

Does this sound like the federal government today? It seems almost every day either new agencies are created or existing ones enlarged. Whether it's the EPA, IRS, DOE, or any of the myriad other federal

---

[35]   United States Constitution, Article III, Section 1.

agencies, they are out looking for violations of their opinions on how we should live our lives. Our lives are being directed, organized, and tracked by the federal government. You might even say the federal government is sending out swarms of officers to harass us, all while the government eats out the substance of the economy for the privilege of this harassment.

*He has kept among us, in times of peace, Standing
Armies without the Consent of our legislatures.*

One of the reasons our Constitution requires the military appropriations be renewed every two years is because of the King's practice of keeping standing armies in peace time. The king determined whether and where armies were stationed regardless of what the colonies wanted, as expressed through their legislatures. Today the president sends troops and engages in "military intervention", often without the consent of Congress. Just like the king, our president is keeping standing armies in other lands without the consent of their representatives.

*He has affected to render the Military independent
of and superior to the Civil power.*

The reason the president is the Commander-in-Chief and the military budget is only two years long, is to be sure the military was under the control of the civilian power. Imagine passing laws only to have the military simply ignore them. If they are independent of, or even worse, superior to your legislature, you live in a military dictatorship and not a free nation.

*He has combined with others to subject us to
a jurisdiction foreign to our constitution, and
unacknowledged by our laws; giving his Assent
to their Acts of pretended Legislation:*

41

Think of the United Nations today. It's bad enough when other nations act like U.N. directives supersede their own laws, but when our lawmakers and judges voluntarily submit us to this foreign jurisdiction, they are doing the same things that drove the colonists to revolt. How long before Washington becomes a neutered government, looking to the U.N. for permission to enact the will of the people?

For Quartering large bodies of armed troops among us:

When I was growing up, it was common to hear the phrase, "A man's home is his castle." The idea that a person was in control of their own property was accepted as natural law. But what good are your property rights if the government can turn your land into a bivouac whenever they want? The federal government may not be quartering troops, but is repeatedly sending inspectors any better? Can you truly be free with Uncle Sam's agents constantly watching over your shoulder?

*For protecting them, by a mock Trial, from
punishment for any Murders which they should
commit on the Inhabitants of these States:*

Not only were the military superior to the local legislature, when they did commit crimes the courts would often protect them over and above the citizens. Imagine a soldier commits a crime, but since the case is seen before a federal judge they are protected from punishment. Yes, at the time the colonists were British citizens, yet Parliament made sure the judges put loyalty to the crown above loyalty to the law.

Administrative courts work much the same way today. Imagine you are wrongly accused by one of the myriad of federal agencies. Your only recourse is to take them to court, but not a regular court. No, you can only go to an administrative law court, a court where the judge and all the lawyers are paid by the federal government. Who do you think has the advantage in that situation? Whether it is judges protecting the military or the federal bureaucracy, this is the type of tyranny that motivated our Founding Fathers to declare themselves free.

For cutting off our Trade with all parts of the world:

Again, this is an example where the king and Parliament were overturning what the peoples' representatives had decided. In this case, the British Parliament passed a law that the colonies could only purchase goods from British merchants. While today the federal government passes restrictions on sales and purchases from certain countries, which is in their Constitutional power,[36] by ignoring the will of their own citizens, Great Britain was exercising complete domination over the colonies.

For imposing Taxes on us without our Consent:

If you ask most Americans why we fought the Revolutionary war, you will hear "taxation without representation!" Yet we are at the 17th reason given for declaring independence when we finally get to the vaunted "taxation without representation." Imposing taxes on the colonists without their consent was a reason we declared independence, but there is so much more. Many people complain about taxes, especially around April 15th, but let's face it, we elected those in Congress who are taxing us. In short, if we don't like the taxes, it's our fault for whom we hired.

For depriving us in many cases, of
the benefits of Trial by Jury:

Why is a trial by jury so important? Imagine your fate in the hands of a judge, someone who was appointed by the government, is paid by the government, and is ultimately responsible to the government for their job. Do you think you're going to get a fair, unbiased review of your

---

36   United States Constitution, Article I, Section 8, Paragraph 3.

case from someone like that? Do you think you would be considered innocent until proven guilty by someone paid by the same government as the prosecution?

One little talked about legal doctrine is that of jury nullification:

> *A sanctioned doctrine of trial proceedings wherein members of a jury disregard either the evidence presented or the instructions of the judge in order to reach a verdict based upon their own consciences. It espouses the concept that jurors should be the judges of both law and fact.*[37]

The idea is that ultimately it is the people who judge not only the facts of the case, but the law itself is an important part of the ideal behind trial by jury. Have juries abused this power in the past? Absolutely. Think about the show trials against accused minorities in the Jim Crow south. However, if you think abuse of jury nullification is a thing of the past, look at some of the trials of famous celebrities in the last few decades. Whether you believe O.J. Simpson was guilty or not, ask yourself which would you prefer: A trial by a jury of your peers or by a judge who may have an agenda of his or her own?

> *For transporting us beyond Seas to be tried for pretended offenses:*

Colonists could be charged with a crime without proof, which is bad enough, but the crown would take some of these people to Canada for trial. Why would they remove those charged from family, friends, and community? Because it also took them away from witnesses and evidence, placing the thumb of government on the scales of justice. Governments may not transport the accused to foreign nations, but they do abuse judicial tactics like gag orders and rules of evidence to the same ends.

---

[37] The Free Legal Dictionary https://legal-dictionary.thefreedictionary.com.

For abolishing the free System of English Laws in a neighboring Province, establishing therein an Arbitrary government, and enlarging its Boundaries so as to render it at once an example and fit instrument for introducing the same absolute rule into these Colonies:

I've often heard, "We are a nation of laws and not men", but at the time of our founding, the crown set up a province with a government of men. Laws were what the powerful said they were and no one was held accountable for his actions if he had enough money and influence. There was concern that this same type of absolute rule would be set up for the colonies.

We see examples of this "arbitrary government" today, where officials are only called to account if they are from the other party and where the law is applied differently to those with money and lawyers than it is to the rest of us. In effect, they have turned the law into an instrument of politics. Add to that a legal system that routinely ignores the written laws, including the words of the Constitution, and I ask you: Are we still a nation of laws?

For taking away our Charters, abolishing our most valuable Laws, and altering fundamentally the Forms of our Governments:

The colonies had local governments, but any law they passed could be vetoed by the king. Rules established by the colony's charter and laws created by its government were regularly vetoed by the king, sometimes for no other reason than he didn't like them or the precedent they established. Some of the most important laws overturned by the king were those restricting and abolishing slavery. That's right, one of the reasons we declared independence was because the king would not allow the colonies to free slaves. Today the federal government violates the sovereignty and constitutions of the states, either directly by enacting laws that infringe on them or by bribing them with promises of money if they do what Washington tells them. Does this not fundamentally alter the forms of government the people adopted via the Constitution?

> *For suspending our own Legislatures, and*
> *declaring themselves invested with power to*
> *legislate for us in all cases whatsoever.*

Imagine having your local legislature suspended and your right to effective representation simply overruled by a remote government. This didn't just happen in 1775, it is happening today as the federal government takes on more and more responsibilities, many of which are actually forbidden in the Constitution. While state and local legislatures may not be banned, many federal bureaucracies and courts are overruling state laws due to an extremely faulty understanding of the supremacy clause in the Constitution. Only federal laws created "in pursuance" of the Constitution are supreme. However, if you look at the Constitution, you will find that much of what Washington does uses powers not delegated to it and thereby, under the Tenth Amendment, are powers left to the states. When the federal government exercises a power not delegated to it, it is effectively suspending the power of state and local legislatures, just as King George and Parliament did.

> *He has abdicated Government here, by declaring us*
> *out of his Protection and waging War against us.*

The king had stopped protecting the colonies and was in fact using troops under his command to violate the rights of his own citizens. Abandoned and abused, is it any wonder the colonies declared themselves no longer a part of the British empire? Now look at Washington today. Is it doing its duty to protect our unalienable rights? Has it not abdicated this responsibility in favor of dictating every aspect of our lives? Is the federal government not waging war against our liberties with secret courts, unconstitutional warrants, land confiscation, and overruling constitutionally passed state and local laws? King George had not officially declared war on the colonies, but his actions were acts of war. If we look at the state of the federal government, do we not see the same ruthless and flagrant disregard for rights, liberties, and the rule of law? I pray this does not become a shooting war, but we need to recognize we are once again fighting for our lives, our liberties, and our sacred honor.

> *He has plundered our seas, ravaged our Coasts, burnt*
> *our towns, and destroyed the lives of our people.*

Every day, the federal government confiscates or regulates anything and everything you can imagine. Some people say every American commits three federal felonies every day. While our towns aren't burnt down (unless you count wildfires that rage because federal forestry regulation), your lives are plundered every day and many of them are destroyed either by being regulated into the ground or simply taken under some pretense.

> *He is at this time transporting large Armies of*
> *foreign Mercenaries to compleat the works of*
> *death, desolation and tyranny, already begun*
> *with circumstances of Cruelty & perfidy scarcely*
> *paralleled in the most barbarous ages, and totally*
> *unworthy the Head of a civilized nation.*

Not only were British troops terrorizing the colonists, but the king was bringing in mercenaries to supplement the force. Would you be surprised if, someday, the United Nations monitors our elections?

> *He has constrained our fellow Citizens taken Captive*
> *on the high Seas to bear Arms against their Country,*
> *to become the executioners of their friends and*
> *Brethren, or to fall themselves by their Hands.*

Many of us remember the days of the draft. Young men are still required to enroll in the selective service on their 18th birthday. Now imagine this draft, were it to come back, not be used in foreign wars, but locally. If that sounds outrageous, ask yourself how often the National Guard has been activated to enforce some law or court decision? Is Washington really that far away from using federal law enforcement against their fellow citizens for standing up for their rights? How long before they call for the military and militia to take up arms against their fellow citizens?

> *He has excited domestic insurrections amongst us,*
> *and has endeavoured to bring on the inhabitants*
> *of our frontiers, the merciless Indian Savages,*
> *whose known rule of warfare, is an undistinguished*
> *destruction of all ages, sexes and conditions.*

Not only was King George bringing in mercenaries, British generals were making agreements with the local native Americans to fight their own citizens.

> *In every stage of these Oppressions We have*
> *Petitioned for Redress in the most humble terms:*
> *Our repeated Petitions have been answered only*
> *by repeated injury. A Prince whose character is*
> *thus marked by every act which may define a*
> *Tyrant, is unfit to be the ruler of a free people.*

The Continental Congress didn't decide one day to declare independence. For years, they followed the law and petitioned the king and Parliament for relief, only to receive additional and more onerous actions for their efforts.

> *Nor have We been wanting in attentions to our*
> *British brethren. We have warned them from time*

*to time of attempts by their legislature to extend an
unwarrantable jurisdiction over us. We have reminded
them of the circumstances of our emigration and
settlement here. We have appealed to their native
justice and magnanimity, and we have conjured them
by the ties of our common kindred to disavow these
usurpations, which, would inevitably interrupt our
connections and correspondence. They too have been
deaf to the voice of justice and of consanguinity. We
must, therefore, acquiesce in the necessity, which
denounces our Separation, and hold them, as we hold
the rest of mankind, Enemies in War, in Peace Friends.*

These men were not mere rabble rousers looking for trouble. They have been petitioning their government to acknowledge and protect their rights not only as British citizens, but by the charters they had agreed to when they emigrated to the colonies. The British government would not abide by their own laws and agreements, even in face of evidence that the colonies would not put up with these injustices forever.

*We, therefore, the Representatives of the united States
of America, in General Congress, Assembled, appealing
to the Supreme Judge of the world for the rectitude of
our intentions, do, in the Name, and by Authority of
the good People of these Colonies, solemnly publish
and declare, That these United Colonies are, and of
Right ought to be Free and Independent States;*

This was not the action of a few men, but men representing the states and the people of these new united States. They appealed to a power higher than government as proof of the rightness of their intentions. They declared these colonies free and independent states, not in their own name, but in the name of the people they represented.

> *that they are Absolved from all Allegiance to the British*
> *Crown, and that all political connection between them*
> *and the State of Great Britain, is and ought to be totally*
> *dissolved; and that as Free and Independent States, they*
> *have full Power to levy War, conclude Peace, contract*
> *Alliances, establish Commerce, and to do all other Acts*
> *and Things which Independent States may of right do.*

These new states were no longer a part of the British empire; they would no longer follow its laws nor submit to its rule. They also had all the powers of other states: To declare war, sue for peace, make treaties and alliances, and establish commerce with whatever other states they wanted. In short, these men announced that they were rightfully putting these 13 new states on par with Great Britain and all the other states of the world.

> *And for the support of this Declaration, with*
> *a firm reliance on the protection of divine*
> *Providence, we mutually pledge to each other our*
> *Lives, our Fortunes and our sacred Honor.*

These men were not fools. They knew that by signing this document, they were committing treason against the British crown. They knew they did not have the military resources to stand toe to toe with the British army. They looked to divine providence to protect them and help their cause, yet they also knew it would take more. If they were caught, they would be sent to England and almost certainly be hung. Knowing this, they pledged their lives, fortunes, and sacred honor to the cause of liberty and independence. It is deplorable that most Americans today will not even pledge the effort to vote, much less to bother researching the candidates first.

Independence today

"We are ready to accept almost any explanation of the present crisis of our civilization except one: that the present state of the world may be the result of genuine error on our own part and that the pursuit of some of our most cherished ideals has apparently produced results utterly different from those which we expected."

— *Friedrich A. Hayek, The Road to Serfdom*

This document, forming 13 nations that would soon bind themselves together under the Articles of Confederation, is a powerful example of the strength and fortitude of those who fought for our liberty. We see that rather than the "rich, white, slave owning men" they are often portrayed as, these men of substance were willing to risk everything to regain the freedoms they had been promised as British citizens. While some did own slaves, research shows that many did so only because it was illegal to free them. The stain of slavery took many years before it was outlawed, but the seeds of that victory were planted by these men and watered by the blood and tears of countless more.

It saddens me that while the owning of another human being is illegal, we as citizens have become enslaved to the larges of our governments, submitting to their tyranny for the scraps they leave us and bowing to the wisdom of the nine high-priests in black robes who dictate law from the bench.

I believe it is time for us to rediscover the ideals that birthed this nation, to recognize in our current government the similar abuses that led to our dissolving the political bands that tied us to Britain, and to again strive for liberty. I fear that American ignorance and apathy regarding both the Declaration of Independence and the Constitution will mean we will simply slip further and further toward tyranny, until we either submit to it or rise to fight against it. I would much rather we re-declare our independence, not through war but through citizenship, and rediscover the idea of self-government, self-reliance, and the tools our founders gave us to defend ourselves against a tyrannical government. It has taken over one hundred years to fall so far from the liberties that have been bought for us, which means we will not regain them quickly or easily.

In fact, the question is: What will you pledge not only to regain your freedom, but that of your children and their children?

The greatness of America lies not in being
more enlightened than any other nation, but
rather in her ability to repair her faults.

– Alexis de Tocqueville

Preamble to the Bill of Rights

Congress OF THE *United States*
begun and held at the City of New-York, on Wednesday the fourth
of March, one thousand seven hundred and eighty nine.

THE *Conventions of a number of the States, having at the time*
of their adopting the Constitution, expressed a desire, in order
to prevent misconstruction or abuse of its powers, that further
declaratory and restrictive clauses should be added: And as
extending the ground of public confidence in the Government,
will best ensure the beneficent ends of its institution.

RESOLVED *by the Senate and House of Representatives of the*
United States of America, in Congress assembled, two thirds of
both Houses concurring, that the following Articles be proposed
to the Legislatures of the several States, as amendments to the
Constitution of the United States, all, or any of which Articles,
when ratified by three fourths of the said Legislatures, to be valid
to all intents and purposes, as part of the said Constitution; viz.

ARTICLES *in addition to, and Amendment of the Constitution*
of the United States of America, proposed by Congress, and
ratified by the Legislatures of the several States, pursuant
to the fifth Article of the original Constitution.

How Many Amendments are in the Bill of Rights?

The first ten amendments to the Constitution are called the Bill of Rights, but did you know there were originally twelve proposed amendments? The first two, one to set the number of representatives in the house and the other to regulate pay raises, did not pass – at least not at first. Actually the second of those proposed amendments, the one regulating pay raises for Congress, wasn't ratified until 1992!

Why a Bill of Rights

During the state ratification debates over the Constitution, there was a question about whether the Constitution needed a written guarantee of certain freedoms and rights: A Bill of Rights. As with congressional debates today, this division was along party lines.

The Federalists

One group, called the Federalists, was led by Alexander Hamilton. Hamilton, along with John Jay and James Madison, wrote a series of essays under the pseudonym "Publius" in favor of the Constitution and in general preferred a strong centralized government. Both Hamilton and Madison argued that a Bill of Rights was not needed since the Constitution did not give the central government any power with which to restrict rights. In fact, they were concerned that having a list of rights in the Constitution would give future members of the government the mistaken impression that they had the authority to regulate those rights.

The Anti-Federalists

The Anti-Federalists, while not as organized as the Federalists, were concerned with the Constitution as it was written, complaining that a strong central government threatened the sovereignty of the states and threatened the peoples' liberties and would fail to protect their rights. The Anti-Federalists wanted protections for both individual rights and state sovereignty, and therefore supported a Bill of Rights. Many of the

Anti-Federalists wrote essays under different pseudonyms which were later collected into the Anti-Federalist Papers. The most well-known Anti-Federalist was Patrick Henry.

The Massachusetts Compromise

There were many compromises in the Constitution, but the one related to the topic at hand is not only why we have a Bill of Rights, but why it is contained in the amendments rather than the original document.

The debate in the states about ratification of the Constitution at times got heated, almost breaking out in civil war in Rhode Island. In neighboring Massachusetts, two Anti-Federalists came up with a compromise: The Anti-Federalists would support ratification of the Constitution with the understanding they could put forth amendments should the document be ratified. The Federalists agreed to support those amendments, specifically a Bill of Rights. After Massachusetts ratified the Constitution, four of five states, who also subsequently ratified, included recommendations for amendments. Thus, another hurdle to the creation of this republic was passed.

The Purpose of the Bill of Rights

THE Conventions of a number of the States, having at the time of their adopting the Constitution, expressed a desire, in order to prevent misconstruction or abuse of its powers, that further declaratory and restrictive clauses should be added: And as extending the ground of public confidence in the Government, will best ensure the beneficent ends of its institution.

Specifically listed in the preamble, the Bill of Rights was adopted to prevent misconstruction (wrong interpretation of words or things[38]) or abuse of powers. The Anti-Federalists wanted no confusion about what powers were being delegated to the central government and what limits were specifically put on those powers. They wanted to make sure that when they said that Congress "shall" or "shall not", they knew the people meant it.

Restrictive Clauses

President Barack Obama once said that the Constitution was a "charter of negative liberties." In a sense, this is true in that the Constitution was meant to restrain the central government from many activities. The first three articles say, among other things, what the federal government can do and the Bill of Rights say what the government can't do. The last amendment of the Bill of Rights says, if it's not listed in the Constitution, the central government can't do it. The Bill of Rights was meant to

---

[38] Webster's 1828 Dictionary http://webstersdictionary1828.com.

bolster this idea of a limited central government by specifying several rights upon which the government cannot infringe. Unfortunately, today the state and federal governments treat these restrictions like speed limit signs, i.e., merely a suggestion.

Public Confidence

Remember that debate about ratifying the Constitution? One purpose of the Bill of Rights was to help the public feel more confident that they were not replacing one dictator in England with a group of them in New York (later Washington, D.C.).

How Far We Have Fallen

Unfortunately, Washington, D.C. and the state capitals have ignored those restrictive clauses and in so doing destroyed the public confidence. How else do you explain an approval rating for Congress averaging in the high teens?[39] We put our faith in men and women to go to Washington, D.C. to protect our liberties and instead they have trampled them, often at our bidding. The Federalists may have been right, by listing rights in the Constitution, our elected officials believe they have the authority to regulate them.

We cannot change the past, and wishing and wanting will not change the present. It is time to stop waiting for those in Washington to fix themselves and to start honoring their oaths to support the Constitution. It is time we used our powers to change Washington, D.C. by how we vote, what we demand of our representatives, and how we hold them accountable. To do that, we need to know and understand what our Founding Fathers actually gave us in this Constitution. If you've read this far, I hope you are ready to become a self-taught patriot yourself.

---

[39] Congress and the Public, Gallop http://www.gallup.com/poll/1600/congress-public.aspx.

Amendment I

*Congress shall make no law respecting an establishment
of religion, or prohibiting the free exercise thereof; or
abridging the freedom of speech, or of the press; or
the right of the people peaceably to assemble, and to
petition the Government for a redress of grievances.*

The First Amendment guarantees us five freedoms: Religion, speech,
press, assembly, and petition. Collectively these rights of conscience
ensure we can both live and act in accord with our beliefs.

Restrictions on Congress

It is important to note that this amendment places restrictions on
Congress. Since all legislative power is vested in Congress, the phrase
"Congress shall make no law ..." makes sense. Today Congress has "delegated" much of its lawmaking authority to the executive branch (which
is not legal), and the courts have taken to themselves the authority to
determine "established law" (another unconstitutional act) since our
Constitution requires all federal laws be created by Congress. Although
Article VI makes the Constitution and federal laws made in pursuance
to it the supreme laws of the land (Supremacy Clause), the wording of the
First Amendment makes it abundantly clear that its restrictions apply
to Congress, and by extension, the federal government.

Freedom of Religion

Some people reference this as Freedom of Worship, but that's not an accurate description. Freedom of worship means you can worship how you want, but that's it. Freedom of religion guarantees not only that we can believe what we want without government coercion, but that we can exercise that belief in public. Freedom of worship says you can go to church, but freedom of religion, as enshrined in the First Amendment, means you can live your religion as you see fit, both by how you live and what you decide to do or not do. The only restriction that should be placed on this freedom is not using it to infringe on the freedoms of others. This protection comes in the form of two clauses: The establishment clause and the free exercise clause.

Establishment Clause

Congress shall make no law respecting
an establishment of religion

Congress cannot establish a religion through law. Courts today say that anything that benefits a religious organization, and in some cases even recognizes a person's belief, is a violation of the establishment clause. For example, voluntary student prayer is banned in public schools (although some say that as long as there are tests, there will always be prayer in schools!) Nursing home residents were not allowed to pray over their meals because of "separation of church and state." Veteran memorials have been covered up or taken down because they are in the form of a cross. Business owners are being fined and shut down because they won't participate in events that violate their religious beliefs. Do these opinions stand up in the light of what the Constitution actually says?

The 1828 Webster's dictionary defines establish as "To found permanently; to erect and fix or settle; . . . To enact or decree by authority and for permanence; . . . To make firm; to confirm; to ratify what has been previously set or made."[40] Does allowing a child to pray in school or after a sporting event build a religion or bring it to a firm or stable base? Does a monument erected with private funds cause a religion to be accepted, or just recognized? Does the public expression of belief equate to the government endorsing a certain religion?

On the contrary, requiring people to put aside their beliefs and espouse a secular viewpoint in order to be recognized and included is the true violation of the establishment clause. Requiring someone by law to do something based on a belief is an establishment of religion and a violation of the establishment clause.

How can a secular requirement made for public benefit be an establishment of religion? Isn't secularism the opposite of religion? Not according to dictionary.com, which defines religion as:

> *A set of beliefs concerning the cause, nature, and purpose of the universe, especially when considered as the creation of a superhuman agency or agencies, usually involving devotional and ritual observances, and often containing a moral code governing the conduct of human affairs; a specific fundamental set of beliefs and practices generally agreed upon by a number of persons or sects.*[41]

Secularism, naturalism, and scientism are also all beliefs concerning the cause, nature, and purpose of the universe, or as one of the 1828 Webster's dictionary definitions says, "Any system of faith and worship."[42] Evolution, though rarely acknowledged as such today, is still a theory unproven by the scientific method about the cause and nature of the universe. Requiring the espousing of these beliefs and practices is the definition of establishing a religion. Should these beliefs be banned

---

[40] Webster's 1828 Dictionary http://webstersdictionary1828.com.

[41] Dictionary.com https://www.dictionary.com.

[42] Webster's 1828 Dictionary http://webstersdictionary1828.com.

from schools or public view? Absolutely not, but neither should other beliefs that compete with them.

At one time these infringements on our rights would have been unthinkable; today they are quite common and considered "established law" by the courts.

Free Exercise Clause

Congress shall make no law ... prohibiting the free exercise thereof;

If the establishment clause protects us from the federal government establishing religion, then the free exercise clause allows us to live our beliefs in public.

When a school prevents students from praying, it is infringing on their right to exercise their religious beliefs. It was reported that, in the case Santa Fe v. Jane Doe, a federal judge decided that graduation prayers must not include any mention of "Jesus" or other "specific deities" and that any student offering such a prayer would face immediate arrest and up to six months in jail. While I was not able to find a referable example of this quote, if true it would point to a serious violation of Jane Doe's and, in fact, the entire student body's, First Amendment right to exercise their religion without federal government interference. This type of opinion not only violates the free exercise clause, but by establishing standards for prayers, it is most definitely establishing religious standards.

When it comes to infringing on people's religious freedom rights, I've seen everyone from courts, to politicians, to everyday citizens, claim "separation of church and state". If freedom of religion includes only the establishment and free exercise clauses, where does this term "separation of church and state" originate?

The story starts with the election of Thomas Jefferson and a group of Baptists from Danbury Connecticut. Jefferson was the first anti-federalist elected to the presidency. (The anti-federalists were a group of

Founding Fathers concerned with the amount of power being delegated to the federal government. Contrary to popular opinion, they were not against the Constitution, but only against some of the provisions that gave power to the United States and the lack of protections for individual rights.) Being generally anti-federalist themselves, this pleased many Baptists. However, there was a group of Baptists in Danbury, CT who were concerned. In a letter to the president congratulating him on his electoral win, they expressed concern that, since they were a minority religion in their state, others could suppress their freedom of religion. Jefferson's response to this concern was:

> *"I contemplate with sovereign reverence that act*
> *of the whole American people which declared that*
> *their legislature should "make no law respecting*
> *an establishment of religion or prohibiting the*
> *free exercise thereof," thus building a wall of*
> *separation between Church and State."*[43]

Rather than being concerned about the infringement of their rights, Jefferson said the First Amendment built a wall of separation between church and state, thus protecting them from state intervention.

For almost 150 years, the courts recognized this need to keep the government out of the affairs of the church. On the few occasions when courts did cite Jefferson's letter, they quoted the whole letter and identified it as personal correspondence, a way to put the First Amendment language in context. Then, in the 1947 case *Everson v. Board of Education,* the supreme Court opinion only quoted the separation phase and used that language to say that no government can participate in the affairs of any religious organization.[44]

For 150 years, the establishment clause meant that government couldn't prefer one sect or religion over another. Then, overnight, the court said government could have nothing to do with religious

---

[43] Jefferson, Writings, Vol. XVI.
[44] Everson v. Board of Education, 330 U.S. 1 (1947).

organizations and it did so by quoting out of context someone who wasn't even in the country for the debate on the First Amendment. Subsequent courts and legal opinions have taken this further to the point that many states have amendments in their constitutions, called Blaine amendments, that prohibit any tax money going to religious organizations. These amendments have been used to prevent educational vouchers from being used in religious schools, religious day-cares being denied access to programs funded by state mandated fees and, as we've already seen, courts determining what can be included in graduation prayers under pain of arrest and jail time. Jefferson's wall, originally described as protecting the church from the state, has instead become a prison fence attempting to keep religious organizations "in their place".

Together, the establishment clause and the free exercise clause were designed, as Jefferson said, to erect a wall between church and state. Not to protect the public from religion, but to protect the conscience of all Americans from the government. Together these clauses are meant to insure the federal government cannot force you to do something against your conscience or to prevent you from exercising it.

Freedom of Speech

Congress shall make no law ... abridging
the freedom of speech,

Freedom of speech and freedom of the press are closely related in that both involve people's right to express themselves. In the chapter on the Declaration of Independence, we mention that the only legitimate rights we can exercise do not infringe on the rights of others. We used the example of yelling "Fire" in a crowded theater. While freedom of speech means I can say what I want in public, it does not protect me from the consequences of using that right to infringe on the rights of other. (In this example, if there was a fire I cannot be prosecuted, but if there was no fire, then I can be sued for the injury and damages I caused.)

Many claim a freedom not to be offended, but this amendment plainly points out the fallacy in such a claim. There is no need to protect speech that no one finds offensive, only speech that might offend someone. So any claimed "right" to not be offended must infringe on someone else's right to speak freely. As stated above, the First Amendment cannot protect you from the illegitimate use of that right, which is why we have slander and defamation laws. Webster's dictionary defines defamation as "The uttering of slanderous words with a view to injure another's reputation"[45]. So I can say what I want, but the First Amendment does not protect me for being sued for making false statements about someone.

We see this freedom being infringed in many ways. Frequently, calls to allow "free speech" are not so much a call to the First Amendment, but for the infringement on the rights of others. Take for example the recent spate of demonstrations against certain speakers. The protesters claim the right of "free speech" when what they are doing is infringing on the free speech and assembly rights of others. The demonstrators are more than welcome to express their point of view, right up to the point they interfere with someone else's rights. What about the rights of those who come to listen to the speaker? Do they have the right to not have their assembly disrupted by those who disagree? By all means, stand outside (on public land) and scream, make difficult points, and ask difficult questions, but do not claim the right to free speech while you deny it to others.

Public vs. Private

Let's also look at "Free Speech Zones" on college and university campuses. Does an institute of higher education have the right to restrict speech to certain areas? I'm sure most of you have an immediate gut reaction of "NO!" Before you commit to that answer though, there is a very important question you need to ask before you can correctly answer this one. Is the college or university a public or private school? If the institution in question is a public school, or more accurately a

---

45   Webster's 1828 Dictionary http://webstersdictionary1828.com.

government run or funded school, then your gut reaction is correct, because they have no right to infringe on the free speech rights of their students. (This is a topic we'll cover in more detail in our discussion of the Fourteenth Amendment and the "Incorporation Doctrine".) If it is a private school though, things are different. As a private organization, (meaning it is neither run by or gets funding from a government) its members have the right to assemble or associate freely, without anyone forcing them to do so in a certain way. You may think a private school's policies, free speech zone, hiring practices, or classes offered are wrong, and you are perfectly free to say so, but you have no right to force the school to comply with your opinions, nor do you have the right to get the government to enforce them for you.

Freedom of the Press

Congress shall make no law... abridging
the freedom...of the press;

While freedom of speech deals with our right to express ourselves verbally, freedom of the press is our right to express ourselves to others en masse. You can get on your soapbox and talk to a large audience if you can get that many to listen to you. However, if you want to express yourself to large numbers of people, you need another method of communication. In the 18th century that method involved the printing press.

Today's corporate media often decries the amateur reporter, claiming that freedom of the press is for the professional media. Is that what our Founding Fathers were trying to protect? Webster's 1828 Dictionary defines press as, "The art or business of printing and publishing. A free press is a great blessing to a free people; a licentious press is a curse to society." In addition to newspapers, a common way for people in colonial times to get news and information was from a printed sheet called a broadside. These documents, designed to be posted and shared, delivered everything from the latest news, government proclamations, and public service announcements, to advertisements and opinions. If you wanted to share your opinion far and wide and didn't own a newspaper or a printing press, you just needed to find someone who would print your broadside and the money to pay them.

Many of our Founding Fathers wrote pamphlets, unbound books either with no cover or only a paper cover. Probably the most famous pamphlet of revolutionary times is Common Sense by Thomas Paine.[46] Unlike more scholarly books, this pamphlet was written in plain language for all to read and understand. This pamphlet challenged the legitimacy of British rule in the colonies and inspired many to join the cause of the revolution.

Compare this to media today. Sure, we still have newspapers and books, but isn't a blog the modern equivalent of a colonial broadside? Isn't an online publication similar to a pamphlet with its simple form and common language? While corporate media may denigrate the blog writer or internet publisher and challenge their qualifications as "press" for First Amendment protection, is this from a reverence of liberty or the protection of their jobs? Just as colonial writers found other paths to distribute their ideas, so do today's bloggers and alternate news sites. Just as newspapers now share the journalist's road with radio and television, more and more they are relying on the Internet to distribute their content, whether printed, audio, or video.

Freedom of the press is not so much about the ability to put words to paper, but to encourage and protect the public marketplace of ideas. It is to insure that anyone, rich or poor, scholar or not, can promote, discuss, and debate their ideas in public. This freedom gives everyone a chance to investigate public figures and present their findings to anyone who will read or listen. "The press" is often described as the "fourth estate", acknowledging their influence on public events and figures. While they claim to have the only job protected in the Constitution, freedom of the press protects anyone exercising the art or business of publication in any form. Our need to vet and hold accountable those who are supposed to

---

[46] Common Sense by Thomas Paine http://www.ushistory.org/paine/commonsense/.

report the news is just as important whether the reporter works for a corporate news organization or out of his or her basement.

Freedom of Assembly

> *Congress shall make no law ... abridging ... the right of the people peaceably to assemble,*

If freedom of speech and press protect our rights of expressing ourselves, the freedom to assemble allows us to gather with others of like opinion. We think of the freedom to assemble when we see public demonstrations, but as Inigo Montoya[47] asked, does that mean what you think it means?

Take the "Occupy Wall Street 'demonstrations'" a few years ago. There was a group of people who wanted to get together and express their disgust with how they viewed Wall Street and its impact on our economy, but was this a demonstration? More important, was it a peaceable assembly? If any part of this freedom gets forgotten, it is the right to "peaceably" assemble. Whenever you see an assembly threatening people, destroying property, and preventing others from going about their business, it is not a peaceable assembly; that is not a demonstration, it is a riot. Whether politically motivated, in response to a court verdict, or a team winning a championship, your right to peaceably assemble does not protect you from the consequences of criminal acts.

The flip-side of this right has to do with permits. Does any government have the authority to determine whether a group is allowed to peaceably assemble? Remember, the First Amendment helps protect our right to peaceably assemble, but it places those restrictions on Congress, not the states or other governments. However, I believe all state constitutions include similar protections of our right to peaceably assemble. Does that mean a city requiring a permit for a parade or demonstration is a violation of our rights? Yes, but with a caveat. My issue is not with a group expecting a large number of people notifying the city or state

---

[47]   Inigo Montoya is a character from the movie *Princess Bride.*

authorities so they can be prepared; that's only common courtesy. My issue is with the laws giving these government agents the "authority" to deny a group their right to assemble before they have had a chance to become unruly.

Freedom to Petition

Congress shall make no law ... abridging the freedom ...
to petition the Government for a redress of grievances.

"Let them eat cake!" Whether Marie Antoinette actually said this phrase or not, it has come to mean a disdain the ruling class has for the ordinary citizen. Our Founding Fathers understood the frustration of repeatedly asking your government to resolve a grievance, only to be ignored. Recognizing the tendency of those in power to dismiss the concerns of others, our right to petition our government is listed in the First Amendment.

How do we petition our government for a redress of grievances? The simplest and easiest way is to contact those we've hired to represent us. We have the right to get our representatives involved in what we think. As with any right, there comes responsibility. I may think everyone should wear a seat-belt when in a car, but should I petition the government to deal with it? It could be argued that it is an authority of your state under the Tenth Amendment, but nowhere will you find an enumerated power for the federal government to regulate traffic laws. You may be concerned about the poor, the elderly, the sick, or the student, but none of those powers are under the purview of the federal government. Should we address these concerns to our state or local governments? That is debatable, but it is a discussion we should have.

What about grievances where our right to petition has been effectively denied? Do you have a disagreement with the EPA, IRS, or any of the other myriad of three letter agencies that make up Washington, D.C.'s bureaucracy? Sure, you can petition the government for a redress of your grievance, but everyone else in the administrative law court where your case is heard work for the federal government. Have assets seized under civil asset forfeiture? You can complain, but the agency has no requirement to answer your challenge unless you spend thousands of dollars to fight them in court. And remember, those courts work for the government and they have more money than you do.

What about a grievance against someone other than the government? Could our right to petition for a redress include the right to take someone to court who has harmed us? I haven't heard this mentioned as part of our right to petition, but I think it's worthy of discussion.

Conclusion

I think the most important thing we can do with our 'conscience rights' is to spend some time thinking about them, how they are being infringed, and how we try to use them to infringe on the rights of others. Remember, this amendment is designed to restrain the federal government from infringing on our rights, not for us to infringe on the rights of others. I suggest you take some time to think about these rights and how they are being used or infringed. Most importantly, think carefully about those claiming these rights. Are they using a legitimate exercise of their rights? Are they being used to infringe on others' rights? I wonder, if we took the time to analyze people's rights' claims, would we put up with some of the foolishness we see in the news today?

Amendment II

A well regulated Militia, being necessary to the security of a free State, the right of the people to keep and bear Arms, shall not be infringed.

Probably one of the most argued about, misquoted, and outright mangled amendments to our Constitution is the Second Amendment. Why is that? I think it has to do with the emotional reaction to guns, even though this is not an amendment solely about them.

Basic English

Part of the misunderstanding of the Second Amendment appears to deal with the basic construction of the sentence itself. I'm not an English major, but I did grow up around writers and editors, married a writer and editor, and helped raise a daughter who is a writer and editor. So when considering this amendment, if you break down the sentence, you find two phrases, an establishing statement and a command.

The Militia

A well regulated Militia, being necessary to the security of a free State

How often have you heard someone say "The Second Amendment is about the militia!" The term "militia" is definitely in the amendment, but it's part of an establishing statement, not the instruction of the amendment. What is an "establishing statement"? It is simply a statement establishing the context for whatever comes next. For example: "Susie is a great student; she is applying to Harvard next year." Or "Johnny is a good boy; he would never do something like that." Or "Murder is wrong, and it should receive the harshest punishment possible." All these sentences start with an establishing statement explaining why the rest of it makes sense. The establishing statement in the Second Amendment explains why we need the command that will follow. The statement is broken up into two sections, an object and an observation.

The "well regulated Militia" is an entity being described, not the subject of the amendment. It is "necessary to the security of a free State," nothing more, nothing less. What is this entity that a free state's security depends on? Webster's dictionary defines militia in two ways:

> *Militia: The body of soldiers in a state enrolled for*
> *discipline, but not engaged in actual service except*
> *in emergencies; as distinguished from regular troops,*
> *whose sole occupation is war or military service.*
> *The militia of a country are the able bodied men*
> *organized into companies, regiments and brigades,*
> *with officers of all grades, and required by law to*
> *attend military exercises on certain days only, but at*
> *other times left to pursue their usual occupations.*[48]

At its core, a state militia is a group of citizens who are able to serve, but only in emergencies. They differ from a national militia (militia of a country) in that persons enroll in the state militia and only serve during emergencies. A state militiaman has no duties except to serve when needed. The national militia are all able-bodied men, are organized, and are required by law to attend exercises.

I've often heard people say "the National Guard is the militia," and they are partially correct. Of the two types of militia, state and national, which sounds more like the National Guard? The militia was not called

---

[48] Webster's 1828 Dictionary http://webstersdictionary1828.com.

the National Guards until 1916. These militias are organized by state and they are voluntary, but they are required to attend military exercises on certain days, are organized in companies, regiments, and brigades, and while they can be activated by a governor in times of emergency, they can also be nationalized and placed under the command of the President.

> *The President shall be Commander in Chief of the Army and Navy of the United States, and of the Militia of the several States, when called into the actual Service of the United States;*[49]

There are two different types of militias, state and national, or as federal law refers to them, the organized and the unorganized militias.

> *(a) The militia of the United States consists of all able-bodied males at least 17 years of age and, except as provided in section 313 of title 32, under 45 years of age who are, or who have made a declaration of intention to become, citizens of the United States and of female citizens of the United States who are members of the National Guard.*
>
> *(b) The classes of the militia are—*
>
> *(1) the organized militia, which consists of the National Guard and the Naval Militia; and*
>
> *(2) the unorganized militia, which consists of the members of the militia who are not members of the National Guard or the Naval Militia.*[50]

---

[49]   United States Constitution, Article II, Section 2.

[50]   10 U.S. Code § 246 - Militia: composition and classes.

The militia needs to be well regulated, but what did that mean to the people who signed and ratified the amendment? I found an excellent article by Brian T. Halonen at *The Constitution Society*. Mr. Halonen describes the use of the term "well regulated" as follows:

> *The phrase "well-regulated" was in common use long before 1789, and remained so for a century thereafter. It referred to the property of something being in proper working order. Something that was well-regulated was calibrated correctly, functioning as expected. Establishing government oversight of the people's arms was not only not the intent in using the phrase in the 2nd amendment, it was precisely to render the government powerless to do so that the founders wrote it.[51]*

In short, the term "well regulated" referred to something being in proper working order, not something overseen (or regulated) by a government.

Whether the organized militia (National Guard and Naval Militia) or the unorganized militia (all other able-bodied persons or those enrolled in an unorganized state militia), they are necessary to a free state. Why? The answer is simple: Who else will keep the peace?

Let's talk about that "free state" first. When we declared our independence from Great Britain, we created thirteen free and independent states:

> *That these United Colonies are, and of Right ought to be Free and Independent States;[52]*

What is a free state?

---

[51] Constitution Society article "The meaning of the phrase 'well-regulated' in the 2nd amendment" http://www.constitution.org/cons/wellregu.htm.

[52] Declaration of Independence.

> *FREE: In government, not enslaved; not in a state of*
> *vassalage or dependence; subject only to fixed laws,*
> *made by consent, and to a regular administration*
> *of such laws; not subject to the arbitrary will of a*
> *sovereign or lord; as a free state, nation or people.*[53]

If our states are not vassals of the federal government, if we are not dependent on others except for laws made by consent, if we are not subject to arbitrary rules, then we are free. If we do live in free states, who will maintain our security? We could put troops on every corner to protect us, but then we'd be living in a police state, not a free one. We could create laws barring us from the tools to maintain our security, but that would make us subject to arbitrary laws (since I've never seen a gun control law that does not exempt law enforcement) and dependent on the government for our protection. Which also means we would not be free. If we are to remain free and secure, we need an armed citizenry so we can protect ourselves.

I'm sure you've heard it said that we have police today, so we don't need people running around with guns to protect themselves. In my experience, this is usually someone who has not had to wait anxiously for the police to respond to a 911 call, hoping the armed law enforcement officer will get there before the criminal finds them. Who protects the neighborhood when the police can't respond? Make no mistake, I hold most law enforcement officers in the highest regard; they risk their lives every day trying to protect us from the worst elements of society. However, they cannot be everywhere, all the time, and we really don't want to live in that sort of police state. When the riots broke out in Ferguson, Missouri and Baltimore, Maryland, who protected their neighborhood while the police fought the rioters? It was the armed citizen. Riots are rare; what about the rest of the time? The U.S. Bureau of Justice Statistics, in their National Crime Victimization Survey, frequently estimate defensive gun use at a little over 100,000 times per year,

---

[53] Webster's 1828 Dictionary http://webstersdictionary1828.com.

and that is the low end of the range for similar studies. Also, it doesn't take into account other arms like knives, pepper spray, and stun devices. If at least 100,000 people a year protect themselves using firearms, does that not show how the right to keep and bear arms is necessary to the security of a free state?

Another situation where a militia is necessary to the security of a free state: When government is corrupt. I wrote an article for the website entitled "The Battle of Athens, TN" where I tell the story of the 1946 election and how a group of WWII veterans used their right to keep and bear arms to expose and stop election fraud and racketeering in their county. Appeals to both state and federal authorities for help went unanswered, leaving the citizens as the only line of defense. While the Battle of Athens, TN was an extreme example, watching mayors and governors ordering police to not engage with violent criminals makes me wonder how long before the people will need to take up arms for their own defense.

Lastly, if a state is to be free, it cannot be a vassal of another government. While states today have submitted themselves to the control of the federal government (in violation of the Constitution), if they are not to be vassals, they must be able to defend themselves. If Congress can call up a state's organized militia, how is a state to defend itself? The answer is the unorganized militia.

Right of The People

> *the right of the people to keep and bear*
> *Arms, shall not be infringed.*

Now, for the command part of the amendment. It seems simple to me, but apparently a lot of people are confused by this part of the amendment.

The People

Back to those who claim the Second Amendment only applies to the militia. Even though the unorganized militia consists of all able-bodied people, the Second Amendment clearly states that it's the right of the people. Nowhere else in the Constitution does the term "the people" refer to anything but the individual citizen.

> *The House of Representatives shall be composed of Members chosen every second Year by the People of the several States[54]*

> *or the right of the people peaceably to assemble[55]*

> *The right of the people to be secure in their persons, houses, papers, and effects, against unreasonable searches and seizures, shall not be violated[56]*

> *The enumeration in the Constitution, of certain rights, shall not be construed to deny or disparage others retained by the people[57]*

> *The powers not delegated to the United States by the Constitution, nor prohibited by it to the States, are reserved to the States respectively, or to the people[58]*

If these other references to "the people" mean individuals, why would it mean something different in this one amendment? The short answer is because people are looking for justification for their position rather than what the Constitution says. Otherwise, only certain people

---

54   United States Constitution Article I, Section 2.
55   United States Constitution Amendment I.
56   United States Constitution Amendment IV.
57   United States Constitution Amendment IX.
58   United States Constitution Amendment X.

would have the right to assemble, only special people would have the right against unreasonable search and seizure, and rights would only be reserved to the elite.

Keep and Bear Arms

I remember talking with one person who stated quite bluntly that we don't have the right to carry a firearm. I asked him simply, "What do you think the word 'bear' means, an animal in the woods?" You have the right to own and carry arms for the simple reason it is necessary to maintain a free state.

Notice it does not say "firearm" but arms. That includes knives, swords, and chemical sprays; in fact, it includes anything that can be considered a weapon. We talk about gun control laws, but what about knife control laws or laws against carrying pepper spray or stun guns? Did you know that in the state of New York, it is illegal to carry a knife that can be opened one handed?

Shall No Be Infringed

"Shall not" is a simple, obligatory statement, yet people and governments repeatedly find ways to infringe on our rights and get courts to agree with them. As George Orwell said, "There are some ideas so absurd that only an intellectual could believe them." The Second Amendment doesn't say maybe not, or should not, it says shall not. That means any infringement on our right to keep and bear arms is a violation of the right protected by the Second Amendment and is therefore illegal. What does it mean to infringe?

> INFRINGE: 1. To break, as contracts; to violate, either positively by contravention, or negatively by non-fulfillment or neglect of performance.
>
> 2. To break; to violate; to transgress; to neglect to fulfill or obey; as, to infringe a law.

3. To destroy or hinder; as, to infringe efficacy.[59]

To break, violate, destroy, or hinder. What does this say about states that make it almost impossible for someone to own a gun or carry a firearm, knife, or pepper spray? What about limiting what guns they can own or how much ammunition they carry? Courts have issued opinions that, as long as there is some way to carry a firearm, your rights haven't been infringed, but that doesn't match the plain English language used in the Constitution.

Back to Basic English

Speaking of plain English, if we look at the language used in this amendment it is very simple. The militia, which consists of all able-bodied citizens, is necessary for a state to remain free. We the people individually have the right both to own (keep) and carry (bear) arms. While this seems plain and simple, there is one other argument used against our rights.

Hyperbole and Straw-men

It seems the argument of last resort against the Second Amendment is to use hyperbole and straw-men.

> *HYPERBOLE: In rhetoric, a figure of speech which expresses much more or less than the truth, or which represents things much greater or less, better or worse than they really are. An object uncommon in size, either great or small, strikes us with surprise, and this emotion produces a momentary conviction that the object is greater or less than it is in reality.*[60]

---

[59] Webster's 1828 Dictionary http://webstersdictionary1828.com.
[60] Webster's 1828 Dictionary http://webstersdictionary1828.com.

I've heard a lot of hyperbolic arguments against the plain reading of the Second Amendment. By far the most ridiculous was a question posed during my first Constitution Study: "What about nuclear arms? Do you think someone should be allowed to own a nuclear weapon?" My guess is that the person believed there were arms so powerful and so destructive they should not be in the hands of the public. But is that what the Constitution says?

We should start by going back to our original discussion about rights. Remember, we define a right as something a person possesses and can only be legitimately used when it does not infringe on the rights of others. While I understood the person's point, if I cannot think of any legitimate reason someone would want to own a nuclear weapon, does my reasoning determine someone's right? Since the Constitution not only recognizes our right to keep and bear arms, but protects it by specifying that it shall not be infringed, it is not up to me to determine what arms you may or may not possess. It is constitutional to own a nuclear bomb, as long as the owner doesn't infringe the rights of others.

> *STRAW MAN: a weak or imaginary*
> *opposition (such as an argument or adversary)*
> *set up only to be easily confuted*[61]

The other argument, when all else fails, is to come up with ridiculous situations and use those extremely unlikely situations to justify the infringement of others' rights. I've heard people say, "If a citizen uses a firearm to defend themselves, they may injure or kill an innocent bystander!" Of course, lost in that argument is the fact that for people to legally defend themselves with lethal force there must be an imminent threat of death or serious injury to an innocent party. In other words, their life is already in danger.

I remember after the Sandy Hook mass-murder, a school in Staten Island wanted to place armed retired New York Police Department

---

[61] Merriam-Webster's Online Dictionary https://www.merriam-webster.com.

officers in the schools for security. Parents went to the media terrified that a retired police office, in the stressful situation of a mass shooting, might shoot an innocent child. Let's think about that for a moment. Your child is in school and his or her life is being threatened by a criminal, possibly deranged person, but these parents don't want an armed retired police officer to protect their child; they'd rather wait for an armed active duty police officer to arrive. I don't mean to demean the pain of anyone who has lost a loved one to any form of illegal violence, but would the parents in this situation feel better if their child was killed by a criminal while they were waiting for an armed officer to respond? No, it's a straw man, one in a long line of ridiculous statements trying to justify their own fears and ignorance about firearms and personal safety.

People Don't Need . . .

While hyperbole and straw men may be the most ridiculous objection to our rights, they are not the most prevalent. I often hear it said "people don't need . . ." such and such item. It could be "assault weapons" (which is a made-up term used to scare people), 30 round magazines, hollow-point bullets. or even semi-automatic rifles. I've even heard gun people say people don't need "one of those". We live in America, which I thought was a free country. So, if I don't infringe on another's legitimate rights, I can own and carry any weapon I want. If I want to walk through downtown with a fully-automatic pistol, a suppressed AR-15, a Celtic broad sword, a mace, and a giant canister of pepper spray while dragging a cannon and a catapult behind me, nothing should stop me until I threaten someone. (Carrying a weapon in public is not threatening someone, nor does it infringe on anyone's legitimate rights, since the right to "not see weapons" must, by definition, infringe on someone's recognized right to bear arms.)

The problem is, it seems to be human nature to define right and acceptable by our own standards, along with a desire to force others to live the way we think they should, but that's not the way rights work. I have no right to tell someone else how to live or what they can do unless what they are doing violates a legitimate right of my own. The ability to tell someone else how to live, and to impose my view on others who have done me no harm, is not liberty, and it's not freedom; it is tyranny, plain and simple.

I think we've been so poisoned by the "gun-control" propaganda that we've lost sight of what our rights are and how they can be exercised. The idea that people might want to carry a tool to protect their own safety has become "uncivilized", but that is a relatively new development in this nation. There's a reason, until recently, you used to be able to buy a gun in the hardware store, order one through the mail, or carry your hunting rifle to school. Any weapon is a tool, but it does not possess intent on its own. It is only when a human being uses that tool that they bring intent to the situation, and its intent and actions that infringe on rights, not tools or inanimate objects.

Also on the subject of liberty, why is punishing the innocent the proper way to deal with criminal behavior? If the purpose of government is to secure our rights, how can it be a legitimate function for said government to restrict the rights of those who have violated no law, in the name of reducing crime? Again, that is not liberty, it is tyranny.

I am repeatedly told I must sacrifice my rights because someone might do something bad. I'm told I can't have certain guns and accessories because someone might use them to do harm. (Oddly enough, rarely would those restrictions hinder someone with criminal intent.) I cannot take my personal protection tools to certain locations because someone may commit a crime there. I have never threatened or hurt someone with a weapon in my life, yet there are those, both inside the various governments of this nation and outside them, who feel they have the right not only to infringe on my liberty but to infringe on my rights because they are afraid that I, or someone like me, might do something bad. By that logic we should ban the printing press, free speech, the media, and all public assemblies, because someone MIGHT say or do something bad.

The next time you hear someone claim we must do something that infringes on someone's rights in the name of security, remind them the infringement of one right leads to the infringement of all rights, including their own right to make such a statement.

> *"They who would give up an essential liberty for*
> *temporary security, deserve neither liberty or security."*
>
> *–Benjamin Franklin*

Conclusion

Today's discussions around the second amendment focuses on the use or control of firearms, but the focus of this amendment is American's right to protect their own freedom. Whether it's protecting yourself and your family, or protecting your state, our individual right to keep and bear arms of all kinds is unique in the world. Rather than looking for how or under what circumstances we can infringe on them, maybe we should return to the original intent of our Founding Fathers and focus on keeping ourselves free. Only then, when we are free to provide for our own safety will we truly be free. Instead, we are told to depend on government to provide for our safety, making us vassals of the entities we created. Maybe that is why so many work so hard to find ways to infringe on this right.

Amendment III

No Soldier shall, in time of peace be quartered in any house, without the consent of the Owner, nor in time of war, but in a manner to be prescribed by law.

We aren't being forced to quarter soldiers, but this amendment is important for us to study. While the First Amendment focused on conscience and the Second on security, the Third Amendment begins to enshrine the idea of private property into the Constitution. What I see here is not only a protection of your home, but also the idea that you not only own your home, but have control over it. If the government wants to house soldiers in your home, they need your consent.

Why is this important? Imagine what would happen if government quartered soldiers in your home. How willing would you be to speak freely knowing a soldier could be reporting what you say to their superiors? Would your right to keep and bear arms be of any use with armed military in every household?

Remember, when this amendment was adopted, we didn't fly soldiers into fire-bases, or even drive them to the front; armies marched wherever they needed to go. We all (hopefully) remember the facts of the winter at Valley Forge. Would it be surprising that an army on the march, especially in winter, would see value in housing its soldiers in warm buildings rather than cold tents? The one exception to this limitation is in time of war, but even then, the military has to abide by the laws created by the peoples' and the states' representatives. This amendment means the military cannot invade your private property except in the circumstance of war, and then only based on laws created by your representatives.

Conclusion

If a man's home is his castle, then he must be in control of it. Let's not skip over this amendment because it's not immediately obvious why it matters today. Instead, let's take to heart this idea of owning and controlling property and that the purpose of government is to protect that right, not to infringe on it.

Amendment IV

The right of the people to be secure in their persons, houses, papers, and effects, against unreasonable searches and seizures, shall not be violated, and no Warrants shall issue, but upon probable cause, supported by Oath or affirmation, and particularly describing the place to be searched, and the persons or things to be seized.

The right of the people to be secure in their persons, houses, papers, and effects shall not be violated. Think about what this is saying: You have the RIGHT to be secure from unreasonable government search or seizure. The government cannot invade your house, confiscate your effects, or accost your person without a warrant, with some reasonable exceptions.

Unreasonable Search and Seizure

What is an unreasonable search or seizure? The answer is in the text: One without a valid warrant or reasonable grounds why a warrant could not be procured in a sufficiently timely manner. (We'll talk more about what is required for a warrant to be valid later in this chapter.) I'm sure you've all watched a police drama at some point it your life, and you know that the police cannot search your home without a warrant. Did you realize that NO government official can even enter your home without your permission unless they have a valid warrant? That means any government representative, from law enforcement to code enforcement, or from dog catcher to child welfare, cannot legally enter your home without your permission unless they have a valid warrant.

Before we declared independence, British officials would routinely search people's homes and businesses using "writs of assistance". Merriam-Webster's defines a writ of assistance as "a writ used especially in colonial America authorizing a law officer to search in unspecified locations for unspecified illegal goods".[62] Imagine having your house invaded by government officers without limit, your property searched and even destroyed, all based on a judge's suspicion that you might have done something wrong but without any evidence. This happened to Mr. Entick in Middlesex England in 1765. His house was invaded, his property destroyed and confiscated. The use and abuse of these general-warrants led our Founding Fathers to create the Fourth Amendment to protect us from the government fishing around in our lives, looking for something with which to charge us. In the colonies, James Otis railed against the practice of writs of assistance in his speech "James Otis: Against Writs of Assistance".

> *And I take this opportunity to declare, that ... I will to my dying day oppose, with all the powers and faculties God has given me, all such instruments of slavery on the one hand, and villainy on the other, as this writ of assistance is. It appears to me ... the worst instrument of arbitrary power, the most destructive of English liberty, and the fundamental principles of the constitution, that ever was found in an English law-book.[63]*

These protections have been under assault for many decades, in a doctrine known as the "reasonableness exception" to the Fourth Amendment. The supreme Court has found that warrantless police action may comply with the Fourth Amendment if it is reasonable under

---

[62] Merriam-Webster's Online Dictionary https://www.merriam-webster.com.

[63] "James Otis: Against Writs of Assistance" - http://www.azquotes.com/quote/892998.

the circumstances. Why did the supreme Court find this way? According to FindLaw.com "The exceptions made to the Fourth Amendment's warrant requirement reflect the Court's reluctance to unduly impede the job of law enforcement officials."[64] However, the purpose of government is to protect the rights of its citizens[65], not make government officials' lives easier. This is a perfect example of why every citizen needs to read and understand our Constitution, to protect us from such foolish, or dare I say criminal, abuse of a public position. I can understand to some degree, that there are situations where getting a warrant before taking someone into custody would be unreasonable. For example, the arrest of someone caught in the act of a felony. However, I'm also sure our Founding Fathers would not find all of what the supreme Court finds "reasonable."

The Supreme Court's Opinion of Reasonableness

What does the supreme Court find reasonable? According to FindLaw.com there are seven situations where either a search or seizure without a warrant is considered "reasonable":

1. A warrant is not required for a felony arrest in a public place or if the officer is in "hot pursuit" of a fleeing felon. This makes sense to me as you can't ask a felon, especially one that is running away, to wait while you get a warrant. If, however, there was time for law enforcement to get a warrant but didn't, to me that is not reasonable.
2. During a lawful arrest, an officer may search the person and immediate vicinity of the suspect. This is justified on the grounds that it is necessary for the officer to protect himself or herself from hidden weapons. To that extent this, too, makes sense, if the arrest itself is legal, including constitutionally.

---

[64] FindLaw https://criminal.findlaw.com.
[65] Declaration of Independence paragraph 2.

3. Automobiles may be stopped if the officer has a "reasonable and articulable suspicion" that the motorist has violated a traffic law. The question here again is how do you define reasonable? Wouldn't different people define reasonable differently? Would an officer that knows you're a "lead-foot" have a reasonable suspicion that you had violated a traffic law? Once stopped, the officer can search the inside of the vehicle but not the trunk, unless the officer has "probable cause" to believe it contains contraband. However, Merriam-Webster's Dictionary defines probable cause as "a reasonable ground for supposing that a charge is well-founded"[66]. Once again, we're back to what is reasonable and, more importantly, who must prove the cause is reasonable. An officer can say he or she smelled alcohol or you seem impaired, but where is the requirement that the officer show proof? If it's a you-said vs officer-said, what makes the officer's word more valid than yours?

4. If an officer reasonably believes that criminal conduct is happening in public, he or she may stop the suspected participant and conduct a limited search of the suspect's outer clothing for weapons. The officer may ask for identification, but the suspect is not technically required to provide it. I say "technically" because refusal to provide identification can be used to support probable cause for arrest (as in Officer says: "No, you don't have to give me ID. I'll just arrest you!")

    While this is colloquially called "Stop and Frisk," it is more accurately called a "Terry Stop" or "Terry Frisk" from the supreme Court case "TERRY v. OHIO (1968)".[67] In this case, Terry and two others were stopped and searched by a Cleveland, OH detective after he observed what he described as suspicious behavior. The court found that what the detective found during

---

[66]   Merriam Webster's Online Dictionary https://www.merriam-webster.com.

[67]   Find Law https://caselaw.findlaw.com/us-supreme-court/392/1.html.

the search could be used as evidence against the plaintiffs since the search was done during a lawful arrest.

My concern is not so much with the search, or even the eligibility of evidence in this case, but whether calling for a stop because of what a law enforcement officer believes is suspicious behavior is a lawful arrest. What one person calls suspicious another may reasonably call being prepared or aware. Mr. Terry was stopped because he and his cohorts were observed repeatedly returning to a store window to stare inside, and to me that does seem somewhat suspicious.

However, when I was a child living in New York City, I was taught to regularly brush my hip pocket to make sure my wallet was still there and discourage potential pick-pockets from targeting me. Would that type of activity, frequently referred to as a smuggler's move, be considered suspicious by someone who didn't grow up in a big city? Besides that, when in public, I like to sit where I can observe the entrances. Would someone consider that suspicious?

So, if a court decides that the officer did not have sufficient reason to make the stop, where does the victim of an illegal stop go to get his or her time and money back? How are law enforcement officers to know what any one judge may find reasonable vs unreasonable? How can someone exercising his or her right not to provide ID or continue an interview with minimal evidence and no warrant, have it considered "probable cause" that they have committed a crime?

5. Exigent circumstances may justify a warrantless search. (Exigent: "circumstances that are of such urgency as to justify a warrantless entry, search, or seizure by police when a warrant would ordinarily be required".[68]) For there to be exigent circumstances, the situation must be so urgent that waiting for

---

[68] Find Law - https://dictionary.findlaw.com/definition/exigent-circumstances.html.

a warrant would be unreasonable, such as shots being fired, screams being heard, or fire coming from a building.

Once again, we're back to proof of exigent circumstances. The vast majority of law enforcement officers are honest and hard-working people. However, every department I know has some sort of oversight group, internal affairs, or office of professional conduct, because they know that some officers will not be honest. Is that same consideration given to the alleged criminal? Are their rights protected as strongly as the officers? On the other side, I'm sure most people do not want the scales of justice tilted so far in favor of the defendant that justice cannot be found for the victim.

6. Roadside checkpoints to find illegal aliens or drunk drivers have been found to be reasonable exceptions to our Fourth Amendment protections. However, the court has also found that checkpoints to detect ordinary criminal activity to be unconstitutional. This is a blatant violation of our Fourth Amendment protected rights since being stopped and potentially searched without a legitimate warrant or reasonable and articulable suspicion of exigent circumstances is, by definition, unreasonable. None of us want drunk drivers on the roads. Then again, none of us want criminals to break into our homes either. I doubt you would find it reasonable for government officials to enter your home to check to see if criminals are inside though, so why should we find it reasonable for them to search our vehicles without cause?

7. Searches, seizures, and arrests made pursuant to a defective warrant may be justified if the officer was proceeding in "good faith".[69] In other words, if the officer believes they have a valid warrant but it is later found that the warrant is invalid, the search, seizure, or arrest is still considered valid. In UNITED

---

[69] Find Law - https://criminal.findlaw.com/criminal-rights/the-fourth-amendment-reasonableness-requirement.html.

STATES v. LEON (1984) the court found "An examination of the Fourth Amendment's origin and purposes makes clear that the use of fruits of a past unlawful search or seizure works no new Fourth Amendment wrong."[70] In other words, the police can illegally search your place, then use whatever they find in court as long as they "thought" it was legal. By that logic, when a criminal steals your car and sells it, they should be allowed to keep the proceeds since the "fruits of a past unlawful" act should not color the legality of subsequent acts.

Founding Father's Opinion on Reasonableness

How did those who wrote and ratified this language define reasonable? According to the 1828 edition of Webster's Dictionary, reasonable is defined as "Having the faculty of reason; endued with reason"; and "Conformable or agreeable to reason; just; rational."[71] Based on this, something is reasonable when it is clothed (endued[72]) with reason, just, and rational. The questions I like to ask myself when trying to decide if something is legally reasonable are: "Is it just?" "Does it conform to rules of justice?" "Does it equally apply justice to all involved?"[73] Lastly, "How would I react if it happened to me?" If "governments are instituted among men to secure [the citizen's] rights," then shouldn't "reasonable" favor the citizen over the government?

The Difference Between the Two

It seems clear to me, based on my reading of the Constitution, our Founding Fathers' opinion and the supreme Court's opinion on the different perspectives of reasonableness can be boiled down to who is being protected. Our Constitution is designed to protect the citizen from the intrusions of government. A search or seizure is reasonable if it is just

---

[70] *United States v. Leon* (1984) No. 82-1771 summary 1(a).

[71] Webster's 1828 Dictionary http://webstersdictionary1828.com.

[72] IBID

[73] IBID

and protects the rights of the citizen. Meanwhile, the supreme Court, and in fact government in general, find a search or seizure reasonable if it makes the government representatives' lives easier. I'm reminded again of the quote attributed to Thomas Jefferson, "When governments fear the people, there is liberty. When the people fear the government, there is tyranny."

Legitimate Warrant

In order to get a warrant, the government has to provide two main things: Cause and scope.

Cause

> *no Warrants shall issue, but upon probable*
> *cause, supported by Oath or affirmation*

Once again, we have "probable cause", which I've shown previously to be defined as "a reasonable ground for supposing that a charge is well-founded".[74] What is important here is that the cause MUST be supported by oath or affirmation. (As a side bar, the phrase "by oath or affirmation" is a nod to religious freedom, since some religions do not allow their adherents to swear an oath.) In other words, a warrant cannot be issued unless someone states the cause and does so publicly. Why is this important? Why must there be a public statement of why the warrant is being issued? Because who says you've done something wrong can be as important as what they claim you've done. An estranged spouse, disgruntled former employee, or political opponent, may have a viewpoint that sees the worst in you and assumes anything you're doing is nefarious. It is also quite reasonable that someone with this point of view might have less than honorable reasons for swearing out a warrant against you. So to protect your rights as the accused, not only the what but the who of the accusation must be given before the warrant is issued.

---

[74]   Merriam-Webster's Online Dictionary https://merriam-webster.com.

Scope

*and particularly describing the place to be
searched, and the persons or things to be seized.*

The warrant must be specific about what or who is to be searched or seized. Why so specific about what must be included in the warrant? The answer is to avoid the British practice at the time for "general warrants". US Legal, Inc defines a general warrant as "a warrant providing a law-enforcement officer with broad discretion or authority to search and seize unspecified places or persons."[75] In colonial times, British soldiers and officers would be issued warrants to search homes, farms, and I believe even whole towns, looking for "contraband". Imagine living your life where a law enforcement officers could show up at your door with a general warrant, search anywhere they want, for anything they want, trying to find something for which to arrest you.

Third-Party Doctrine

The supreme Court has held that a person has no legitimate expectation of privacy, and therefore no Fourth Amendment protections, for information they willingly expose to a third-party. Referred to as the "Third-Party Doctrine", this attempt to describe the limits of the Fourth Amendment has been used as a modern-day equivalent of a "general warrant".

In the supreme Court case *Katz v. United States*, the concurring opinion of Justice Harlan included:

> "What a person knowingly exposes to the
> public, even in his own home or office, is not a
> subject of Fourth Amendment protection."[76]

---

[75] US Legal https://uslegal.com.

[76] *Katz v. United States*, 389 U.S. 347 (1967) - https://supreme.justia.com/cases/federal/us/389/347/case.html.

This idea that what you knowingly make public does not fall under your Fourth Amendment protection did not originate with Katz. Instead, Katz is the logical conclusion of previous rulings that the police can use publicly available information in their investigations.

In the 20th century, the court found in several cases that recordings of undercover agents did not violate the defendant's Fourth Amendment rights since they were not being used to intercept communication, but to validate the testimony of the agent.

Then, in the 1976 case *Miller v. United States*, the court found that providing the records and documents necessary to do business with a bank (checks, deposit slips, and statements) was exposing them to the banks employees and taking the risk that they could reveal them to the government.

> *The Fourth Amendment does not prohibit the*
> *obtaining of information revealed to a third party*
> *and conveyed by him to Government authorities.[77]*

A similar case in 1979, *Smith v. Maryland*, involving the recording of phone numbers dialed, expanded the third-party doctrine.

> *First, we doubt that people in general entertain*
> *any actual expectation of privacy in the numbers*
> *they dial. All telephone users realize that they*
> *must "convey" phone numbers to the telephone*
> *company, since it is through telephone company*
> *switching equipment that their calls are completed.*
> *All subscribers realize, moreover, that the phone*
> *company has facilities for making permanent records*

---

[77]   *United States v. Miller*, 425 U.S. 435 (1976) - https://supreme.justia.com/cases/federal/us/425/435/case.html.

> *of the numbers they dial, for they see a list of their
> long-distance (toll) calls on their monthly bills.*[78]

These two cases together show the foundation of the third-party doctrine. According to the court, the fact that you know that the businesses you deal with keeps records of your transactions with them is sufficient for you to assume the risk that they *may* make them public, thereby making any search of those records reasonable. The Smith court doubted you would have any expectation that the telephone company, while using the records they collect for their own business purposes, would not share them with others. Recent controversies regarding the federal government collection of telephone metadata shows that, in this opinion, the court was wrong. People in general do not expect companies they do business with to share their records without the permission of the parties involved.

> *even if petitioner did harbor some subjective
> expectation of privacy, this expectation was not one
> that society is prepared to recognize as "reasonable."*[79]

Apparently, even if you have an expectation of privacy, the court can determine if society (or more accurately, if the court) will recognize that as reasonable.

Subsequent cases in the federal court system have expanded the use of the third-party doctrine to most modern-day communications, making what appears to be an arbitrary distinction between content and non-content parts of communication. What you emailed to your mother is protected by the Fourth Amendment, but the fact that you emailed your mother on her birthday is fair game. While there is some rationale for the distinction that the content of your communication is

---

[78]   *Smith v. Maryland*, 442 U.S. 735 (1979) - https://supreme.justia.com/cases/federal/us/442/735/case.html.

[79]   *United States v. Miller*, 425 U.S. 435 (1976) - https://supreme.justia.com/cases/federal/us/425/435/case.html.

private while the information needed to deliver it is not, especially to those who are more familiar with snail mail than email, the amount of data collected about us by phone companies, Internet Service Providers, and application developers and retailers (both physical and virtual), makes this a distinction with little difference. Modern big-data analytics can probably learn more about you from this metadata than from the content of your messages. This brings up a couple of interesting questions: What belongs to you? And what expectation of privacy do you have when dealing with other private entities?

Over the last several years, there has been a lot of discussion about whether the federal government's collection of "your" phone and internet records (metadata) is a violation of your rights protected by the Fourth Amendment. Are those records yours? Take your telephone call records. You sign a contract with a phone company to provide you with a service for phone calls. As part of this service, the phone company must keep track of what calls you make and how long they last. In the case of a cell phones, they track what towers the call ran through, and to assist us in an emergency, we've asked the phone company, through our legislatures, to include GPS information collected from the call. (This was to help 911 dispatchers to direct emergency services to the correct location in the event of an emergency call from a cell phone, since, unlike a landline, it is not tied to a physical location.)

I'm sure we can all agree that this information is *about* you, but is it *your* information? Did you create this information? Yes, you made the phone call, but you didn't record the information about that call; you expected the phone company to do so. And yes, you wrote, addressed, and sent an email, but you expected your Internet Service Provider (ISP) to use the "send to" information to direct the email correctly. So the claim that this is, in fact, your information is false, since you didn't record any of this information; a private entity (your phone company or ISP) did.

This brings up whether your expectations are that the private entities you do business with will keep the information they have about you private. Have any of us read the "Terms & Conditions" page when we install software on our computers or sign up for a new service? How about the privacy policy of the websites we do business with? Me neither. However, that legal contract determines the companies' requirements to keep information about you safe and what expectations of privacy you legally have.

When the government presents a subpoena to your phone company, ISP, or bank, requesting their records about the transactions you've had with them, they must decide how to respond to it. Since they have no vested interest in keeping information about you private and have no wish to go through the expense and hassle of requiring a warrant (not to mention other possible repercussions), most companies simply turn over the data. This may be a violation of their terms and conditions or their privacy policy, but that is a matter of contract law, not a Constitutional one. You can sue them for damages, but the cost of that litigation to a major company is nothing when compared to fighting the government in court, or worse, fighting a vindictive bureaucracy that has taxpayer money to support it and no individual accountability.

Between the questionable ownership of these records and the dramatic disparity of the consequences, is there any wonder almost everyone from phone companies to online retailers simply turn over records when faced with a subpoena? Even so, there is one area where the federal government has dealt with the privacy issue of information about you: HIPAA.

Health Insurance Portability and Accountability Act

Passed by Congress and signed into law by President Clinton in 1996, and better known as HIPAA, this law was an attempt by the federal government to deal with issues of coverage, privacy, security, and fraud in the healthcare industry. (If you're thinking that the Constitution does not give Congress the authority to pass laws regarding healthcare, then congratulations, you're starting to think like a Constitutional Patriot!)

The privacy aspects of this law focused mainly on concerns that with the advent of electronic medical records, the risk of those records being compromised would greatly increase. HIPAA privacy rules also established guidelines for when and how healthcare information can be shared. (Most of the summary information I've found about HIPAA refers to a "person's healthcare information". However, the law defines healthcare information as information "created or received by" various healthcare professionals. This language shows that the information is about the patient, but it is not owned by the patient.)

As with most laws, especially federal laws created outside the pursuance of the Constitution (Article VI, Paragraph 2), this act created a bloated, complicated, and extremely costly solution to what was a relatively simple problem to fix. Instead of recognizing that custody of records about an individual or entity should be shared between the private parties involved, Congress created a gigantic bureaucracy and regulatory system, a system that costs (and continues to cost) healthcare providers billions of dollars every year in compliance alone. Yet this system did little to either protect a person's privacy or facilitate their ability to share information among those who should legitimately have access to it. In other words, rather than addressing a simple shortcoming in the Fourth Amendment, Congress took a mess and made it bigger, slower, and more expensive. The next time you have to fill out that HIPAA notice for the umpteenth time, or have to jump through hoops just to get your spouse's or child's test results, you can thank Congress.

Solving the Third-party Doctrine issue

While the fix to the third-party doctrine is simple, I doubt I will see it happen in my lifetime, because it would require Congress and the states to willingly give up governmental power. My recommendation is an amendment to the Constitution to expand Fourth Amendment protection to include information created for or about private individuals or entities.

The right of the people to be secure in their
persons, houses, <u>documents,</u> papers, and effects,
<u>including data and records created by them or</u>

> *about them,* against unreasonable searches and
> seizures, shall not be violated, (emphasis mine)

This simple change would mean your emails, text messages, medical records, and buying habits could not be turned over to, searched, or reviewed by government officials unless you voluntarily turned them over to a government entity or they obtained a legitimate warrant. In other words, your medical test results would be private unless you gave access to Medicare or Medicaid. Since these are government entities, any information handed over to them becomes public record and subject to government rules about information sharing. It also means that data recorded about you, like phone, ISP, or bank records, and data collected by the apps we all have on our phones, would require a warrant for the government to have access to them. By including "data ... created by them," storing your documents in the cloud would no longer expose them to warrantless government search.

Civil Asset Forfeiture

> *Under state and federal civil asset forfeiture laws,*
> *law enforcement agencies can seize and keep*
> *property suspected of involvement in criminal*
> *activity. Unlike criminal asset forfeiture, with civil*
> *forfeiture, a property owner need not be found*
> *guilty of a crime—or even charged—to permanently*
> *lose her cash, car, home or other property*[80]

The most serious abuse of the Fourth Amendment I can think of in the 21st century is civil asset forfeiture. Condemned by the ACLU, Cato Institute, and National Review, this set of local and federal laws allow property to be seized simply for being suspected of being involved in a

---

[80]   Policing for Profit the Abuse of Civil Asset Forfeiture by Marian R. Williams, Ph.D. Jefferson E. Holcomb, Ph.D. Tomislav V. Kovandzic, Ph.D. Scott Bullock. Institution for Justice.

crime. Put another way, if a law enforcement officer can make a "reasonable" assertion that he or she suspect your property was involved in a crime, it is taken and sold without you even being charged with a crime. No warrant, no due process, and no "innocent until proven guilty," just the raw application of police state power. And it's all being done under the guise of keeping you safe. To add insult to injury, most of these laws are written in such a way as to encourage governments to steal your assets.

In the case *United States v. Seventeen Thousand Nine Hundred Dollars in United States Currency,* New York couple Angela Rodriguez and Joyce Copeland lost the above-mentioned $17,900 to police in a case in which no charges were ever filed against them. (And if the thought that a specific amount of money can be party to a crime doesn't make your head explode, I don't know what will.) When they sued to recover their money, a federal court found they lacked standing to sue for possession of their own assets.

Imagine police taking your money (or your car, your house, or any other asset) without charging you with any crime. They make you sue to get your money back, only to have a court tell you that you don't have the authority to sue to get your own money back. Does that sound like a reasonable seizure? But what is a citizen to do, when we've turned our Constitution over to acolytes of "justice," as well as all the tools to keep our governments in check.

Conclusion

Ultimately, the question of cause and scope comes down to the interpretation of a judge. A judge determines if the stated evidence meets the requirements for probable cause, a judge will decide if the description of the items to be seized and places to be searched are sufficiently specific and, of course, it is at the discretion of a judge whether it is even reasonable for a warrant to be required. Those we have elected to represent us not only do not fulfill their responsibility to keep the judicial branch in check through oversight and impeachment, but they pass laws that take our most basic concepts of justice, reasonable seizures, legitimate warrants, and due process, and throw them out the window. And what do We the People do? Nothing!

Since our elected officials seem reluctant to hold our judges accountable, we've seen our Fourth Amendment protections erode to the point that our protections are in the hands of a judge and not the Constitution or the actual law of the land. Now does that sound reasonable to you?

Amendment V

No person shall be held to answer for a capital, or otherwise infamous crime, unless on a presentment or indictment of a Grand Jury, except in cases arising in the land or naval forces, or in the Militia, when in actual service in time of War or public danger; nor shall any person be subject for the same offense to be twice put in jeopardy of life or limb; nor shall be compelled in any criminal case to be a witness against himself, nor be deprived of life, liberty, or property, without due process of law; nor shall private property be taken for public use, without just compensation.

We've all heard about someone "pleading the fifth", but what does that mean? It means they are invoking their Fifth Amendment protected right against self-incrimination. The Fifth Amendment doesn't say that though, and besides, it includes so much more.

The Grand Jury

No person shall be held to answer for a capital, or otherwise infamous crime, unless on a presentment or indictment of a Grand Jury,

You cannot be taken to court for a capital or infamous crime without the indictment of a Grand Jury. What is a Grand Jury?

Grand Jury: A panel of citizens that is convened by a court to decide whether it is appropriate for the government to indict (proceed with a prosecution against) someone suspected of a crime.[81]

The job of a Grand Jury is to review the government's case and determine if it is appropriate for them to proceed with prosecution or if the prosecution is malicious. (This is opposed to a trial jury, which determines if the accused is guilty.) We see here that once again our Founding Fathers put the people above the government. The government can investigate and put a case together, but in the case of a serious crime it's still up to We the People to determine if their case has sufficient merit to proceed with prosecution. The ordinary citizens of the Grand Jury also have the responsibility to determine if the case is so bad the government lawyers should be indicted themselves (a presentment).

I've heard it said that a good prosecutor can get a Grand Jury to indict a ham sandwich. This is another of those truisms that shows just how little Americans know about the system created under our Constitution and the rights and responsibilities they have. Put yourself in this situation: The government has investigated you for some crime, they've put together their case, and got a prosecutor to file charges. Now it's in the hands of the Grand Jury. This group of ordinary citizens are charged with reviewing the government's case and determining whether it is sufficient to disrupt your life, put you through the emotional and financial turmoil of putting up a defense, and possibly throwing your family into chaos, all with the possibility of jail time or worse. Now imagine you have been called for this duty. Do you think it should be so easy to convince you to prosecute someone that you would indict "a ham sandwich"?

If indicting someone is so upsetting to their lives, why is it so easy for it to happen? I believe it's because most Americans neither know nor care about the responsibilities they have as citizens and especially

---

[81]   The Free Legal Dictionary https://legal-dictionary.thefreedictionary.com.

as members of a jury. The role of the Grand Jury is to be a check on government's prosecutors' power, and they are there to help ensure that nuisance, libelous, or malicious cases are not allowed to proceed and injure innocent people.

Have you ever heard the saying, "You're not tried by a jury of your peers, but by 12 people who couldn't figure out how to get out of jury duty?" Let's face it, most of us don't like jury duty; it's time consuming, disruptive to our lives, and generally something we'd rather not do. What happens when you are the defendant though, and find out that nobody with a basic understanding of the law and the Constitution could be bothered to serve on your jury? When the government brings serious charges against you, your life is literally in the hands of these people. Think about that the next time you receive that jury summons.

Double Jeopardy

> *nor shall any person be subject for the same offense*
> *to be twice put in jeopardy of life or limb;*

How many chances does the government get to prosecute you for the same crime? The answer is once, mostly. There are two important phrases in the text we need to understand if we are to be good citizens.

Jeopardy

The first question that needs to be answered in a question of double jeopardy is when are you put in jeopardy?

> *For jury trials, jeopardy attaches when the jury*
> *is sworn. In criminal cases tried by a judge*
> *without a jury, jeopardy attaches when the first*
> *witness is sworn in. If a defendant enters a plea*
> *agreement with the prosecution, jeopardy does*
> *not attach until the court accepts the plea.*[82]

---

[82]   Find Law https://findlaw.com.

Once the jury or first witness is sworn in, you are officially in jeopardy, or in legal terms, "jeopardy attaches." Of course, when jeopardy stops is just as important to understand as when it begins. Jeopardy ends when you are acquitted, the charges are dismissed, the court grants a mistrial, or you appeal a conviction. Once jeopardy attaches, you cannot be tried or even arrested for the same offense. This does not mean you cannot be sued for the action for which you were just acquitted. There is a difference between criminal trials and civil suits. We will talk more about suits in the chapter on the 7th Amendment.

Life or limb

Does the term "life or limb" mean that double jeopardy is only related to capital crimes or to other offenses that threaten life or body? You might think so, but ask yourself what is, "jeopardy of life or limb"? When your well-being is threatened, or there is a risk of death, it makes sense. But what about when your liberty is at stake? When the government punishes you with imprisonment, fines, or even in the case of probation, your life as you knew it is most likely over. The courts have routinely found that "jeopardy of life or limb" is not simply physical punishment, but any punishment the government can mete out.

Separate Sovereignty

One aspect of Double Jeopardy that doesn't get talked about very much is the courts' theory of "separate sovereignty". This is the idea that there is an exception to the Fifth Amendment's Double Jeopardy clause that allows both state and federal prosecution for the same crime because the prosecuting parties are "separate sovereigns".

> *Under this doctrine, the prohibition on double jeopardy does not prevent dual prosecution when the prosecutions are each by separate sovereigns. Thus, a criminal defendant can be prosecuted by a state court and then by a federal court (or*

> *the other way around). A criminal defendant*
> *may be tried by two separate state courts.*[83]

This theory confuses "separate sovereigns" with "overlapping sovereigns". In the situation where an action is both a state and a federal crime, we have overlapping sovereigns, two entities claiming sovereignty over a single act. However, the Constitution specifically prohibits this situation:

> *The powers not delegated to the United States by the*
> *Constitution, nor prohibited by it to the States, are*
> *reserved to the States respectively, or to the people.*[84]

If a power is not specifically delegated to the United States, what we now call the federal government, then it is reserved either to the states or the people. This amendment reinforces not only the idea that we have separate sovereigns, but that their sovereignties do not overlap.

Self Witness

> *or shall be compelled in any criminal*
> *case to be a witness against himself*

We've all heard it, usually in some courtroom drama or high-profile hearing, where the defendant will "plead the fifth." What they mean is that they cannot be forced to testify against themselves. We've been taught that a Fifth Amendment plea is against self-incrimination; however, in reality, the Fifth Amendment protects our right against self-witness, not self-incrimination. That means in a criminal case you cannot (legally) be forced to testify about yourself, not for any reason or for no reason at all. Imagine living in a country where the government can force you to testify, even if doing so is harmful to you and your case or even just because you don't want to.

---

[83] WEX Legal Dictionary https://www.law.cornell.edu/wex.

[84] United States Constitution Amendment X.

Let's look at this from the other side, that of a juror who must decide the case. How does he or she interpret a witness pleading the fifth? Our first instinct may be to attach guilt to someone who does so, but pleading the fifth is NOT an admission of guilt, only an exercising of a right to not be a witness against yourself. It is a dangerously false argument to say, "But if they have nothing to hide, they should testify." There can be many reasons why someone does not want to testify against himself or herself, and not all of them involve self-incrimination. Since you never have to say why you will not testify, there is no way for anyone else to know if it has anything to do with the case at hand. Maybe your testimony will reveal something about yourself you'd rather keep secret, or maybe your testimony would harm someone you love. Whatever the reason, you cannot be forced to testify against yourself.

You can though, be compelled to be a witness against someone else.

> *In all criminal prosecutions, the accused shall*
> *enjoy the right ... to be confronted with the*
> *witnesses against him; to have compulsory*
> *process for obtaining witnesses in his favor*[85]

Why can you be compelled to testify against others if you cannot be forced to testify against yourself? The accused's right to put up a meaningful defense is protected. Remember, a legitimate exercise of a right cannot infringe on the rights of others. If I am a witness to something and my testimony would help the defense, then I am not only honor bound, but legally required, to provide that testimony unless the testimony is against myself. Could this put people in the difficult position of protecting themselves or another? Of course. Part of the responsibility of living in a free country is not only understanding our rights, but our responsibilities as well, which means making the hard choices when they come up. Putting the exercise of my right against self-witness above

---

[85]   United States Constitution Amendment VI.

the defendant's right to compel witnesses may infringe on the rights of another, but it is legal.

It's important to note the right of exemption from self-witness does not extend to civil cases (where you sue someone or are sued by someone), but only criminal cases.

Due Process

> *nor be deprived of life, liberty, or property,*
> *without due process of law;*

So what is "due process"?

> *Due: Proper; fit; appropriate; suitable; becoming;.* [86]

> *Process: In law, the whole course of proceedings,*
> *in a cause, real or personal, civil or criminal,*
> *from the original writ to the end of the suit.* [87]

So, due process of law is the proper and appropriate legal proceedings from the original writ or warrant to the end of the case. It is not enough that a process is followed, but that process must be proper. This part of the Fifth Amendment is meant to protect your right to a fair trial and against "drumhead trials" or "kangaroo courts."

> *Kangaroo Court: An unfair, biased, or hasty judicial*
> *proceeding that ends in a harsh punishment; an*
> *unauthorized trial conducted by individuals who*
> *have taken the law into their own hands, such*
> *as those put on by vigilantes or prison inmates;*
> *a proceeding and its leaders who are considered*
> *sham, corrupt, and without regard for the law.* [88]

---

[86]   Webster's 1828 Dictionary http://webstersdictionary1828.com

[87]   IBID

[88]   The Free Legal Dictionary https://legal-dictionary.thefreedictionary.com

What good are laws if you cannot depend on them to defend your life, liberty, or property? In their draft of the Massachusetts Constitution, John Adams, Samuel Adams, and James Bowdoin explained that the purpose of what they were creating was "to the end it may be a government of laws and not of men." The Fifth Amendment's Due Process clause not only protects your rights, but helps establish a legitimate legal system, one in which the rules and procedures are followed and the goal is to ensure a proper and fit verdict is rendered.

Eminent Domain

> *nor shall private property be taken for*
> *public use, without just compensation.*

Our Founding Fathers saw a time when it may be necessary for private property to be used for public purpose. While I am certain they did not foresee freeways, airports, or other modern-day public uses, they did include a plan to create a federal city which would require land for a capital, not to mention the need for forts, magazines, and arsenals.

> *To exercise exclusive Legislation in all Cases*
> *whatsoever, over such District (not exceeding ten*
> *Miles square) as may, by Cession of particular States,*
> *and the Acceptance of Congress, become the Seat of*
> *the Government of the United States, and to exercise*
> *like Authority over all Places purchased by the*
> *Consent of the Legislature of the State in which the*
> *Same shall be, for the Erection of Forts, Magazines,*
> *Arsenals, dock-Yards, and other needful Buildings;*[89]

What the founders did want to do was protect the citizens from the government simply taking land from them, for whatever purpose they

---

[89]   United States Constitution, Article I, Section 8, Paragraph 17.

desired. If property was taken, it was to be for public use and a just or fair compensation was to be paid.

Public Use

One of the most well-known recent cases involving the question of public use is the case Kelo v. City of New London where the city condemned the property of several individuals who would not willingly sell their property to the city for its integrated development plan. Susette Kelo sued the city, claiming that their plan did not constitute a "public use."

> *While the government may take their homes*
> *to build a road or a railroad or to eliminate a*
> *property use that harms the public, say petitioners,*
> *it cannot take their property for the private use of*
> *other owners simply because the new owners may*
> *make more productive use of the property.*[90]

The point Kelo brings up is that though the government may take land for public use, condemning land to give it to another owner is not public use. What protection of private property is there if the government can take land and give it to someone else? Where does the government get the authority to determine what the best use of your property is? We would effectively only own our land as long as the government thought we were making the best use of it.

The supreme Court found against Kelo, in part because the "Court long ago rejected any literal requirement that condemned property be put into use for the . . . public." Isn't it wonderful how our unelected high-priests in black robes can simply reject the idea of following the language of the Constitution they have sworn to uphold? If the Constitution doesn't mean "public use" when it says "public use", then what does it mean? This case is a perfect example of why all citizens

---

[90] *Kelo v City of New London* – O'Connor Dissent.

need to read and study the Constitution, and their need to hold their elected representatives accountable. When the court can simply decide not to follow the literal words of the law they are, in effect, legislating from the bench, which is a power granted solely to Congress. There is a reason federal judges "hold their Offices during good Behaviour"[91] and Congress has the power to impeach them.

Just Compensation

If the government is going to take your property, they are to give you "just compensation." What is "just compensation"?

Just: Conformed to rules of justice[92]

Justice: The virtue which consists in giving to every one what is his due[93]

If you own property that is taken for public use, the government should pay you the full value for it. The act of condemning Ms. Kelo's property, while evidently done to gain the ability to take it, also decreased its value and thereby relieved the City of New London from the burden of paying its full value. Anytime a government agency manipulates the value of a property it is about to take, it becomes a violation of the just compensation clause of the Fifth Amendment.

This case not only violated Ms. Kelo's Fifth Amendment right to not have her property taken, but also her due process rights to a fair trial, while calling into question Congress' legislative authority. Why should we be surprised? Congress will not hold the justices of the supreme Court accountable and we will not hold our elected officials accountable.

---

91   United States Constitution, Article III, Section 1.

92   Webster's 1828 Dictionary http://webstersdictionary1828.com.

93   IBID.

Conclusion

The Fifth Amendment protects the rights of the people in legal circumstances from the abuse of government power. You cannot be indicted for a serious crime except by a Grand Jury made up of other citizens. You cannot be tried twice for the same crime. You cannot be forced to be a witness against yourself. And you must allow the proper process of law, whether in criminal cases or the taking of your property by the government.

We have seen that we cannot depend on others to protect our rights. We must take action, we must know our rights, and we must use that information to hold those we send to Washington to represent us accountable to do the job the Constitution set for them and nothing more. If those who represent us will not fulfill their duties we must look for those who will. The job of our representative includes overseeing and, when necessary, prosecuting the other branches of government. If we want to once again live in a nation of laws not of men, we need to elect better people to represent us. People who are more focused on fidelity to the Constitution and less on what government "pork" they'll send to their home district?.

Amendment VI

*In all criminal prosecutions, the accused shall enjoy
the right to a speedy and public trial, by an impartial
jury of the State and district wherein the crime shall
have been committed, which district shall have been
previously ascertained by law, and to be informed of
the nature and cause of the accusation; to be confronted
with the witnesses against him; to have compulsory
process for obtaining witnesses in his favor, and to
have the Assistance of Counsel for his defense.*

Amendment VI continues the protection of rights in the legal system, this time focusing on criminal prosecutions.

Speedy and Public Trial

*In all criminal prosecutions, the accused shall
enjoy the right to a speedy and public trial, by an
impartial jury of the State and district wherein the
crime shall have been committed, which district
shall have been previously ascertained by law*

If you are being prosecuted for a crime, the Sixth Amendment protects your right to a speedy and public trail. Why is it important that your trial be both speedy and public?

The answer to the need for a speedy trial should be obvious. Between your indictment and trial, your life is effectively on hold. You may be held in jail or placed under bond to appear in court. You must engage counsel, and the longer this goes on the more it costs. During this time your name and reputation are under attack. If you are innocent, you want to get this over quickly and with the correct verdict. If the government can drag out the proceedings, not only do you pay the emotional and financial costs, but they can use delaying tactics to help persuade you to take a deal in the government's favor.

However, if your reputation is on the line and embarrassing information may come out, why is it so important for the trial to be public? To start with, you want to make sure everything the government is doing in prosecuting you is out in the open and legitimate. If your trial is in secret, what proof do you have of any malfeasance committed by the government? Since everything done in a criminal court has to be recorded and made public, those outside your defense team who wish to help can know what's going on. Maybe they can verify or find evidence contrary to the statement of a witness. They may be able to provide information to your counsel to help your defense. Most importantly, if the government does anything to violate your right to a fair trial, they can bring it to light.

This brings up the question of "gag orders" and when they should be issued during a trail.

> *Gag order: a judicial ruling barring public disclosure*
> *or discussion (as by the press) of information related*
> *to a case; broadly: a similar nonjudicial prohibition*
> *against the release of confidential information or*
> *against public discussion of a sensitive matter*[94]

There are times when information is so sensitive or prejudicial to the **defense** that it should not be discussed in public, especially while

---

[94] Merriam-Webster's Online Dictionary https://merriam-webster.com.

the case is in progress. But I have two serious concerns with judicial gag orders: Freedom of speech and the right to a public trial.

If my right to freedom of speech shall not be violated, where does a judge, who by definition, is an employee of the government, have the authority to restrict my speech? Again, we have two (potentially) competing rights here: The right to free speech and the right of the accused to an impartial jury. It would be an illegitimate use of someone's free speech rights to interfere with the defendant having an impartial jury. (As we've discussed in the chapter on the Declaration of Independence, for an exercise of a right to be legitimate it cannot infringe on someone else's unalienable right.) Therefore, is it legitimate for a judge to restrict someone's right to free speech in order to preserve the accused's right to an impartial jury? Since the government is in the process of trying someone, I believe a case can be made that their need to insure due process for the accused would allow a limited and temporary restriction on the free speech of others to do so.

The other concern I have with gag orders is their ability to shield from the public any misdeeds of the government in either the investigation or the prosecution of a case. Since the judge strictly controls the information the jury is allowed to see or hear (a topic for another time), the restriction of information can seriously harm the case of the defense. For example, it would certainly harm the defense if the judge disallows evidence that the police may have violated the defendant's rights during the collection of evidence. If the judge also orders that the defense not be allowed to discuss this in public, then the defendant's right to a public trial has been infringed.

So how should these competing rights be handled? First, before the judge issues a gag order, he or she should be required to show that it is to protect the right of the defendant to have an impartial jury. Second, when a gag order is violated, the person who violated the order should be allowed to show that the order was not protecting the rights of the defendant, and how his or her actions were. Again, it is important to remember that it is the proper role of government to protect people's rights, not to assist other parts of the government.

By an Impartial Jury

We often hear that we are tried by a "jury of our peers", though nowadays it seems more like we are tried by a jury of 12 people who couldn't get out of jury duty. Jury duty is one of the most important duties a citizen has. While it is the government that investigates and tries a case, it is a jury of everyday citizens that determine not only the guilt or innocence of the defendant, but whether the law itself is appropriate in the case.

Jury Nullification

> *The traditional approach in U.S. court systems is for jurors to be the "triers of fact," while the judge is considered the interpreter of law and the one who will instruct the jury on the applicable law. Jury nullification occurs when a jury substitutes its own interpretation of the law and/or disregards the law entirely in reaching a verdict.*[95]

If you've served in a jury or watched a courtroom drama, you've probably heard the judge give the jury instructions. This is the idea that while the jury is the "trier of fact," it is the judge who determines what the law is. However, is that what the people who wrote the Constitution had in mind?

> *JURY: A number of freeholders, selected in the manner prescribed by law, empaneled and sworn to inquire into and try any matter of fact, and to declare the truth on the evidence given them in the case. Grand juries consist usually of twenty four freeholders at least, and are summoned to try matters alleged in indictments. Petty juries, consisting usually of twelve men, attend courts to*

---

[95] Free Legal Dictionary https://legal-dictionary.thefreedictionary.com.

> *try matters of fact in civil causes, and to decide*
> *both the law and the fact in criminal prosecutions.*
> *The decision of a petty jury is called a verdict.*[96]

The definition of jury starts with a group of free people who are sworn to inquire and try a matter of fact. Notice that with both the grand jury and the petty jury in civil cases, their role is only to decide the facts of the case. However, juries in criminal prosecutions determine both the facts and the law of the case. In a criminal case, the jury must determine not only if the facts of the case meet the requirements of the law, but whether the law itself is justified in this case. Notice that a jury cannot overturn a law, but only determine if the law should be applied in the case before them.

In most modern legal writings, the instructions given by most judges and even supreme Court opinions, have denied the right of jury nullification. In the case of *Sparf and Hansen v. United States*, the court found, "I hold it the most sacred constitutional right of every party accused of a crime that the jury should respond as to the facts, and the court as to the law." This is hardly a surprising position for the courts to take. After all, wouldn't you like to decide the rules of the court? But is that what the founders had in mind?

If we go back to the 1828 Webster's dictionary definition of jury, we see that it is "to decide both the law and the fact in criminal prosecutions." Remember, the states declared their independence from an oppressive federal government in large part due to judicial infringements on their rights as British citizens. From the opening of the preamble to the enumeration of powers being heavily weighted toward the representatives of the people in the House of Representatives, we see a focus on protecting people's rights and giving the people power to protect themselves from an oppressive government.

With those facts in mind, I find it quite logical that our founders wanted to give the people the final say when applying criminal laws

---

[96]   Webster's 1828 Dictionary http://webstersdictionary1828.com.

against their fellow citizens. Why else would the Constitution require a criminal trial be by jury (Article III, Section 2, Paragraph 3 and here in Amendment VI)? Also, since a jury verdict of not guilty cannot be appealed (Amendment VII), we see that our founders have truly put the future of the accused in the hands of not the state, but of the people. (Since the Constitution places restrictions on governments and not people, the process of a trial can be appealed, but the jury verdict cannot. If the trial is found to have not provided due process, the trial itself is nullified.) Therefore, telling a jury that they are not allowed to consider the applicability of the law to the case in front of them subjugates the will of the people in the jury to the state and federal governments. In a perfect world, prosecutors would never view a case through their own political or personal viewpoints, but we don't live in a perfect world, and prosecutors have been known to "grandstand" to make political or professional points. That is why our Constitution puts the final decision of both fact and law in the hands of the people. Remember that the next time you receive that jury summons in the mail.

Where the Crime Was Committed

Why is it important that a criminal be prosecuted in the state and district where the crime happened? There are several reasons. Remember in the Declaration of Independence, one of the grievances the colonist brought against the king was that he was transporting criminals overseas for trial. This not only took the accused away from home and community support, but away from evidence that may exonerate him. Moving the trial away from the location of the crime also meant the jury pool would not consist of people who lived in the community where the crime happened and thereby would not have the same shared values and history. Of course, the downside of that would be that it may also be hard to find an impartial jury if the crime impacted a large portion of the community.

Informed of the Accusation Against You

and to be informed of the nature
and cause of the accusation

The remaining sections make sure the accused can prepare an effective defense. This part of the amendment starts with the accused being informed of what he or she is accused. Imagine walking into the courtroom on your first day of trial and only then finding out what you're being charged with. How can you prepare an effective defense it you don't know the accusations against you up front?

Confronted with Witnesses Against You

to be confronted with the witnesses against him

When you hear that someone has accused you of something, isn't the first question you ask: Who said that? Did the person misinterpret something you said or did? Does the person have something against you? Was the person even there or are they reporting what they heard from someone else? This is all information you will need to mount your defense.

This is also why I view anonymous accusations with great concern. I understand the desire of someone who knows something to not want to be named, especially if they are afraid of the person they are accusing. I also understand the desire of law enforcement and prosecutors to offer anonymity to help get information to build their case. But at what point does the anonymous tip violate the accused's right to confront witnesses against them? Which is why I believe anonymous tips and information should be viewed with a certain amount of suspicion.

Compel Witnesses for Your Defense

to have compulsory process for
obtaining witnesses in his favor

The accused doesn't only have the opportunity to call witnesses, it also has a process to compel them to testify. This comes in handy when the defendant's witness/witnesses are less than eager to testify. Someone may not want to testify for many reasons, but the right to compel witnesses in the accused's favor helps them mount a defense. Of course, a defendant cannot force someone to answer, but he or she can make sure the witness comes to court and publicly state that he or she will not testify. And should it be found that the witness lied on the stand, perjury charges should await them.

Assistance of Counsel

and to have the Assistance of Counsel for his defense.

Have you ever tried to read legal documents? They claim they are written in English, but it seems like some other language to me. I read court opinions for the Constitution Study blog and podcast, and I can tell you, it's not much fun. Having someone who knows the law to provide counsel can make all the difference in the world. Their experience in dealing with judges and juries, their familiarity with legal processes, as well as their knowledge of the law, are all very important to the defendant. I guess Abraham Lincoln was right when he said, "He who represents himself has a fool for a client."

Conclusion

Your right to a fair trial is protected by the Sixth Amendment. Whether it's the right to a speedy and public trial, an impartial jury, compelling witnesses, or the assistance of counsel, making sure that the process the government uses to try and convict someone is due and proper is extremely important to a free people.

Amendment VII

In Suits at common law, where the value in controversy
shall exceed twenty dollars, the right of trial by jury
shall be preserved, and no fact tried by a jury, shall
be otherwise reexamined in any Court of the United
States, than according to the rules of the common law.

W hile the Sixth Amendment protected the rights of the accused in a criminal trial, the Seventh Amendment protects both parties in civil cases that arise from common law. What is common law?

Unwritten or common law: *a rule of action which*
derives its authority from long usage, or established
custom, which has been immemorially received
and recognized by judicial tribunals. As this law
can be traced to no positive statutes, its rules or
principles are to be found only in the records of
courts, and in the reports of judicial decisions.[97]

The 1828 Webster's Dictionary defines common law as those which are established by custom rather than legislation and are generally unwritten. Modern interpretations of the Seventh Amendment similarly define common law, but with certain important issues.

---

[97] Webster's 1828 Dictionary http://webstersdictionary1828.com.

121

*The Seventh Amendment continues a practice from
English common law of distinguishing civil claims
which must be tried before a jury (absent waiver by the
parties) from claims and issues that may be heard by a
judge alone. It only governs federal civil courts and has
no application to civil courts set up by the states when
those courts are hearing only disputes of state law.*[98]

Notice that Cornell's Legal Information Institute teaches that common law distinguishes civil claims which must be tried by a jury as opposed to those heard by a judge alone. Based on the language of the amendment, the distinguishing factor is the value of the controversy being greater than $20. The law school also teaches that the Seventh Amendment only applies to federal courts in a common legal interpretation and that the Bill of Rights only applied to the federal government until the Fourteenth Amendment "incorporated" portions of it to the states. This position, however, completely ignores the supremacy clause in Article VI of the Constitution, which clearly states that all judges are bound to the supreme law of the land. (You can read more about this in the chapter on Article VI.)

*This Constitution, and the Laws of the United
States which shall be made in Pursuance thereof;
and all Treaties made, or which shall be made,
under the Authority of the United States, shall be
the supreme Law of the Land;* **and the Judges in
every State shall be bound thereby, any Thing
in the Constitution or Laws of any State to the
Contrary notwithstanding** *(emphasis mine).*[99]

---

[98] Legal Information Institutehttps://www.law.cornell.edu/constitution/seventh_amendment.

[99] United States Constitution, Article VI. - (Emphasis added)

Contrary to current jurisprudence, the Constitution requires that all civil cases valued at over $20 must be tried by a jury unless waived by both parties to the suit. (FYI, $20 in 1793 would be worth about $1,200 today, but since the Constitution did not put a cost of living increase into this amendment the value of $20 stands.) While the courts today routinely ignore this amendment, you have a constitutionally protected right to a jury trial for civil suits. Since I doubt anyone would go through the pain and expense of suing someone for as little as $20, I also assume any case is eligible for a jury trial.

Why is the right to a jury trial so important? As we saw in the Sixth Amendment, jury trials place the outcome of the case in the hands of its citizens instead of the government. Our founders wanted to make sure the people had the tools to keep governments in check. Without the right to a jury trial, the fate of your case would be in the hands of a judge who works for the government. By exercising your right to a trial by jury, you can place your case in the hands of other citizens who may have a different point of view than a judge.

The preeminence of the people over government is further enhanced by the language that protects a jury's verdict regarding the facts of the case from future review. In other words, if you win your civil case before a jury, the government nor the other party in the case can appeal the decision, only the process that was used.

Conclusion

Once again, we see our founders placing their faith and the ultimate power in the hands of the people over those of the government. It's too bad that most people go to such great lengths to get out of their duty to protect the rights of their fellow citizens. Maybe if we put ourselves in the position of those in the case, we would see jury duty as a burden worth bearing. You should hope that if the day comes when we are the ones being tried, those in the jury box will feel the same.

Amendment VIII

Excessive bail shall not be required, nor excessive fines imposed, nor cruel and unusual punishments inflicted.

The Eighth Amendment continues what was started in the Fifth: Protecting the rights of the accused. In this amendment, punishments both for the accused and the convicted are limited.

Excessive Bail

Bail: 1. To set free, deliver, or liberate from arrest and imprisonment, upon security given that the person bailed shall appear and answer in court.

2. The security given for the release of a prisoner from custody; as, the man is out upon bail[100]

Bail is a security given to persuade the person to appear in court. Let's face it, without some form of security most people who are charged would not appear in court if they were released. Sure, some people have demonstrated such character that they are released on their own recognizance, but most people would not appear on their court date without having given some sort of security.

What is the purpose of bail? It allows the accused but not yet convicted, to be released from jail. If we are truly innocent until proven guilty, then allowing an accused defendant who has not yet been convicted to go home is the right thing to do. They can be with their family,

---

[100] Webster's 1828 Dictionary http://webstersdictionary1828.com.

earn money to pay not only their bills but for their defense, and most importantly, they can better aid that defense if they are not locked up. It saves the state the cost of incarcerating the accused before trial, but with the Bill of Right's focus on protecting the citizen from the state, I think it's much more likely our founders wanted to protect the citizen than save the state money. That said, it would be quite easy for a judge to set bail so high the average American would not have the money. Hence the Eighth Amendment's protection against excessive bail. The question is: What is excessive bail?

> *EXCESSIVE: Beyond the established laws of morality and religion, or beyond the bounds of justice, fitness, propriety, expedience or utility; as excessive indulgence of any kind.*[101]

Excessive bail is that which is beyond the laws of morality, beyond the bounds of justice, fitness, propriety, expedience, or utility. If that doesn't exactly clear it up for you don't feel bad; it's still rather questionable to me, too. What is "beyond the bounds of justice"? Is setting bail higher than the accused can afford beyond the bounds of justice? What if the person is accused of violent and dangerous acts? Would setting bail low enough for the accused to pay be unjust to their victims or those the accused may have threatened? We're back again to what people, or more importantly, what the judge finds reasonable. I'm sure most of us could agree that $1,000,000 bail for petty theft is excessive, but what about for someone accused of fraud valued in the billions? What if the person is accused of assault, rape, or even murder? What would be excessive bail in that situation?

This would probably be less of an issue if judges were held accountable for their decisions. Remember, federal judges serve for the duration of their good behavior.

---

[101] Webster's 1828 Dictionary http://webstersdictionary1828.com.

The Judges, both of the supreme and inferior Courts,
shall hold their Offices during good Behaviour[102]

If judges were held accountable for their bad behavior, then questions about excessive bail could be dealt with. Should someone believe the bail was excessive or insufficient, then the actions of that federal judge could be reviewed by those we sent to Washington, D.C. to represent the people: The members of The House of Representatives. I'm sure judges would give greater consideration to the bail they set if they thought their decisions might be reviewed by the House. Especially if they might lose their jobs if they were found to have behaved badly.

Excessive Fines

FINE: A sum of money paid to the king or state
by way of penalty for an offense; a mulet; a
pecuniary punishment. Fines are usually prescribed
by statute, for the several violations of law; or
the limit is prescribed, beyond which the judge
cannot impose a fine for a particular offense.[103]

A fine is a penalty paid to the state for an offense. So the question I ask myself is: What is an appropriate fine to pay the government for an offense?

Let's start with a very basic question: What did the offense cost the government? That, to me, is the basis of determining if the fine is excessive. Howard Stern was fined $2.5 million for using offensive language on the air. While there's a lot to talk about in that case, when discussing the Eighth Amendment my question is: Why should the government make $2.5 million, minus whatever costs they actually incurred, to punish Mr. Stern? While $2.5 million may not be much to the federal

---

[102] United States Constitution, Article III, Section 1.
[103] Webster's 1828 Dictionary http://webstersdictionary1828.com.

government, the idea that said government can profit from judicial proceedings disturbs me.

The other question we should ask is: Why is the fine paid to the government? If the government was the one harmed, then a fine makes sense. But what if the harm came to someone else? JPMorgan was fined over $2 billion for its actions in the Bernie Madoff case, but did the government lose that much money because of their actions? What about the people who were harmed by what JPMorgan did?

Fines are a punishment, but if the basis for a fine is simply how much the judge wishes to punish the guilty, what limits are there? How do you define excessive if the only limit is a judge's personal ethics? Does punishing someone by paying a fine to the government rather than the injured party impact your opinion of what is excessive?

Cruel and Unusual Punishment

Like the rest of this Amendment, cruel and unusual seems to be in the eye of the beholder. Some see the death penalty as cruel while others see it as an effective deterrent. Some think it is cruel to incarcerate someone for a crime where no one else is hurt, others see it as the legally established punishment for those crimes. What some call cruel others call just, and what some call unusual others call effective.

What is cruel and unusual punishment? I think our founders looked at what western society thought was acceptable. There are countries in the world today where punishments include the amputation of the offender's hand, death by stoning, or being thrown off a building. In the west, we find these punishments cruel and unusual.

Conclusion

The last of three amendments dealing with the judicial system, Amendment VIII focuses on the treatment of the accused and convicted. The accused will not be subject to excessive bail, giving them the opportunity to be home and to help in their own defense. As for the convicted, they cannot be given a cruel or unusual punishment, including an excessive fine. This amendment is meant to protect the accused and the convicted from government exuberance in prosecuting and sentencing.

Amendment IX

*The enumeration in the Constitution, of
certain rights, shall not be construed to deny
or disparage others retained by the people.*

The Bill of Rights enumerates several rights that the government is not allowed to infringe upon, but is that all the rights the government was created to protect? According to the 9th Amendment the answer is no. The rights listed in the Constitution are neither the complete list of rights, nor is it to be used to deny other rights, which are retained by the people.

The phrase "retained by the people" is interesting, especially in the 18th century. Governments then were based on the divine right of kings and the right of the aristocracy to rule the people. What rights you received were from the ruling classes, and you were expected to be happy with them. Here we see that people retain the rights. In order for you to retain your rights, you must have them in the first place. While this amendment is short and very simple, it should carry a lot of weight, yet today this amendment is practically ignored.

I have a right to liberty and to live without pressure or influence from the government except for the enforcement of natural law. According to this amendment, the rights that are listed in the Constitution do not deny me my right to liberty, yet the government can't seem to go a day without passing some law or regulation that tells me how I must live my life. Maybe if we learned more about this amendment We the People would defend those rights our government so regularly disparages.

Amendment X

The powers not delegated to the United States by the Constitution, nor prohibited by it to the States, are reserved to the States respectively, or to the people.

The Constitution, as a contract, delegates powers to the United States itself, the union states and their central, or as we now call it, federal government. If these powers are delegated, who delegates them? Remember the Declaration of Independence?

> *We, therefore, the Representatives of the United States of America, in General Congress, Assembled, appealing to the Supreme Judge of the world for the rectitude of our intentions, do, in the Name, and by Authority of the good People of these Colonies, solemnly publish and declare, That these United Colonies are, and of Right ought to be Free and Independent States;*[104]

This document declares that the colonies "are, and of Right ought to be Free and Independent States." If these are free and independent states, under whose authority did these representatives declare them to be so? The people of those states. So the representatives of the states, in the name and under the authority of the people of those states, declared the states to be free and independent. Then another group of representatives of the states, under the authority of the people of those states, contracted

---

[104]   United States Declaration of Independence.

together to create a central government. As part of that contract, the states delegated SOME of their authority to that central government. To make sure there was no question about this delegation of powers, Congress and the states amended the contract to make clear that any powers not specifically delegated to the central government remained with the states. In a case where a power was not delegated to the central government but was prohibited to the states, then the people directly retained the power.

Why is it so necessary for us to understand this delegation of powers? I went to the website "A-Z Index of U.S. Government Departments and Agencies"[105] and did some calculations. This website lists 659 U.S. government departments and agencies. A little research also found that this list included all 50 states, six territories, two houses of Congress, five courts, and 53 duplicate agencies. Removing those duplicate and non-agencies entities leaves us with 537 departments and agencies in the federal government. Using somewhat generous definitions, I found 49 agencies where I could find a delegated power in the Constitution.

So, if any power not delegated to the United States remain with the states or the people, that means more than 90% of federal departments and agencies are unconstitutional and therefore illegal. Imagine how much less painful April 15th would be if the IRS only took from us the money needed to do the work the federal government was authorized to do? Then imagine how much easier life would be if we didn't have to spend it stumbling over these federal agencies that have neither a legal nor legitimate reason for being.

The fact that the list of U.S. Government Departments and Agencies included the states really bothers me. First I thought, "How stupid. Can't the government get an accurate count of its own departments and agencies?" Then it dawned on me; the federal government orders how the states draw up their Congressional districts, how to spend their education money, what environmental and licensing laws they can have, and on and on. That means the federal government treats the states as

---

[105]   https://www.usa.gov/federal-agencies/.

if they were departments of itself! And since the states long ago abandoned standing up for their own sovereignty, why wouldn't the federal government treat them like colonies rather than states?

Conclusion

Why is this so amendment important? Because if we don't understand the Constitution, we believe that politicians are exercising a legal authority when they pass legislation that violates the Tenth Amendment. We accept, and then maybe even expect it, when our state representatives genuflect to the federal government rather than stand up for the rights of their citizens.

If you want to get money out of politics, if you want to get Washington, D.C. under control, and if you want to return control of the federal government to the states and the people, you must first understand the limitations placed on that government and be willing to hold all our elected representatives accountable to enforce it.

We the People – Preamble

We the People of the United States, in Order to form a more perfect Union, establish Justice, insure domestic Tranquility, provide for the common defense, promote the general Welfare, and secure the Blessings of Liberty to ourselves and our Posterity, do ordain and establish this Constitution for the United States of America.

Lost History

At one time every elementary school student in the country memorized this preamble. Today I think we'd be lucky if most high school or college graduates would recognize the famous introduction. After studying the Constitution, I find this one of the most moving parts of the document. As we go through it, think about what is being said and what our Founding Fathers blessed us with.

Why did they do it?

We the People of the United States are some of the most famous words in American history. They should be a reminder of the fact that in this country the people are sovereign. Ultimately, it is We the People who formed this country and We the People who are responsible for the condition it is in now.

Remember, when this document was written there was not a single nation. There were 13 States, individual sovereign countries with all the rights and privileges thereof (see the last paragraph of the Declaration of Independence). These states united together to form this federation and in this structure rests the power with the people and the political bodies they formed into states.

So why did these 13 states band together this way?

In order to form a more perfect union

What we call the "United States of America" was not the first union formed after we declared independence from Great Britain. After declaring independence in July 1776, the states proposed the "Articles of Confederation" in November of 1777; however, they weren't ratified until March of 1781. This was the first union formed by the newly freed colonies. While the name of this union was the "United States of America", the "united" part was a bit of a misnomer, as these states didn't work together so well.

This union had issues, like the collection of taxes and managing relations with other nations. When representatives of the states got together in 1787 to "fix" the Articles of Confederation, they figured out it would be easier to begin again. One of the main reasons we have the constitution we do is the work of the Constitutional Convention trying to make a better, or more perfect, union. This new union had a purpose.

Establish justice

Notice it doesn't say establish "social justice," "racial justice," or even "economic justice," but simply "justice." The Webster's Dictionary of 1828 defines justice as

> *"The virtue which consists in giving to every one*
> *what is his due; ... Distributive justice belongs to*
> *magistrates or rulers, and consists in distributing to*
> *every man that right or equity which the laws and the*
> *principles of equity require; or in deciding controversies*
> *according to the laws and to principles of equity."*[106]

---

[106] Webster's 1828 Dictionary http://webstersdictionary1828.com.

In other words, justice is the idea we are all equal before the law or, as it's sometimes put, the rule of law not of men. I often hear news reports about this or that demonstration with a crowd shouting "No Justice, No Peace." I find this odd since this is almost always people who don't like the outcome of the justice system yet cannot show evidence of an actual injustice. Rioting because you don't get the decision you want is not justice, it is prejudice. Justice means looking at all the facts and coming to a just decision based on law, not a person's color, ethnicity, religious beliefs, or any other criteria. While we have never been perfectly just, this document was created to form a government where justice was established for all.

Think of all the concepts incorporated into our laws to help insure that everyone has a chance at a just outcome. The framework for equal justice includes your right to to sue for damages, to a trial by a jury, to trial council, to compel witnesses, against self-witness, against unreasonable search and seizure, and against cruel and unusual punishment. Does it work perfectly? Of course not. When there are people with money and influence there will be attempts to tilt the scales of justice in their favor. And as long as there are those who are willing to publicly put agenda before justice, we will have to work to insure pure justice rather than the social, racial, or other "justices" people call for today. Only then will we have a chance to fulfill Rev. Martin Luther King Jr's dream.

> *I have a dream that my four little children*
> *will one day live in a nation where they will*
> *not be judged by the color of their skin but*
> *by the content of their character.*[107]

---

[107] Rev. Martin Luther King's "I Have a Dream" speech, 1963 https://www.archives.gov/files/press/exhibits/dream-speech.pdf.

Insure domestic tranquility

Remember we had 13 individual states, each with its own agenda. Part of the reason our Founding Fathers created this constitution was to avoid fights or even wars between the states. Imagine a fight between New York and New Jersey about traffic on the Hudson River? Or a dispute between North Carolina and South Carolina over their border. Such situations were not only possible, but some had happened under the Articles of Confederation, so part of the design of the Constitution is to avoid such conflicts and insure tranquility between the states. Part of how they planned to do this was through the next two clauses: Provide for the common defense and promote the general welfare.

Provide for the common defense

Just as we don't want fights between states, we don't want them to have to fight foreign forces alone. As fledgling nations, the states, especially the smaller ones, had little power to repel any armed forces that may wish to impose themselves. Just as animals may come together to defend themselves from a common threat, this constitution provides for the defense of all the states as a whole. The Constitution provides for individual state militias coming together when necessary to fight as one. The federal government was also given the authority to negotiate with foreign nations with the approval of the states through the Senate (a topic discussed in the chapter on Article II). This common defense scheme allowed us to repel the British when they invaded in the war of 1812 and to assist other nations in the great wars of the 20th century.

Promote the general welfare

Contrary to what appears to be popular belief, "general welfare" doesn't mean sending a check to everyone who lives here. "General welfare" is a term that means the government that will be formed by this constitution needs to treat all the states the same. This new government was not to pass laws to favor one state or region over another. The Constitution sets up a system where states large and small can insure legislation that benefits all of them. (We'll go into more detail about the phrase when we cover the general welfare clause in Article I Section 8.)

Secure the blessings of liberty for ourselves and our posterity

Of all the phrases in the preamble of the constitution, this seems to be the one we've lost the most in this country. Today we seem to think more about freedom, the ability to do what I want without consequences, than liberty. We act as if liberty is the natural condition of man though history shows us that even today most people live under the control of government, but since we elect those in that government we think we are free. "When government fears the people, there is liberty ..."[108] The liberty to live our lives as we see fit, as long as we don't infringe on the rights of others, is a blessing. The Founding Fathers wanted to secure these blessing not only to themselves, but to their posterity. In other words, to us. Too often, it seems we look to government to tell others how we think they should live their lives, forgetting that any government that can force others to live as we like can force us to live as they want.

Liberty is never secure. As Ronald Reagan said,

> *"Freedom is never more than one generation away*
> *from extinction. We didn't pass it to our children*
> *in the bloodstream. It must be fought for, protected,*
> *and handed on for them to do the same, or one day*
> *we will spend our sunset years telling our children*
> *and our children's children what it was once like*
> *in the United States where men were free."[109]*

Our Founding Fathers created a Constitution to secure these blessings not only to themselves, but to us. It is our duty and responsibility to insure our posterity (our descendants) enjoys them as well.

---

[108] Often attributed to Thomas Jefferson, though there is some dispute since no written record exists to my knowledge.

[109] Ronald Reagan, Speech to the Phoenix Chamber of Commerce, March 30, 1961.

The blessings of liberty we inherited from our predecessors are not being taken away, they are being given away, piece by piece and yard by yard. Every time we ask government, especially the federal government, to do something for us we give away our liberty. Every time we demand the government tell others how to live, we give away our liberty. Every time we vote for someone because they promise to give us something, we sell our liberty and our children's liberty for the price of a few coins.

Conclusion

Today the limited government designed by our forefathers has become the overbearing behemoth many feared it would be. Now, rather than being asked to take our liberties, Washington, D.C. demands them, and too often we cheer. Republican and Democrat, Conservative and Progressive, Congressman, President, and Justice alike have turned the enumerated power in the Constitution into wax, molding it into whatever they desire.

Every year an email makes the rounds listing things high-school graduates have never seen. Think about the children in your life and remember: They have never seen a land where the government hasn't determined if a church was truly a church, if a prayer was acceptable in public, where the government didn't dictate what our children have to learn in school, or how we may use our land. We borrow against our children's future, enslaving them with mountains of debt no generation could pay off. In short, we have sold their blessings of liberty for our own ease, comfort, and greed. Our Founding Fathers pledged their lives, fortunes, and sacred honor to this new nation. What will you pledge to restore the blessings of liberty to your posterity?

Creating the Federal Government

How it came into being

There are several common myths in America, like that federal government has three co-equal branches, federal judges have lifetime appointments, and that the President is elected by the people. Not only are these statements false, but they perpetuate ignorance about the Constitution, the people's role in it, the power they have, and their responsibility for our government.

The first three articles of the Constitution create and organize the federal government. It not only establishes the three branches of the federal government, but determines how each will run and the limits of their powers. Articles 4-6 provide additional rules and limits on the federal government, as a whole, and lastly, Article 7 determines what is necessary for the Constitution to go into effect.

Article I – Legislative Branch

A rticle I of the Constitution establishes the legislative branch of the new government. It also determines how this branch is to be made up, how it is to operate, and what specific powers it has.

Section 1 – Legislative Power

All legislative Powers herein granted shall be vested in a Congress of the United States, which shall consist of a Senate and House of Representatives.

While I'm sure we all know what legislative powers are, let's look at the Webster's 1828 dictionary to see how it is defined:

LEGISLATIVE: Giving or enacting laws; as a legislative body.

Capable of enacting laws; as legislative power.[110]

If ALL legislative power (the power to create laws), is granted to Congress, what about all these regulations with the force of law being created by executive agencies and unelected bureaucrats?

LAW, noun

---

[110] Webster's 1828 Dictionary http://webstersdictionary1828.com.

> *A rule, particularly an established or permanent*
> *rule, prescribed by the supreme power of a*
> *state to its subjects, for regulating their actions,*
> *particularly their social actions. Laws are*
> *imperative or mandatory, commanding what*
> *shall be done; prohibitory, restraining from what*
> *is to be forborn; or permissive, declaring what*
> *may be done without incurring a penalty.*[111]

If laws are rules for regulating the actions of those subject to them, how can an agency such as the EPA, BATFE, or the Department of Labor create rules, especially those that may incur a penalty for violating them? Over the years, Congress has figured out that, if they create a federal agency and give it the tasks of effectively making laws, then they don't have to take the heat for difficult decisions. Add to that the fact that congressmen can blame the agency they created, and ostensibly oversee, for these problems and that the American people won't hold them accountable, and you can see why they do it. Sounds like a pretty nice deal, unless of course, you believe in the rule of law and the supremacy of the Constitution. What we see right off the bat is that Congress, by delegating rule-making power (a power that they have no authority to delegate) is violating their primary purpose: That of making laws.

We also see that Congress is divided into two houses, the Senate and the House of Representatives. Why did our Founding Fathers give us a bicameral (or two house) legislative body?

The first, and most common, answer I found is representation. Not surprisingly, the smaller states wanted an equal representation per state as the larger states, while the larger states wanted representation determined by population. I say this is not surprising since the larger states would get more representatives if they were chosen by population, and the people of the smaller states would have greater influence per-capita if each state had the same number representatives. Connecticut delegate

---

[111] Webster's 1828 Dictionary http://webstersdictionary1828.com.

Roger Sherman proposed the two chambered, or bicameral body, which was acceptable to the delegates of both small and large states and became known as the great compromise of 1787. That is where most commentators on the subject stop.

Looking a little farther into the Constitution itself though, we see that the bicameral legislature our founders set up does more than balance the interests of large and small states, they also balance the interests of the people and the states, as we'll see in sections two and three.

Section 2 – The House of Representatives

The first of the two houses of Congress created by the Constitution is the House of Representatives. Sometimes referred to as "The People's House", this body is not only designed to represent the people of the United States of America, but given specific powers to wield in that capacity.

Clause 1 – The People's House

The House of Representatives shall be composed of
Members chosen every second Year by the People of
the several States, and the Electors in each State shall
have the Qualifications requisite for Electors of the
most numerous Branch of the State Legislature.

The members of the House of Representatives are to be chosen by the people and are to serve two-year terms. Since members of the House are chosen by the people, they are expected to represent the people themselves. And the people were expected to hold their representatives accountable. As Rufus King said in the Massachusetts ratification debates:

It seems proper that the representative should be
in office time enough to acquire that information
which is necessary to form a right judgment; but
that the time should not be so long as to remove

from his mind the powerful check upon his conduct,
that arises from the frequency of elections, whereby
the people are enabled to remove an unfaithful
representative, or to continue a faithful one.[112]

We also see that the electors are to have the same qualification as the largest branch of the state legislature. In other words, the qualifications for someone to vote in an election of a House seat, such as age and residency, had to be at least the same as for your state legislature.

Clause 2 – Requirements for House Member

No Person shall be a Representative who shall not
have attained to the Age of twenty five Years, and
been seven Years a Citizen of the United States,
and who shall not, when elected, be an Inhabitant
of that State in which he shall be chosen.

To serve in the House of Representatives, a person had to be at least 25 years old, a resident of the United States for at least seven years, and be an inhabitant (resident) of the state which he was to represent. This requirement shows a concern not only about the maturity of House members, but their experience as a United States citizen.

The construction of this sentence is awkward, and can make for some odd deductions if read out of context. Rather than a list of qualifications, this is a list of disqualifications. So, when you read "who shall not, when elected, be an inhabitant of that state," it sounds like you must elect someone from another state. While my father would cringe at my using such a double negative, what this clause is saying is, if you're not at least 25, or not a citizen of the U.S. for at least seven years or not a resident of the state you wish to serve, you cannot be representative for

---

[112] Debates in the Convention of the Commonwealth of Massachusetts, on the adoption of the federal Constitution. In convention, Boston, January 9, 1788.

that state. I hope this makes sense, because explaining this made my head hurt.

Clause 3 – Apportionment

> *Representatives and direct Taxes shall be apportioned among the several States which may be included within this Union, according to their respective Numbers, which shall be determined by adding to the whole Number of free Persons, including those bound to Service for a Term of Years, and excluding Indians not taxed, three fifths of all other Persons. The actual Enumeration shall be made within three Years after the first Meeting of the Congress of the United States, and within every subsequent Term of ten Years, in such Manner as they shall by Law direct. The Number of Representatives shall not exceed one for every thirty Thousand, but each State shall have at Least one Representative; and until such enumeration shall be made, the State of New Hampshire shall be entitled to chuse three, Massachusetts eight, Rhode Island and Providence Plantations one, Connecticut five, New York six, New Jersey four, Pennsylvania eight, Delaware one, Maryland six, Virginia ten, North Carolina five, South Carolina five, and Georgia three.*

Both the number of representatives and the amount of direct taxes were to be apportioned to the states based on their population. (Direct taxation was changed with the 16th Amendment.) How the total representation was to be determined has been misrepresented often over the years, leading many to claim that the Constitution was pro-slavery or that the founders viewed black men as less than human, but a plain reading of the text shows the error in both points of view.

While I believe most of the slaves at the time of the founding were black, looking at the language used, "the whole Number of free Persons, including those bound to Service for a Term of Years, and excluding Indians not taxed, three fifths of all other Persons." All free persons and those who had a time of limited services were to be counted. Those Indians who were not taxed were not counted, and three-fifths of everyone else was to be counted. So, all free black men were counted and three-fifths of any one who was not free, regardless of their race, were counted. What was the purpose of this three-fifths clause?

Every state wanted as many representatives in the House as possible. The southern states, where slave holding was common, sought to do this by counting all their slaves for representation even though they were considered property and not free to participate in the representative republic that was being set up. This bothered the abolitionist, who countered that if the southern states wanted to count their property for representation, then they would count their horses, cattle, and pets. It is no surprise the southern states did not like this idea. As a compromise, it was determined that only three-fifths of slaves would be counted toward representation. This limited the representation of slave holding states in the House, weakening their ability to pursue pro-slavery legislation, at least for a time. With the ratification of the 14th Amendment the three-fifths clause was rescinded.

How were we to determine the number of persons in each state? Congress first met on March 4, 1789, and the first census was taken in 1790. While the term "census" does not exist in the Constitution, the enumeration of the population of the states has happened every ten years since, although lately with some controversy.

You see, Congress and the Census Bureau have taken the language, "in such Manner as they shall by Law direct" to mean not only the manner of the census, but the content as well. The Constitution clearly says the purpose of the enumeration is to apportion representatives and direct taxes, not to do societal research or political gerrymandering. So now, rather than asking how many people live in each household, the Census bureau wants to know who works, what you do, how much you make, what kind of dwelling you live in, your telephone number, your sex, your date of birth, and your race, and that's just the short form.

If you happened to get the long form, the Census bureau also wanted to know your marital status, your level of education, your ethnicity, what language you spoke at home, where you were born, where and what type of dwelling you lived in five years ago, a partial medical history, did your grandchildren live with you, did you serve in the military and if so how long, were you were employed and where, when, and how you got to work and with how many people, how much money you made ten years ago, detailed information about what type of dwelling you lived in, whether you owned or rented, and how much you spent on your mortgage, rent, and utilities.

What does any of that have to do with apportioning representation or directing taxes? Instead, what it is, is another example of those in Washington, D.C. poking their nose into something that isn't their business so they can place more of your freedoms under their control.

One other interesting thing to note is the number of representatives in the House. The Constitution clearly states "The Number of Representatives shall not exceed one for every thirty Thousand." That means after the 2010 census, with a population of almost 309,000,000 people, the House of Representatives could have no more than 10,300 members. If you think floor debates are crazy now with 435 members, imagine a House almost 24 times the size. So why do we have 435 members instead of thousands? The Permanent Reapportionment Act of 1929[113] set the number of representatives at 435 and it hasn't been changed since. Just another example of those in Washington, D.C. ignoring the Constitution and the American people letting them.

---

[113]   https://history.house.gov/Historical-Highlights/1901-1950/The-Permanent-Apportionment-Act-of-1929/.

Clause 4 – Vacancies

> *When vacancies happen in the Representation from*
> *any State, the Executive Authority thereof shall*
> *issue Writs of Election to fill such Vacancies.*

When a vacancy happens in the House of Representatives, the executive authority of the state, the governor, calls a special election to fill the vacancy. Compare this to how a vacant Senate seat is filled in Section 3. Since a member of the House represents the people of their district, it's up to the people to fill the vacancy. The only role the state's governor has is to call for the election.

Clause 5 – Officers of the House & Impeachment

> *The House of Representatives shall choose*
> *their Speaker and other Officers; and shall*
> *have the sole Power of Impeachment.*

The House of Representatives chooses their own officers. The only officer specified in the Constitution is the Speaker. How the House chooses its officers exposes a sea of corruption and influence peddling, but that's the fodder for another book. As ugly as it may be, it is constitutional for the House to pick its officers in any way they want. If we don't like how they do it, it is our responsibility to change those in the House.

The House also has the sole power of impeachment. Talking to many people today, I get the impression that they think impeachment is conviction of a crime. However, impeachment is an accusation of a crime. Similar to a grand jury indictment (see the chapter on the Fifth Amendment), the House has the power to charge federal officers (President, Vice President, federal judges, and other federal officers), with offenses worthy of being removed from office. Since the House has sole power of impeachment, they can choose the reason they will impeach a person.

Section 3 – The Senate

Sometimes erroneously refer to as "the upper house," the Senate is the representation of the states in Congress. Compare the powers delegated to this house with those delegated to the House of Representatives and you'll find what was supposed to be an interesting balancing act of forces and objectives within Congress.

Clause 1 – The State's House

The Senate of the United States shall be composed of two Senators from each State, chosen by the Legislature thereof, for six Years; and each Senator shall have one Vote.

Originally the Senators were chosen by the legislatures of the states they would represent. As I mentioned in section one, each state getting two senators, each with one vote, was to balance the desires of large and small states. However, in 1913, with the ratification of the 17th Amendment, the method of choosing Senators changed, and so did the relationship between the states and the federal government.

When the federal government was formed, the way the members of the two houses of Congress were chosen were different for a reason. Members of the House were chosen by the people and were meant to represent the people. Senators were chosen by the state legislatures because they represented the states. This meant that for any legislation to pass Congress, it had to be approved both by the representatives of the people and those of the states. Remember, when we declared independence from Great Britain, we created thirteen independent states. The Constitution does not change the fact that the states are independent; it created a new entity, the United States government, and delegated to it certain powers. The Tenth Amendment confirms that any power not delegated to the central government, which we now call the federal government, was retained by the states or the people. Therefore, it makes sense that the thirteen states wanted to keep a hand in what the federal government is doing. Sadly, with the ratification of the 17th Amendment, the states have effectively lost any direct say in what the federal government does.

Clause 2 – Senators Terms Rotated

> *Immediately after they shall be assembled in Consequence of the first Election, they shall be divided as equally as may be into three Classes. The Seats of the Senators of the first Class shall be vacated at the Expiration of the second Year, of the second Class at the Expiration of the fourth Year, and the third Class at the Expiration of the sixth Year, so that one third may be chosen every second Year; and if Vacancies happen by Resignation, or otherwise, during the Recess of the Legislature of any State, the Executive thereof may make temporary Appointments until the next Meeting of the Legislature, which shall then fill such Vacancies.*

With House members serving two years while Senators serve six, our founders wanted to make sure that one-third of Senators stood for election every time the House members did. To accomplish this, the first group of Senators were divided equally into three groups. The first group's term would expire in two years, the second in four years, and the third at six years.

Vacancies for Senators were to be filled by the state's legislature. If, however, the legislature was not in session, then the governor could make a temporary appointment until the legislature was back in session. With the ratification of the 17th Amendment the way Senate vacancies are filled changed as well. Now when a Senate seat is vacant, the governor calls a special election. The state legislature may give the governor the ability to make temporary appointments until the election happens.

Clause 3 – Requirements for Senators

> *No Person shall be a Senator who shall not have*
> *attained to the Age of thirty Years, and been*
> *nine Years a Citizen of the United States and*
> *who shall not, when elected, be an Inhabitant*
> *of that State for which he shall be chosen.*

While a person may become a member of the House at the age of 25, he or she cannot be a Senator until they reach 30. A House member needs to be a citizen for seven years, but a Senator must be one for nine. Why the difference? We'll see as we go through Article 2 that the duties and responsibilities of the two houses of Congress are different. The House focuses on issues such as taxation and spending, while the Senate deals with treaties and the appointment of government officials. Our founders seemed to think that while 25 years was sufficient life experience to deal with the responsibilities in the House, a bit more would be needed to fulfill the responsibilities of the Senate.

As with the list of qualifications for a member of the House of Representatives, what we have here is a list of disqualifications for Senator and the same painful double negative language, but by now I hope we have a good understanding of how it works.

Clause 4 – President of the Senate

> *The Vice President of the United States shall*
> *be President of the Senate, but shall have no*
> *Vote, unless they be equally divided.*

It shouldn't take more than elementary school math to realize that with two Senators per state there is a chance for there to be a tied vote in the Senate. To deal with this eventuality, our founders made the Vice President the President of the Senate, but gave him no vote unless there is a tie.

Today, this ability to break a tie in the Senate is used for partisan purposes, but when the Constitution was first ratified, the Vice President was not the President's running mate, he was the second-place finisher in the presidential election. With the ratification of the Twelfth Amendment the electors began casting separate ballots for President and Vice President.

Clause 5 – Officers of the Senate

The Senate shall choose their other Officers, and
also a President pro tempore, in the Absence
of the Vice President, or when he shall exercise
the Office of President of the United States.

Just as in the House, the Senate chooses its own officers. However, where the House has a Speaker, the Senate has a President pro tempore, which is Latin for "for the time being." The President pro tempore of the Senate was to act as President of the Senate in the absence of the Vice President or if the Vice President must act as President.

Clause 6 – Trying Impeachments

The Senate shall have the sole Power to try all
Impeachments. When sitting for that Purpose, they
shall be on Oath or Affirmation. When the President
of the United States is tried, the Chief Justice shall
preside: And no Person shall be convicted without the
Concurrence of two thirds of the Members present.

While the House of Representatives can impeach a federal officer, the Senate tries the case. While the Senate is trying an impeachment, its members are under oath or affirmation, similar to a jury trial. Unlike a jury trial, though, the decision does not need to be unanimous but only a two-thirds majority. In a case where the President is impeached, the Chief Justice of the supreme Court must preside over the trial.

It's important to recognize the distinction made here regarding impeachment. It's the House of Representatives, the representatives of the people, who determine if it's right to bring charges against a federal officer, but it's the Senate, the representatives of the states, who both try the facts of the case and determine if it's worthy of removal from office. Those of us old enough to remember saw this in the impeachment of President William J. Clinton. The house passed articles of impeachment, accusing the President of perjury and obstruction of justice. The Senate found the President not guilty, either because the House did not prove the facts of their case or because they did not believe it was worthy of removal from office.

Clause 7 – Punishment of Impeachment

> *Judgment in Cases of Impeachment shall not*
> *extend further than to removal from Office, and*
> *disqualification to hold and enjoy any Office of*
> *honor, Trust or Profit under the United States:*
> *but the Party convicted shall nevertheless be*
> *liable and subject to Indictment, Trial, Judgment*
> *and Punishment, according to Law.*

The only sentence an impeachment trial can impose is removal from office and disqualification to hold a federal office. That does not mean the convicted person cannot be charged with crimes related to the actions that brought the impeachment, only that the Senate can impose no other punishment. This means that impeachment does not count as jeopardy under the Fifth Amendment's double-jeopardy clause. This is because someone convicted of impeachment is not in danger of financial penalty or imprisonment.

Section 4 – Elections

While the offices are in the federal government, the elections are run by the states because they are state offices. This is not just a formality, but should be a reminder that we are 50 sovereign states and the choosing of those who will represent both our people and our states is a sovereign function.

Clause 1 – Times, Places and Manner of Elections

The Times, Places and Manner of holding
Elections for Senators and Representatives, shall
be prescribed in each State by the Legislature
thereof; but the Congress may at any time by
Law make or alter such Regulations, except
as to the Places of choosing Senators.

The time, place, and manner of holding elections are state functions. In fact, there are no national elections in the United States; they are all held at the state level. This is important for many reasons and I will go into more detail on some of them when I discuss presidential elections in Article II. By having the elections for federal offices controlled by the states, the Constitution not only reinforces state sovereignty, but by distributing the power over elections, it helps reduce the impact of electoral irregularities.

Congress can pass laws regarding those election rules, such as setting a national Election Day, but they cannot change the place of choosing Senators. The 17th Amendment did that.

Clause 2 – Congress' Annual Assembly

The Congress shall assemble at least once
in every Year, and such Meeting shall be on
the first Monday in December, unless they
shall by Law appoint a different Day.

Remember, in 1787 traveling around the states was a lot more difficult than it is now. Imagine having to ride a horse or a coach from Georgia up to New York City, our first capital. After the Capital was moved to Washington, D.C., things didn't get any better. Not only was it a long and difficult ride, but Washington was built on a swamp and summers were unbearably hot and humid. (Maybe that is why our founders selected Washington, to discourage politicians from spending too much time there?) The date of the meeting was changed by the 20th Amendment from the first Monday in December to January 3rd.

Section 5 – Rules for Congress

Every organization needs a set of rules of operation. Section 5 includes some of the rules for Congress, even the rule that they can make their own rules about how they operate, within the limits of the Constitution of course.

Clause 1 – Judgment of Elections, Returns and Qualifications

> *Each House shall be the Judge of the Elections,*
> *Returns and Qualifications of its own Members, and*
> *a Majority of each shall constitute a Quorum to do*
> *Business; but a smaller Number may adjourn from*
> *day to day, and may be authorized to compel the*
> *Attendance of absent Members, in such Manner, and*
> *under such Penalties as each House may provide.*

Each house of Congress judges the elections, returns, and qualifications of its own members. That means if something is shady in an election, the house that member is elected to can judge whether the election is valid and if the member is qualified to serve. Does that mean that Congress can overrule the will of the people or the state? Yes, to some extent. It is this check and balance that is meant to help keep both Congress and the states accountable. If the House were to unfairly dismiss the election of a member, it would not only require a majority of the members to concur, but those members would have to answer to the people who elected them. While that is also true for the Senate today, in 1787 the Senators would be held accountable to the state legislatures.

By having the houses of Congress be the judge of the elections of its members, they can hold the states accountable should there be evidence of a manipulated election.

In order for either house to conduct business, a majority of the members must be present, though a smaller number may be able to adjourn the meeting. That means a house of Congress can be in session even if there aren't enough members to conduct business. We'll see why this is important as we delve deeper into this Article, see that this smaller number of members can compel absent members to attend, and what penalties can be applied for failure to comply.

Clause 2 – Rules of Proceedings

Each House may determine the Rules of its Proceedings,
punish its Members for disorderly Behavior, and, with
the Concurrence of two thirds, expel a Member.

Each house can determine its own rules. Whether you like or hate the filibuster, it's there because the Senate created that rule for itself and only the Senate can change it. Don't like that the Speaker of the House appoints members of committees, then blame the House rules because only the House can change it. Each house also can punish its members for disorderly behavior. What is disorderly behavior? Whatever that house determines it is. Don't think House members should be taking trips overseas on the public dime? It's up the House to determine if that should be punished. Think Senators should not be out campaigning when the Senate is in session? Again, that's the Senate's prerogative.

Also notice, there are only two ways a Congressman can be removed from office: He or she can lose an election or two-thirds of their fellow members can vote to remove them. Technically there is a third way, in that they can be impeached and convicted. However, since it takes both houses to remove someone via impeachment, it's easier just to have one house remove him or her.

Clause 3 – Journal of Proceedings

> *Each House shall keep a Journal of its Proceedings,*
> *and from time to time publish the same, excepting*
> *such Parts as may in their Judgment require Secrecy;*
> *and the Yeas and Nays of the Members of either*
> *House on any question shall, at the Desire of one*
> *fifth of those present, be entered on the Journal.*

Have you ever heard of the "Congressional Record?" That is the journal of proceedings from both houses of Congress. Everything Congress says and does, with the exception of what a majority deems must be kept secret, has to be written down and publicly published. It requires only one-fifth of the members present to request that their votes be recorded in the journal as well. Remember from the Preamble, We the People have formed this union and the legislature works for us, either directly or via the state. That is why what they say and do are public record, so those they work for can oversee them.

Clause 4 – Adjournment

> *Neither House, during the Session of Congress,*
> *shall, without the Consent of the other, adjourn for*
> *more than three days, nor to any other Place than*
> *that in which the two Houses shall be sitting.*

Why would the Constitution deal with how Congress goes into recess? The answer is three-fold. First, they wanted to make sure that one house could not shut down the Congress by making sure they got the consent of the other before leaving. They can adjourn for three days, but beyond that they need to get permission from the other house. The second reason is to make sure both houses meet in the same location. The Senate cannot decide it's going to meet in Chicago; they must meet at the location determined by law for them to be in session. The third isn't stated here, but in Article II, Section 2, the President is given the power to fill vacancies in the executive branch when the Senate is in recess. By ensuring that the Senate cannot go into recess without the House's consent, the leadership of the Senate cannot conspire with the President to make recess appointments they could not get through the full Senate.

Section 6 – Paying Congressmen

The paying of Congressmen can be a contentious issue. On the one hand, paying someone an appropriate amount for their work is right, On the other hand, do we really want career politicians?

Clause 1 – Compensation and Exception from Arrest

The Senators and Representatives shall receive a Compensation for their Services, to be ascertained by Law, and paid out of the Treasury of the United States. They shall in all Cases, except Treason, Felony and Breach of the Peace, be privileged from Arrest during their Attendance at the Session of their respective Houses, and in going to and returning from the same; and for any Speech or Debate in either House, they shall not be questioned in any other Place.

Congressmen get paid for their work. Some think they are paid too much, others think they don't get paid enough, but they are required to be paid out of the U.S. Treasury. Also, with the exception of treason, felonies, and breach of the peace, Congressmen are exempt from arrest while they are attending sessions and while they are traveling to and from their congressional house. This prevents state officials and citizens from interfering with the duties of congressmen. You may think what a congressman does in office is criminal, and it may even be so, but unless it is treason, a felony, or breach of the peace, they cannot be arrested while in session or going to or from session. In addition, Congressmen cannot even be questioned, in a legal sense, for what they say in Congress. You can question what they say or do in Congress, but the legal system cannot. If you don't like what your Congressman says, it's up to you to help get them voted out.

Clause 2 – Emoluments & Holding Office

> *No Senator or Representative shall, during the*
> *Time for which he was elected, be appointed to*
> *any civil Office under the Authority of the United*
> *States, which shall have been created, or the*
> *Emoluments whereof shall have been increased*
> *during such time: and no Person holding any Office*
> *under the United States, shall be a Member of*
> *either House during his Continuance in Office.*

No one can be both a Congressman and hold another office in the federal government. That is why, when a Congressman is nominated for an office in the government, he or she must immediately resign when confirmed and appointed. Vice versa, if someone holding an office in the government runs for a house of Congress, they must resign when they are elected.

One other little twist has to do with Congress' oversight of federal offices. Congressmen cannot be appointed to an office if that office was created or its pay increased while they were in office. That person must wait until his or her term expires before he or she can be appointed to that position. That will prevent a Congressman from taking advantage of his or her position and Congress' ability to control the pay of federal workers.

Section 7 – Legislation

Since the primary power of the legislative branch is the creation of legislation, section 7 describes the process.

Clause 1 – The Power of the Purse

All Bills for raising Revenue shall originate in the
House of Representatives; but the Senate may propose
or concur with Amendments as on other Bills.

Why would our Founding Fathers want all revenue bills to originate in the House? Remember, the Senate is to represent the states and the House is to represent the people. So, the purpose of this clause is to make sure that any bills for collecting money would be created by those who represent the people. When you complain about filling out your tax returns, you should blame your Representative, not the President or your Senator. This idea that raising revenue should start with the people's house has been extended to bills for spending as well, although this is not required by the Constitution.

I've heard people say the Senate and the President have nothing to do with taxation and spending bills, but the language here says that bills must originate in the House. If these bills start in the House, it's logical that they must go somewhere else. We see here that the Senate may propose or concur with amendments as on other bills. For the Senate to be able to propose an amendment, then it must be submitted to them for consideration. Therefore, there are only two options for a revenue bill before the Senate: They may propose amendments to it or they may concur with it. Nowhere does the Constitution say that only the House of Representatives is responsible for revenue bills. This language shows that our founders wanted the people's house to be responsible for creating this legislation, but not to be the sole house responsible for it.

One other question we need to ask is: What does it mean for a bill to originate in one of the houses of the legislature? Remember the Affordable Care Act, also known as Obama Care. This bill started in the House of Representatives (it was given a house bill number) then sent to the Senate, which completely rewrote it. I've heard a lot of people complain that, because the bill raised revenue through fines, and because the bill was rewritten completely in the Senate, the bill didn't originate in the House. Technically, though, the House crafted a revenue bill which they sent to the Senate where amendments were offered, then the bill was returned to the House. The amendments completely rewrote the legislation, but the House approved those changes. If you have an issue with the Senate effectively writing a revenue bill, complain to your representative, since the House approved the rewrite.

Clause 2 – Presidential Involvement

Every Bill which shall have passed the House of Representatives and the Senate, shall, before it become a Law, be presented to the President of the United States; if he approve he shall sign it, but if not he shall return it, with his Objections to that House in which it shall have originated, who shall enter the Objections at large on their Journal, and proceed to reconsider it. If after such Reconsideration two thirds of that House shall agree to pass the Bill, it shall be sent, together with the Objections, to the other House, by which it shall likewise be reconsidered, and if approved by two thirds of that House, it shall become a Law. But in all such Cases the Votes of both Houses shall be determined by yeas and Nays, and the Names of the Persons voting for and against the Bill shall be entered on the Journal of each House respectively. If any Bill shall not be returned by the President within ten Days (Sundays excepted) after it shall have been presented to him, the Same shall be a Law, in like Manner as if he had signed it, unless the Congress by their Adjournment prevent its Return, in which Case it shall not be a Law.

Most Americans are familiar with the basic process of lawmaking in this country. Let's take a closer look at some of the details behind this process.

Every bill that is passed by both the House of Representatives and the Senate goes to the President. If the President approves by signing it, the bill it becomes law. This sounds easy, but remember, each house can make up their own rules for their proceedings (Section 5), so the process for a bill being passed by each house is generally long and difficult. If the President doesn't approve of the bill, he must return it to the house where the bill originated along with a list of his objections. Notice, the President does not just veto a bill, he must give his reasons why he is doing so.

This is an interesting process. If all legislative power is given to Congress, what does the President, the head of the Executive branch, have to do with making law? Since it is the executive branch which must enforce the law, the head of that branch is given the opportunity to approve it or list objections. This check and balance between the branches of government is meant to give the executive branch the opportunity to comment not only on the effectiveness of the bill, but on its constitutionality. When President George W. Bush signed the Bipartisan Campaign Reform Act of 2002, he included a signing statement that stated, "Certain provisions present serious constitutional concerns."

One of the main reasons legislation must go the President before becoming law is for the executive to determine if, in their opinion, it is constitutional or not. By signing legislation he thought had "serious constitutional concerns", President Bush abdicated one of his most important duties as President, that of supporting the Constitution by doing what he can to make sure unconstitutional bills do not become law.

When a bill is returned to Congress, the objections of the President are entered into the journal for the house that originated the bill and then they can reconsider it. This makes sure Congress is aware of the specific issues the President has with the legislation. Congress can then modify the legislation or, if they believe the President is in error, can re-vote on the legislation as is. If two-thirds of both houses believe the bill is acceptable as is, they override the President's veto. This, too, is a check and balance, making sure that a President cannot simply veto any legislation over the will of the representatives of the people and the states.

It is also interesting that while the recording of votes requires one-fifth of the members to vote for it (Section 5), in the case of an override vote all yeas and nays must be recorded in the journal.

What happens if the President ignores the bill? The President has ten days, Sundays excepted, to return a bill, either signed or with objections. First, let's look at the "Sundays excepted" clause. The United States does not have an official religion, but at the founding, most Americans were either some denomination of Christianity or agreed with the Judeo-Christian ethics of the society. In keeping with the true definition of "separation of church and state", and recognizing that many of those in the executive branch would most likely follow Christian standards of conduct, the founders determined to allow the weekly day of devotion to be excluded from the time the President had to return legislation.

If the ten days expires, the fate of the bill is determined by whether Congress is in session. If Congress is in session, then the bill becomes law even if the President does not sign it. However, if Congress is not in session and therefore the bill cannot be returned to them, then the bill does not become law.

We see that, while the process of law-making looks simple, the details can become complicated. With votes and vetoes, reconsideration, overrides, and signing gamesmanship, the process of turning bills into laws can be long and complicated.

Remember, those who wrote and ratified the Constitution wanted a limited and confined central government. They not only wanted to limit what Congress could make laws about, but they wanted to make sure that only the best laws could survive the process. That is why there are so many hurdles for legislation to go through and why so many different entities need to approve it. So, the next time you hear someone complain because Congress isn't passing enough laws, remind them that the system was designed that way for a very good reason.

Clause 3 – Legislation Continued

*Every Order, Resolution, or Vote to which
the Concurrence of the Senate and House of
Representatives may be necessary (except on a question
of Adjournment) shall be presented to the President
of the United States; and before the Same shall take
Effect, shall be approved by him, or being disapproved
by him, shall be repassed by two thirds of the Senate
and House of Representatives, according to the Rules
and Limitations prescribed in the Case of a Bill.*

We've dealt with bills, now we'll deal with orders, resolutions, or votes. We know what votes are, but what about orders and resolutions?

*ORDER: Mandate; precept; command;
authoritative direction.*[114]

*RESOLUTION: The determination or decision
of a legislative body, or a formal proposition
offered for legislative determination.*[115]

The difference between an order and a resolution comes down to outcome. When an order is given, it comes with the authority to enforce it. In other words, violate an order and there will most likely be consequences. Although we don't see many congressional orders, they appear to be meant to enforce a previously passed law. Resolutions, on the other hand, are merely a statement of opinion of Congress or a proposition for another branch to do something. Currently we see a lot of the most feckless of resolutions, the "non-binding resolution", which is little more than a congressional hissy fit since it has neither the force of law nor the expectation that Congress will actually do what they have "resolved" to do.

---

[114] Webster's 1828 Dictionary http://webstersdictionary1828.com.
[115] IBID.

Section 8 – Congress' Enumerated Powers

Section 8 is probably the most important yet least understood section of Article I. Within this section are almost all the powers that Congress has. In fact, when the 10th Amendment was passed on December 15, 1791, this list became the only powers, along with a few other scattered through the Constitution, that Congress could legally use.

> *The powers not delegated to the United States by the Constitution, nor prohibited by it to the States, are reserved to the States respectively, or to the people.*[116]

Sadly, today neither the people nor the federal government seem to bother with the legal limitations on Congress or, in fact, any of the branches of the federal government.

Clause 1 – Taxation

> *The Congress shall have Power to lay and collect Taxes, Duties, Imposts and Excises, to pay the Debts and provide for the common Defense and general Welfare of the United States; but all Duties, Imposts and Excises shall be uniform throughout the United States;*

Congress has the power to collect taxes, along with duties, imposts, and excises (different types of taxes). Some of you may be tempted to blame this clause for your frustration on April 15th. Blame, however, should be placed on the 16th Amendment:

> *The Congress shall have power to lay and collect taxes on incomes, from whatever source derived, without apportionment among the several States, and without regard to any census or enumeration.*[117]

---

[116] United States Constitution, Amendment X.
[117] United States Constitution, Amendment XVI.

Until the 16th Amendment was ratified in 1913, Congress was not allowed to impose taxes on you directly. Before the 16th Amendment, Article I, Section 2 stated that direct taxes (taxes imposed directly on the people of the United States rather than through trade), were apportioned to the States, not the people. In other words, these taxes were divided amongst the states proportional to their population; then the states would collect taxes from their citizens as they chose.

Congress is also empowered to pay the national debts and provide for the common defense and general welfare of the United States. Unfortunately, today Congress seems more interested in increasing the national debt than in paying it off (but more about that later in this chapter).

To understand this phrase, and in fact much of the Constitution, we must ask one important question: What did the signers and the ratifiers of the Constitution mean by the 'United States'? Remember, before the ratification of the Constitution, we had thirteen sovereign and independent states. If you read the Declaration of Independence, you'll see they are referred to as the "united States," where "united" is an adjective describing the states. When drafting the Articles of Confederation, our founders now started referring to the "United States" as a single entity. Does that mean the states were no longer sovereign and independent states? No. Our founding documents and the Federalist and Anti-Federalist Papers indicated the "United States" refers to the central government and the "United States of America" to the union of states as they have compacted together. What the term "United States" does not mean are the citizens of the states themselves. This will become important as we explore the rest of the phrase.

What can Congress collect taxes for? They can collect taxes to pay the debts of the federal government, but not for the individual states. This is important as we see more states and territories in financial trouble looking to Washington, D.C. to bail them out. Congress is also to provide for the common defense of the states as a whole, not the defense of, or within the individual states. This means the Congress is to provide for the defense against a threat to the states from the outside or between states, but not within the states themselves. We have gone to war several times in our history to protect the states, and Congress has allocated untold billions of dollars to defend our nation, but Congress cannot legally provide for the internal defenses of a state. For example, Congress can provide for the defense of our national borders, but it cannot legally pay for law enforcement activities within a state. What defense Congress can provide must be common for all the states.

While there are several phrases in the Constitution that are regularly misrepresented, one of the most common is Congress' power to provide for the "general welfare" of the United States. Let's break down that phrase so we can understand it.

> *GENERAL: Public; common; relating to or*
> *comprehending the whole community; as the*
> *general interest or safety of a nation.*[118]

> *WELFARE: Exemption from any unusual*
> *evil or calamity; the enjoyment of peace and*
> *prosperity, or the ordinary blessings of society*
> *and civil government; applied to states.*[119]

General welfare, when applied to the states, means the exemption from unusual evil or calamity and the enjoyment of peace, prosperity, and the blessings of society for the community as a whole. The next logical question should be: What community?

Notice, the Constitution does not say the general welfare of the people of the United States of America, nor the general welfare of the States, but of the United States. Today, when we think of the United States, we usually think of a nation broken into 50 subdivisions we call states, but when the Constitution was ratified, we had 13 independent states who joined together and delegated some of their powers to a central

---

[118] Webster's 1828 Dictionary http://webstersdictionary1828.com.

[119] IBID.

government called the United States. This distinction may seem trivial, but it is quite important.

If the United States is a single government subdivided into smaller units we call states, then Washington, D.C. rules and your states are really colonies of Washington, D.C., which is not much different from their condition in 1776 as colonies of Britain.

> *The Congress shall have Power To lay and collect*
> *Taxes, Duties, Imposts and Excises, to pay the*
> *Debts and provide for the common Defense*
> *and general Welfare of the United States*[120]

However, the meaning of this quote is different if we are 50 sovereign states who have delegated some of their power to the union, and if the term United States refers to the union and its central government. It means that Congress can collect taxes to pay the debts of the federal government, not those of the states. It means Congress can collect taxes to pay for the defense of the nation as a whole, not the defense of individual states. And most importantly, it means Congress can collect taxes to pay for the general welfare of the union, but not for the people nor for the individual states themselves.

This is not what we've been taught, and you may be thinking I'm pulling this out of thin air. I looked to the words of James Madison, known as the "Father of the Constitution," when he debated the Cod Fisheries bill in the House of Representatives in February, 1792. The bill in question included a provision for the central government to provide bounties to cod fisherman to encourage people to join the profession. During the debate, on February 3rd, a Mr. Giles said:

> *The present section of the bill (he continued) appears*
> *to contain a direct bounty on occupations; and if*
> *that be its object, it is the first attempt as yet made*
> *by this government to exercise such authority;*

---

[120] United States Constitution, Article I, Section 8, Clause 1.

> *-- and its constitutionality struck him in a doubtful*
> *point of view; for in no part of the Constitution*
> *could he, in express terms, find a power given to*
> *Congress to grant bounties on occupations: the*
> *power is neither {427} directly granted, nor (by any*
> *reasonable construction that he could give) annexed*
> *to any other specified in the Constitution.*[121]

No one, not even those who supported the bill, could come up with any reasonable way of showing that the Constitution gave Congress this power. Later, on February 7th, Mr. Madison went into a detailed explanation of why the common defense and general welfare clauses could not be used to justify Congress having the power to spend money in that way.

> *It is to be recollected that the terms "common defence*
> *and general welfare," as here used, are not novel terms,*
> *first introduced into this Constitution. They are terms*
> *familiar in their construction, and well known to the*
> *people of America. They are repeatedly found in the*
> *old Articles of Confederation, where, although they are*
> *susceptible of as great a latitude as can be given them*
> *by the context here, it was never supposed or pretended*
> *that they conveyed any such power as is now assigned*
> *to them. On the contrary, it was always considered*
> *clear and certain that the old Congress was limited*
> *to the enumerated powers, and that the enumeration*
> *limited and explained the general terms.*[122]

In short, never before had it been considered that Congress would have the power to collect taxes to be used for anything it thought was

---

[121] Debate on the On the Cod Fishery Bill, granting Bounties, House of Representatives, February 3, 1792.

[122] IBID.

good or for the general welfare. Mr. Madison went on to describe the dangers of granting Congress such power.

> *If Congress can employ money indefinitely to the*
> *general welfare, and are the sole and supreme judges of*
> *the general welfare, they may take the care of religion*
> *into their Own hands; they may a point teachers in*
> *every state, county, and parish, and pay them out of*
> *their public treasury; they may take into their own*
> *hands the education of children, establishing in like*
> *manner schools throughout the Union; they may*
> *assume the provision for the poor; they may undertake*
> *the regulation of all roads other than post-roads; in*
> *short, every thing, from the highest object of state*
> *legislation down to the most minute object of police,*
> *would be thrown under the power of Congress; for*
> *every object I have mentioned would admit of the*
> *application of money, and might be called, if Congress*
> *pleased, provisions for the general welfare.*[123]

Mr. Madison recognized that if we gave Congress the power to determine what is and is not for the general welfare of the United States, then every portion of your life would be under the control of Congress. We see today, as Congress has routinely delegated their powers to the executive and judicial branches, we now live in a nation where literally everything is a federal case.

> *In short, sir, without going farther into the subject.*
> *Which I should not have here touched at all but for*
> *the reasons already mentioned, I venture to declare*
> *it as my opinion, that, were the power of Congress to*
> *be established in the latitude contended for, it would*
> *subvert the very foundations, and transmute the*

---

[123] IBID.

> *very nature of the limited government established*
> *by the people of America; and what inferences might*
> *be drawn, or what consequences ensue, from such*
> *a step, it is incumbent on us all to consider.*[124]

Mr. Madison was right. As we have seen through history, Congress' appetite for control over the citizenry has grown without limit or restraint. The very idea that there are limitations on the federal government is all but heresy in today's political and judicial environments. Effectively no limitation exists on Congress but what the supreme Court decrees, and the role of the states is no longer considered. I wish previous generation had considered the consequences of giving Congress powers beyond their constitutional boundaries, and can only encourage that we today not only consider them, but begin enforcing those boundaries again.

Clause 2 – Borrow Money

To borrow Money on the credit of the United States;

Notice that it is the Congress that has the power to borrow. Unfortunately, for the last 50 years, Congress has been run by people who don't understand basic math as it applies to borrowing money. Currently, the Congress owes (which means WE owe) $21.49 trillion dollars, or approximately $67,000 per person in the United States, and that does not include the promises Congress has made but for which they have not put aside any money.

As of the writing of this book, the last year with complete Gross Domestic Product (GDP) data for the U.S. is 2017. "Gross domestic product (GDP) is the monetary value of all the finished goods and services produced within a country's borders in a specific time period."[125] In 2017,

---

[124] Debate on the On the Cod Fishery Bill, granting Bounties, House of Representatives, February 7, 1792.

[125] Investopedia https://www.investopedia.com/terms/g/gdp.asp.

the total value of all finished goods and services in the United States was $19.39 trillion[126], or $2.1 trillion less than what we owe through our government. It would be bad enough if you had debts greater than your annual income, but the federal government collected $3.32 trillion in 2017. That means we owe, through our government, almost SIX AND A HALF TIMES more than Washington, D.C. takes in every year. That is ruinous.

If any other entity in the United States, any person, business, state, county, or local government was this deeply in debt, it would have had to declare bankruptcy decades ago. But since people around the world seem to trust that the United States will at least pay the interest on its debts, they keep lending Washington, D.C. money. Congress, like a heroin addict, is more than happy for their next fix. Regrettably, one day we the American people will have to pay for their addiction.

Clause 3 – Commerce Clause

To regulate Commerce with foreign Nations, and
among the several States, and with the Indian Tribes;

As James Madison wrote in Federalist Paper #45, the power of the federal government is to be focused on foreign affairs.

The powers delegated by the proposed Constitution
to the federal government are few and defined.
Those which are to remain in the State governments
are numerous and indefinite. The former will be
exercised principally on external objects, as war,
peace, negotiation and foreign commerce. ... The
powers reserved to the several States will extend
to all the objects which in the ordinary course
of affairs, concern the lives and liberties, and

---

[126] U.S. Debt Clock http://www.usdebtclock.org/.

properties of the people, and the internal order,
improvement and prosperity of the State.[127]

The Commerce Clause here gives Congress the power to regulate commerce among several different sovereign entities, foreign nations, Indian tribes, and among the several states. Remember, when the Constitution was written and ratified, we had thirteen independent and sovereign states that, as James Madison put it, delegated power to the federal government. So, they were sovereign entities just like foreign nations and Indian tribes. If we are going to understand this power to regulate foreign commerce though, there are a couple of words we need to understand.

REGULATE: To adjust by rule, method or established
mode; as, to regulate weights and measures; to
regulate the assize of bread; to regulate our moral
conduct by the laws of God and of society; to
regulate our manners by the customary forms.

To put in good order; as, to regulate the
disordered state of a nation or its finances.

To subject to rules or restrictions; as, to
regulate trade; to regulate diet.[128]

Congress, and only Congress, has the power to regulate, to adjust by, or subject to rules or restrictions, trade with foreign nations, between the states, and with the Indian tribes. If we read the whole definition, the primary idea is to make things regular or to standardize so Congress can create rules to standardize or make regular foreign commerce. They can also standardize things like weights, measures, finances, and taxes

---

[127] Federalist Paper #45 https://www.congress.gov/resources/display/content/ The+Federalist+Papers#TheFederalistPapers-45.

[128] Webster's 1828 Dictionary http://webstersdictionary1828.com.

between the states. Imagine if a gallon of gasoline in Tennessee was different from one in Delaware or if a pound of beef weighed less in Ohio than in Georgia?

> COMMERCE: *In a general sense, an interchange or mutual change of goods, wares, productions, or property of any kind, between nations or individuals, either by barter, or by purchase and sale; trade; traffick. commerce is foreign or inland. Foreign commerce is the trade which one nation carries on with another; inland commerce or inland trade, is the trade in the exchange of commodities between citizens of the same nation or state. Active commerce*[129]

Commerce is the exchange of goods and/or services, either between nations or between individuals. Therefore, the Commerce Clause gives Congress the power to make regular the exchange of goods and services between the states and with foreign nations. What Congress cannot do is regulate commerce within a state, yet our friends at the supreme Court seem to think differently.

For over 150 years, the courts kept in check Congress' repeated attempts to control the economy by abuses of the Commerce Clause. However, in 1942, the case *Wickard v. Filburn* reached the supreme Court. Roscoe Filburn was a farmer in Ohio who grew wheat, including some strictly for the use of his family. This "extra acreage" ran afoul of the federal "Agricultural Adjustment Act", an unconstitutional law regulating agricultural production. Mr. Roscoe sued, claiming that since the wheat was never sold there was no commerce to regulate. The court decided against Mr. Roscoe on the basis that, "This record leaves us in no doubt that Congress may properly have considered that wheat consumed on the farm where grown, if wholly outside the scheme of

---

[129] Webster's 1828 Dictionary http://webstersdictionary1828.com.

regulation, would have a substantial effect in defeating and obstructing its purpose to stimulate trade therein at increased prices."[130]

Even admitting that wheat consumed on the farm where it was grown is wholly outside the scheme of regulation, this court found that it was interstate commerce because it would have a "substantial effect" on the purposes of Congress. However, Congress is not superior to the Constitution. In fact, Article VI says the Constitution and only laws passed pursuant to it are the supreme law of the land.

Congress abuses this power repeatedly by effectively regulating everything from milk to toilets. Congress even abuses this power to regulate gun laws within the states. Since it's obvious the courts will no longer stand up to Congress' abuse of this power, it's time for the states to do so. Unfortunately, they have shown little willingness and even less commitment to protecting the rights of their citizens.

Clause 4 – Naturalization & Bankruptcies

To establish a uniform Rule of Naturalization,
and uniform Laws on the subject of
Bankruptcies throughout the United States;

The Constitution established a union among the several states, but it also stated in Article VI, Section 2:

The Citizens of each State shall be
entitled to all Privileges and Immunities
of Citizens in the several States.[131]

We've lost the idea that we are 50 free, independent, and sovereign states in union together. According to Article VI, we are citizens of the state we reside in just as much as of the United States of America. While the states have delegated the authority to set the rules for nationalization

---

[130] *Wickard v. Filburn*, 317 U.S. 111 (1942) - https://supreme.justia.com/cases/federal/us/317/111/.

[131] United States Constitution, Article VI, Section 2, Clause 1.

to the central government, they have not delegated the power to set the rules for immigration.

> IMMIGRATION: *The passing or removing into a country for the purpose of permanent residence.*

> NATURALIZATION: *The act of investing an alien with the rights and privileges of a native subject or citizen.*[132]

This is an important part of the debate today because we're ignoring the definitions of these words and the federal government has assumed the authority to set rules for both immigration and naturalization. If we followed the Constitution, the states would set their own immigration policy and the federal government would set the naturalization policy.

You may think having different immigration policies in each state would cause confusion, but look at the definition of immigration. States would determine the rules for residency. If someone immigrated to California then wanted to move to Colorado, they would have to follow Colorado's rules if they wanted to become residents of that state. The question then becomes, who determines rules for visiting this nation? Again, since it hasn't been specifically delegated to the central government, it remains with the state.

If the states retained the power to set rules for foreign visitors and immigration, why was the central government delegated the power to determine the rules for naturalization? Because, according to Article VI, citizenship grants both privileges and immunities that are recognized throughout the union. Can you imagine the concerns the states had knowing they would have to grant privileges to citizens of other states that may not have the citizenship standards they require? For example, what if the state an immigrant wanted to settle in, say Massachusetts, required 11 years of residency before they could become a citizen. If another state, say Delaware, only required three years, then the immigrant could simply live in Delaware for three years, gain his or her citizenship,

---

[132] Webster's 1828 Dictionary http://webstersdictionary1828.com.

then move to Massachusetts and be granted all the privileges of being a citizen of Massachusetts. To help deal with this issue, the Constitution delegates the power to establish rules for nationalization to Congress.

Congress is also delegated the power to create uniform bankruptcy laws throughout the United States. This means someone cannot avoid their debts by fleeing to a state with more favorable laws regarding bankruptcies.

Clause 5 – Money, Weights and Measures

> *To coin Money, regulate the Value*
> *thereof, and of foreign Coin, and fix the*
> *Standard of Weights and Measures;*

Congress not only has the power to coin money, but to determine its value, both locally and in relation to foreign currency. I believe many agree with me that Congress has done a pretty poor job regulating the value of money, but it is their job. What we have to do is hold them accountable for how they are doing that job.

Congress also has the power to determine how long a foot is, how much a pound weighs, and any other weight or measure. While the definition of most weights and measures were determined long ago, the clause means the Congress, not the states, determine standard weights and measures. When you buy a pound of butter in Texas it will weigh the same as one from Tennessee. If not, you have a cause for legal action.

Clause 6 – Counterfeiting

> *To provide for the Punishment of counterfeiting the*
> *Securities and current Coin of the United States;*

Congress has the power to determine the punishment for counterfeiting the securities and coin of the United States. I'm sure we're all familiar with the concept of counterfeiting money, but what are these securities the Constitution is talking about?

> *SECURITY: Anything given or deposited to secure*
> *the payment of a debt, or the performance of a*
> *contract; as a bond with surety, a mortgage, the*
> *indorsement of a responsible man, a pledge, etc.*[133]

When the United States borrows money, it issues a bond or bill as a promissory note to pay off the debt it has incurred. Congress can set a punishment for counterfeiting these and other securities of the United States, but not for other securities like corporate stocks and bonds, though that, of course, doesn't stop them from doing it.

Notice that Congress has the power to determine the punishment for counterfeiting securities and coin, but not currency. That's because before 1861, United States dollars were only available as coins, not the "folding money" we know of today. Like bonds, these original bills were redeemable in gold from the United States Treasury, meaning they were on the "gold standard."

As you can imagine, no country wants its money faked, and since the states had delegated the power to coin and regulate the value of money to Congress, it made sense for them to determine the punishment for counterfeiting it.

Clause 7 – Post Offices & Post Roads

To establish Post Offices and post Roads;

We're all familiar with the Post Office. Whether picking up your mail at home or waiting in line at the counter, what is now called the U.S. Postal Service started before we declared independence.

In 1775, Benjamin Franklin became the first Postmaster General. When the Constitution was ratified in 1787, Congress received the power to create post offices and in 1792, President George Washington signed the Postal Service Act creating the United States Post Office Department. In 1872, the United States Post Office Department was

---

[133] Webster's 1828 Dictionary http://webstersdictionary1828.com.

elevated to a cabinet level department. Then in 1971, the Post Office Department was dissolved and replaced with the United States Postal Service, a supposedly independent agency that is controlled by Congress and whose financial shortfalls are covered by our taxes. While Congress is not specifically given the power to run the Postal Service, it is implied with the power to create post offices. Unfortunately, today it seems Congress spends more time naming post offices than dealing with the issues within the postal service.

Congress also has the power to establish post roads. In the 18ᵗʰ century, mail traveled by road and the federal government was expected to create, and presumably maintain, roads for this mail to travel on. However, while the Constitution gives Congress the power to establish post roads, it has routinely been allowed the power to create any public road. Even James Madison was concerned that Congress may take unto itself the power to maintain roads other than post roads[134].

Clause 8 – Patents and Copyrights

> *To promote the Progress of Science and useful*
> *Arts, by securing for limited Times to Authors*
> *and Inventors the exclusive Right to their*
> *respective Writings and Discoveries;*

Congress promotes science and arts in many ways. We have the National Endowment for the Arts, the National Science Foundation, and more grants than can be counted, all done to "promote the progress of science and the useful arts." There's just one problem: That is not how Congress is supposed to promote science and art.

Congress is supposed to secure, for limited times, exclusive rights to writings and discoveries. In short, copyrights and patents. The idea is simple; it takes time and money for someone to write a book, develop a new process, drug, or invention, so they should have exclusive use

---

[134]   Debate on the On the Cod Fishery Bill, granting Bounties, House of Representatives, February 3, 1792.

for a period of time. If we want these scientific discoveries, new books, or other pieces of art, then we must have a method to allow those who invest in these things to recoup those investments. Congress can only legally promote science and art through granting exclusive rights for a time. Today we call these rights patents and copyrights.

> *PATENT: the exclusive right granted by a government*
> *to an inventor to manufacture, use, or sell an*
> *invention for a certain number of years.*[135]

> *COPYRIGHT: the exclusive right to make copies,*
> *license, and otherwise exploit a literary, musical, or*
> *artistic work, whether printed, audio, video, etc.*[136]

Rather than restraining themselves to their constitutional role of protecting copyrights and patents, Congress has created numerous agencies which illegally spend money "promoting the arts and sciences". These agencies include the Institute of Education Sciences, National Science Foundation (NSF), Office of Science and Technology Policy, Commission of Fine Arts, Indian Arts and Crafts Board, John F. Kennedy Center for the Performing Arts, National Endowment for the Arts (NEA), and the U.S. Commission of Fine Arts. All these agencies, when Congress only needs one: The U.S. Patent and Trademark Office. Rather than promoting the arts and sciences, these agencies restrict them by using their money to influence not only what gets studied, but what outcome the government would prefer. I'm sure we've all heard the saying, "He who pays the piper calls the tune."

Clause 9 – Federal Courts

> *To constitute Tribunals inferior to the Supreme Court;*

---

[135] Dictionary.com https://dictionary.com
[136] IBID.

Congress, and only Congress, has the power to create federal courts inferior to the supreme Court. Even when the United States was new and small, it would be impossible for a single court to hear all the cases under the jurisdiction of the judicial branch created in Article III. Inherent in the power to create these lower courts is the power to determine both their size and their jurisdictions within the scope of the Constitution. Why would the power to create inferior courts be put in the hands of Congress and not the supreme Court? Because Congress is accountable to the people and the states. This check on the judicial branch, along with the power of impeachment mentioned earlier, means the people ultimately determine, through their representatives, what our federal court system looks like.

Clause 10 – International Crimes

To define and punish Piracies and Felonies
committed on the high Seas, and Offenses
against the Law of Nations;

Congress defines what piracy is, what crimes are considered felonies on the high seas (which today are known as international waters[137]), and what crimes are against the law of nations. Also, Congress determines the punishment for these crimes. This power is restricted to two mains areas, the high seas and the law of nations, meaning the laws not within the states.

Clause 11 – War & Letters of Marque

To declare War, grant Letters of Marque
and Reprisal, and make Rules concerning
Captures on Land and Water;

WAR: A contest between nations or states,
carried on by force, either for defense, or for

---

[137] Dictionary.com https://dictionary.com.

*revenging insults and redressing wrongs, for the
extension of commerce or acquisition of territory,
or for obtaining and establishing the superiority
and dominion of one over the other. [138]*

War Powers

Only Congress can declare war. In 1973, Congress passed "The War Powers Resolution", sometimes referred to as "The War Powers Act".

*SEC. 2. (a) It is the purpose of this joint resolution
to fulfill the intent of the framers of the Constitution
of the United States and insure that the collective
judgment of both the Congress and the President will
apply to the introduction of United States Armed
Forces into hostilities, or into situations where
imminent involvement in hostilities is clearly indicated
by the circumstances, and to the continued use of
such forces in hostilities or in such situations. [139]*

Congress had a problem. With late 20th century technology, war, especially nuclear war, could start so quickly Congress would not have time to respond. They wanted to delegate a portion of their war powers to the President for these imminent emergencies.

Apparently, Congress did not read the Constitution, since it clearly states that only Congress can declare war, whether it's for defensive or offensive purposes.

*(b) Under article I, section 8, of the Constitution,
it is specifically provided that the Congress shall
have the power to make all laws necessary and*

---

[138] Webster's 1828 Dictionary http://webstersdictionary1828.com.

[139] GovInfo https://www.govinfo.gov/content/pkg/STATUTE-87/pdf/STATUTE-87-Pg555.pdf

proper for carrying into execution, not only its
own powers but also all other powers vested by
the Constitution in the Government of the United
States, or in any department or officer thereof.[140]

Article I, Section 8, Clause 18 does give Congress the authority to make laws for executing all the power delegated to the United States.

(c) The constitutional powers of the President as
Commander-in-Chief to introduce United States
Armed Forces into hostilities, or into situations
where imminent involvement in hostilities is clearly
indicated by the circumstances, are exercised only
pursuant to (1) a declaration of war, (2) specific
statutory authorization, or (3) a national emergency
created by attack upon the United States, its
territories or possessions, or its armed forces.[141]

This is where things get hairy. The President is the Commander-in-Chief of the armed forces, but only when they are called into actual service.

The President shall be Commander in Chief of
the Army and Navy of the United States, and of
the Militia of the several States, when called into
the actual Service of the United States;[142]

While the President is the Commander-in-Chief of the armed forces when they are in service to the United States, he is not given the authority to determine what, when, and where that service may be; that

---

[140] IBID.

[141] GovInfo   https://www.govinfo.gov/content/pkg/STATUTE-87/pdf/STATUTE-87-Pg555.pdf.

[142] United States Constitution, Article II, Section 2, Clause 1.

remains with Congress. As I said, the apparent concerns of Congress had to deal with hostilities that progressed faster than they could re-act. Congress wanted the President to have the authority to engage the armed forces in hostilities without having to wait for them.

*SEC. 4. (a) In the absence of a declaration
of war, in any case in which United States
Armed Forces are introduced—*

*(1) into hos'tilities or into situations where
imminent involvement in hostilities is
clearly indicated by the circumstances;*

(2)

*(3) into the territory, airspace or waters of a
foreign nation, while equipped for combat, except
for deployments which relate solely to supply,
replacement, repair, or training of such forces;*

(4)

or

*(3) in numbers which substantially enlarge
United States Armed Forces equipped for combat
already located in a foreign nation;*[143]

By reading into the Constitution the power of the President to "in-troduce United States Armed Forces into hostilities", Congress thought all they had to do was put boundaries around this power. If Congress had followed the Constitution, I believe they could have given the military a limited authority to engage in hostilities without sacrificing their

---

[143] GovInfo https://www.govinfo.gov/content/pkg/STATUTE-87/pdf/STATUTE-87-Pg555.pdf.

control over those hostilities. As Commander-in-Chief, the President has the authority to use the military is any way allowed by Congress, thus getting to the ends Congress wanted, but by Constitutional means. As history has shown, power granted is rarely power returned. Now Presidents of both parties exercise this power to engage in hostilities with limited Congressional oversight and I see little evidence that they will return this power to Congress.

Letters of Marque & Reprisal

> *MARQUE: Letters of marque are letters of reprisal;*
> *a license or extraordinary commission granted by*
> *a sovereign of one state to his subjects, to make*
> *reprisals at sea on the subjects of another, under*
> *pretense of indemnification for injuries received.*[144]

Letters of marque are literally licensed piracy. Congress has the power to grant Americans the authority to attack the vessels of other nations while at sea. While we don't see this much in the 21st century, during the 18th and 19th centuries this was not uncommon. After the Paris Peace Treaty that ended the Revolutionary War, British naval vessels would routinely board American merchant ships to seize American citizens they alleged were Royal Navy deserters. Since the American Navy was very small at the time, Congress issued letters of marque to allow privateers to plunder British vessels in reprisal. Since Congress also has the power to make rules about what is captured, bounties were offered allowing the privateers to profit from what they had taken.

Clause 11 – Standing Armies

> *To raise and support Armies, but no*
> *Appropriation of Money to that Use shall*
> *be for a longer Term than two Years;*

---

[144] Webster's 1828 Dictionary http://webstersdictionary1828.com.

The idea that the federal government raises money to support the Army should not be a surprise, though the fact the Constitution requires that support be limited to a two-year term may be. The colonies that our states came from were familiar with standing armies.

> *He has kept among us, in times of peace, Standing*
> *Armies without the Consent of our legislatures.*[145]

They had seen what can happen when a military force exists outside of civilian leadership, and that is why the President is the Commander-in-Chief of the military. What would happen if the military, either on their own or under the direction of the President, decided they knew better and started acting on their own?

> *A standing military force, with an overgrown*
> *Executive will not long be safe companions to liberty.*
>
> *James Madison*[146]

The Constitution provides two bulwarks against such a coup. First, the funding for the military comes from Congress, and it is required to be renewed every two years. With the money controlled by Congress, even if the executive branch were to try to use the military for their own agenda, where would they get the money? They could bypass Congress and begin collecting money themselves, but that leads us to the second bulwark.

> *Oppressors can tyrannize only when they*
> *achieve a standing army, an enslaved*
> *press, and a disarmed populace.*
>
> *James Madison*[147]

---

[145] United States Declaration of Independence.

[146] James Madison, Speech before Constitutional Convention, 6/29/1787.

[147] James Madison - http://www.famous-quote.net/james-madison-quotes.html.

The second protection is the militia. As we discussed in the chapter on the Second Amendment, an armed populace is necessary for the security of a free state. As James Madison said, tyrants require three things: A standing army, an enslaved press, and a disarmed populace.

Today we have a standing army, with the bi-annual funding bill a mere facade; it is a ridiculous and theatrical cover-up meant to give the appearance of conforming with the law. Meanwhile, to all practical purposes it defies its spirit under the guise of protecting us. What is the purpose of this standing army? There have been times when the nation was in danger and our brave military stood to protect us. Now, however, its effective mission is to project American power around the globe and to force others to live in a manner our political class deems acceptable. The military has been used to repay those who have attacked us, but after the debt has been paid, how many years must we use our military to enforce our will on others? I hold those who serve our nation in extremely high regard. Unfortunately, I hold those in political power over them in extremely low regard, especially when it comes to their use of our military.

> *Whoever, except in cases and under circumstances*
> *expressly authorized by the Constitution or Act of*
> *Congress, willfully uses any part of the Army or*
> *the Air Force as a posse comitatus or otherwise to*
> *execute the laws shall be fined under this title or*
> *imprisoned not more than two years, or both.*[148]

As if the misuse of our military isn't bad enough, today we see the militarization of our police forces. The Posse Commitatus (Latin for "power of the country") Act, first signed into law in 1878 and later updated in 1956 and 1981, makes it illegal to use the Army or Air Force to execute U.S. Law. What does this have to do with standing armies? Today, we not only have a standing army controlled by Washington,

---

[148]   18 U.S. Code § 1385 - Use of Army and Air Force as posse comitatus.

D.C., but the federal government is enabling and encouraging the militarization of our local, state, and federal law enforcement. How long before these militarized police forces start treating the citizens they have sworn to protect like enemy combatants? SWAT teams have already been used to serve warrants on non-violent offenders,[149] arrest suspected child pornographers,[150] and use military tactics to arrest suspects in a criminal investigation.[151] It's one thing to use a Special Weapons And Tactics squad in a special situation and it's quite another to militarize ordinary law enforcement. Because of the tactics they use, when a mistake is made the consequences are often devastating, as the examples I've used will attest.

How safe do you feel knowing that your federal, state, and probably local governments have military forces they can deploy for whatever reason they wish? Think about Article I, Section 8, Clause 12 the next time you encounter police in body armor, using military vehicles and tactics to enforce the law.

Clause 13 – The Navy

To provide and maintain a Navy;

Just as Congress can create and maintain an army, it can also create a navy. Remember in the late 18th century these were the only military forces in existence.

One interesting point, in The Posse Comitatus Act[152] last revised in 1981, only the Army and Air Force are prohibited from enforcing U.S. law, not the Navy or the Coast Guard. Even within the territorial waters of the United States, the Navy and Coast Guard can act as law

---

149 Washington Post http://www.washingtonpost.com/wp-dyn/content/article/2011/01/18/AR2011011806145.html.

150 TechDirt https://www.techdirt.com/articles/20110425/11220014028/swat-team-raids-home-because-guy-had-open-wireless-router.shtml.

151 The Free Thought Project https://thefreethoughtproject.com/swat-team-raids-wrong-house-throws-flash-bang-grenade-6-year-olds-room/.

152 18 U.S. Code § 1385 - Use of Army and Air Force as posse comitatus.

enforcement without violating posse comitatus. Why do you think this exception was made, and continued even in 1981? The primary purpose of the law, when it was enacted, was to prohibit the military occupation of the former Confederate States of America after their loss in the Civil War. It appears that when Representatives and Senators from the former Confederate States went to Washington, they had an agenda to prevent future military occupation of any state. In the 1878 election, when the Democratic Party dominated Congress, they passed the Posse Comitatus Act. Since their concern was on military occupation, they focused on land forces and not naval ones. In 1949, the Air Force was separated from the Army and in 1956 the Posse Comitatus Act was amended to include the new branch of the military. Apparently, no one considered the possibility that naval forces, which includes the Marines, might occupy American territory.

Clause 14 – Rules for the Military

> *To make Rules for the Government and*
> *Regulation of the land and naval Forces;*

Remember this line from the Declaration of Independence?

> *He has affected to render the Military independent*
> *of and superior to the Civil power.*[153]

Our Founding Fathers were concerned about the military not being under the control of the civilian leadership. That's why the President is the Commander-in-Chief of the military, why the funding for the military cannot extend beyond two years, and why Congress is given the power to make the rules and regulations for the military. With Congress in control of both the military's rules and money, the representatives of the people and the states should remain in charge over them. Of course, that assumes Congress bothers with effective oversight of the military.

---

[153] United States Declaration of Independence.

The next time you feel like screaming because of some idiotic military program or rule, don't blame the military. Blame your representative, since they make the rules and authorize the money.

Clause 15 – Calling Up the Militia

> *To provide for calling forth the Militia to*
> *execute the Laws of the Union, suppress*
> *Insurrections and repel Invasions;*

While it is illegal for the military to enforce U.S. law, the militia can. Why can the militia enforce U.S. law when the regular military cannot? Remember from the chapter on the 2nd Amendment, the militia is the armed citizen and is distinct from the rest of the military until called into service of the federal government. Since the militia is made up of "citizen soldiers", they are not considered to represent the same threat of a military coup and a professional military.

Congress, not the President, has the power to call up the militia. There are only three reasons the militia can legally be called up by the federal government: To execute federal law, to suppress insurrection, and to repel invasion. The militia was called up several times in the 1960s to enforce desegregation laws, which is a valid use of the militia. The militia has been used to quell riots, which is proper only if they are called up by the states and not the federal government, since a riot is not an insurrection. Most disturbing was the use of the militia by both Presidents George H. W. Bush and Barack Obama in overseas engagements. Congress has the power to call up the militia to repel invasion, but not to invade another country.

Finally, we get to the biggest issue with the calling up of the militia. There are many examples of the President calling up the National Guard (the organized militia). There's a problem with that though, because the President doesn't have the authority to call up the militia; only Congress can. "But wait," you may ask, "isn't the President the

Commander-in-Chief of the militia?" The answer is yes, but only when they are called into actual service of the United States.

The President shall be Commander in Chief of
the Army and Navy of the United States, and of
the Militia of the several States, when called into
the actual Service of the United States; [154]

The case could be made that the Army and Navy are always in service to the United States, but the militia serves its state, not the United States, until they are called up under the Congressional power of Article I, Section 8, Clause 15. Since the President isn't the Commander-in-Chief of the militia until they are called into federal service, he or she has no authority over the militia until Congress calls them.

As is so often the case, our ignorance of the Constitution allows the federal government to ignore the law and we let them get away with it.

Clause 16 – The Militia

To provide for organizing, arming, and disciplining,
the Militia, and for governing such Part of them as
may be employed in the Service of the United States,
reserving to the States respectively, the Appointment of
the Officers, and the Authority of training the Militia
according to the discipline prescribed by Congress;

Congress has the power to organize, arm, and discipline the militia. Remember the militia is defined as:

MILITIA: The body of soldiers in a state
enrolled for discipline, but not engaged in
actual service except in emergencies; [155]

---

[154] United States Constitution, Article II, Section 2, Clause 1.
[155] Webster's 1828 Dictionary http://webstersdictionary1828.com.

Congress can organize the militia, providing arms and discipline. (Discipline here means setting the rules of conduct and standards of correction, not the actual delivery of training or punishment.) They can also govern the militia, but only when they are in actual service to the United States. As I've said before, the National Guard is the organized militia. It is organized by Congress, armed by Congress, and disciplined by Congress, not the President. The President only becomes Commander-in-Chief of the militia when they are in actual service to the United States, but when they are called into service it's Congress who still has the power and responsibility to govern them.

While Congress has the authority to organize the militia, they actually remain state militias, with the states appointing officers and providing training according to Congress' standards of discipline. Remember, one of the reasons we declared independence from Great Britain was the posting of standing Armies in the colonies. The Constitution provides a balanced approach to competing needs by putting primary control of the militia in the hands of the states while giving Congress the authority to set standards for those militias. The militia, by definition, is not a standing military, so they serve only when called. By putting primary control of the national militia (not to mention the unorganized militia) in the states, they retain a force to defend themselves, not only from criminal or foreign acts, but from a potentially overbearing federal government.

As of July 2019 the Department of Defense reports approximately 1.3 Million active duty personal[156] plus approximately 800,000 in the National Guards and Reserves[157]. With 60% of the organized military in active service it would seem that standing army has a significant numerical advantage. But the National Guards and Reserves only represents the organized militia. U.S. law specifies that all able-bodies

---

[156] Defense Manpower Data Center https://www.dmdc.osd.mil/appj/dwp/rest/download?fileName=rg1907.pdf&groupName=milRankGrade.

[157] Defense Manpower Data Center https://www.dmdc.osd.mil/appj/dwp/rest/download?fileName=DRS_42486_SelRes_201907.pdf&groupName=resRankGrade.

males between 17 and 45 represent the unorganized militia. A 2018 Pew Research Center report[158] approximately 30% of Americans say they own a gun. The Census Bureau reports approximately 64 million American men between the ages of 17 and 45. If 30% of those men age 17 to 45 own firearms, that means the unorganized militia consists of almost 20 million members. If we include women in the militia then the number swells to almost 38 million. With control of the majority of America's fighting forces distributed amongst the states, and loyal to them, it would be hard for those in Washington, D.C. to put together a military that could impose its will over the states by force. And with Congress providing a standardized set of rules for organization, arms, and discipline, the militias of the various states could quickly and easily work together since they were all trained to the same standards.

Clause 17 – Federal Lands

> *To exercise exclusive Legislation in all Cases*
> *whatsoever, over such District (not exceeding ten*
> *Miles square) as may, by Cession of particular States,*
> *and the Acceptance of Congress, become the Seat of*
> *the Government of the United States, and to exercise*
> *like Authority over all Places purchased by the*
> *Consent of the Legislature of the State in which the*
> *Same shall be, for the Erection of Forts, Magazines,*
> *Arsenals, dockyards, and other needful Buildings;--*

Congress, and only Congress, has legislative power in the nation's capital. Over the years, Congress has granted Washington, D.C. the ability to form a city council and propose legislation, but it is up to Congress to turn it into law. When Congress rubber-stamps the will of the city council, it is our fault for letting them abdicate their duties.

---

[158] Pew Research https://www.pewresearch.org/fact-tank/2018/12/27/facts-about-guns-in-united-states/.

Washington, D.C. Representation

Is it unfair for Washington, D.C. to be run by Congress rather than their own city council? Washington, D.C. has a delegate in the house, but they are not allowed to vote on bills and Washington, D.C. has no members in the Senate. The 23rd Amendment, passed in 1961, gave Washington, D.C. electors to vote for President and Vice President, but they still have little representation in Congress. There are repeated calls for Washington, D.C. to be given the same rights and privileges as states. So why did our founders create a capital city with so few rights?

First, we must understand that Washington, D.C.'s only purpose is to be the seat of government. As the seat of government, it must be separate from any state. Why is our nation's capital separate from any state? James Madison explained in Federalist 43:

> *The indispensable necessity of complete authority at the seat of government, carries its own evidence with it. It is a power exercised by every legislature of the Union, I might say of the world, by virtue of its general supremacy. Without it, not only the public authority might be insulted and its proceedings interrupted with impunity; but a dependence of the members of the general government on the State comprehending the seat of the government, for protection in the exercise of their duty, might bring on the national councils an imputation of awe or influence, equally dishonorable to the government and dissatisfactory to the other members of the Confederacy.[159]*

If the seat of the federal government was inside a state, that state and its legislature would be able to exercise power over the nation's capital that no other state could. They could disrupt proceedings, hinder access

---

[159] Federalist Papers # 43 https://www.congress.gov/resources/display/content/ The+Federalist+Papers#TheFederalistPapers-43.

to those in the federal government, and even use this power to sway the votes of others. For this reason, the Constitution required our nation's seat of government be separate from any state, under the sole control of Congress, and therefore a federal city. Calls for D.C. statehood miss the point that our national seat of government should not be subject to any single state's authority, even its own.

Calls for voting rights for residents of Washington, D.C. miss the very important point that it is not a state, therefore it has no place in the Senate which was created to represent the states. Also, since Washington, D.C. was designated as our seat of government, it was meant to be a place to do the business of the federal government. As such, it was expected that should people reside there, it would only be a temporary situation for those who worked in the federal government. Just as those who are residents of U.S. Territories do not have the privileges of states, neither do federal cities.

Some say this is taxation without representation, but there is little to support that position. Since Washington, D.C. is not part of a state, the residents do not pay state tax. While residents do pay federal taxes, they are U.S. Residents, and the fact they choose to reside in a federal territory rather than a state is their choice alone. The 23rd Amendment gave the residents of Washington, D.C. electors for President and Congress has allowed a delegate in the House, although with limited privileges. There may be benefits of living in a federal territory, just as there are for living in a state, but that does not mean the residents of a federal territory have the right to be treated the same as if they lived in a state.

Federal Lands

Washington, D.C. is not the only federal lands authorized by the Constitution. The Congress has the same sole legislative authority over federal lands purchased by the consent of the state legislature for the purpose of erecting forts, magazines, arsenals, dock-yards, and other needful buildings. There are two very important things to notice in this clause: First, the land must be purchased with the consent of the state legislature and second, it must be used for specific purposes.

Consent of the State Legislatures

Did you know that the federal government owns over one-fourth of all the land in America (27.4%[160])? Do you realize the federal government owns most of Nevada (84.9%) and over half of Utah (64.9%), Idaho (61.6%), Alaska (61.2%) and Oregon (52.9%)? Have you ever asked yourself why the federal government owns so much land? Better yet, have you ever asked if it was legal?

In 1803, the United States purchased 827,000 square miles of land west of the Mississippi river. Known as the Louisiana Purchase, this deal brokered by Thomas Jefferson with the help of James Madison was done in an attempt to avert war with France over control of ports and warehouses on the southern Mississippi.[161] While this probably helped avert a war and certainly encouraged America's western expansion, there is just one problem: There is no authority in the Constitution for the United States government to purchase land except from the states and for specified purposes. Even Jefferson recognized this problem:

> *The general government has no powers but such*
> *as the constitution has given it; and it has not*
> *given it a power of holding foreign territory, &*
> *still less of incorporating it into the Union ... In the*
> *meantime we must ratify & pay our money, as we*
> *have treated, for a thing beyond the constitution,*
> *and rely on the nation to sanction an act done for*
> *its great good, without its previous authority.[162]*

---

[160] Ballotopia https://ballotpedia.org/Federal_land_ownership_by_state.

[161] The Jefferson Monticello https://www.monticello.org/site/jefferson/louisiana-purchase.

[162] Letter from Thomas Jefferson to John Dickinson, August 9, 1803.

Jefferson made the deal while believing it was unconstitutional and hoping that the nation would sanction the act ex post facto. James Madison, among others, believed that Jefferson was within his power under the treaty-making clause. However, only treaties made under the authority granted by the United States are binding law according to Article VI.

> *and all Treaties made, or which shall be made,*
> *under the Authority of the United States,*
> *shall be the supreme Law of the Land*[163]

Since the treaty was ratified by the Senate on October 20, 1803, and was never challenged in court, the purchase and its associated precedents are now considered settled.

Once the United States had this land, they sent people to settle it. These new territories eventually petitioned Congress to become states.

New States may be admitted by the Congress into this Union[164]

This is done through an enabling act. Part of these enabling acts was language that required the people of the proposed state to renounce any and all rights and title to unappropriated public lands until the United States extinguishes the title. In short, to enter the Union, a territory had to hand over all its unclaimed public land to the federal government until they decided to do something with it. (It is important to note, this was not a requirement of the Constitution for a state to enter the union, but of Congress.) Since these territories did not have a state legislature at the time, Congress could not get the consent to purchase the land required by this clause. But since the United States has no authority to purchase and hold land in the first place, except for the purposes listed, are you really surprised?

---

[163]   United States Constitution, Article VI, Clause 2.
[164]   United States Constitution, Article IV, Section 3, Clause 1.

Uses of Federal Land

> *to exercise like Authority over all Places purchased by*
> *the Consent of the Legislature of the State in which the*
> *Same shall be, for the Erection of Forts, Magazines,*
> *Arsenals, dockyards, and other needful Buildings*[165]

Along with the seat of government, Congress has the power to exercise authority of all places purchased by the consent of the state's legislature, but only for the purposes listed. Notice what isn't listed: National parks, national forests, or national monuments. The United States has entered into treaties that acquired land, but since the constitutional amendment Jefferson recognized was needed for the purchase and obvious authority over said lands was never even drafted, we again have Washington, D.C. assuming powers which the Constitution gives to the states. So now we have a federal government owning large percentages of the land of some states with no legal authority to do so, using it for purposes they are not authorized to use it for, and frequently using this land to influence state politics. Does this sound necessary and proper to you?

Clause 19 – Necessary and Proper

> *To make all Laws which shall be necessary and*
> *proper for carrying into Execution the foregoing*
> *Powers, and all other Powers vested by this*
> *Constitution in the Government of the United*
> *States, or in any Department or Officer thereof.*

Here we have the infamous "necessary and proper" clause. This has been used for decades to justify just about any act of Congress, since it has the power to make all laws necessary and proper. There's just one little problem: That's not what the necessary and proper clause says.

---

[165]   United States Constitution, Article II, Section 8, Clause 17.

Congress has the power to make all laws which are necessary and proper, but necessary and proper for what? To execute the powers vested by the Constitution in the United States. That means if a power is not delegated to the United States, Congress has no power to make a law granting, controlling, or regulating that power. My research on the 10th Amendment revealed that 90% of federal departments and agencies do not conform to a power delegated to the United States. That not only means those agencies are illegal, but those in Congress who voted for these agencies, and who continue to vote to fund them, have violated their oaths of office by making laws that are not necessary and proper for the powers delegated to the United States.

While we rarely think about this clause, our representatives in Congress have done far more damage to the republic and our rights than the executive and judicial branches. They have abused this power to give false cover not only to their illegal acts, but those of the government as a whole.

To summarize, Article I, Section 8 lists the majority of the powers delegated to the legislative branch of government. With the passage of the 17th Amendment (which has a chapter all to itself), all congressional seats are selected by a vote of the people, and therefore are accountable to us. It has become quite obvious that our general lack of knowledge about the Constitution and the unwillingness of the American people to hold elected officials accountable to their oath to uphold it, has led to the situation we have today where details like what the Constitution actually says means very little.

Section 9 – Restrictions on the United States

While section 8 of this article defines the powers delegated to Congress, section 9 focuses on specific restrictions on them.

Clause 1 – Migration and Importation

> *The Migration or Importation of such Persons as any*
> *of the States now existing shall think proper to admit,*

> *shall not be prohibited by the Congress prior to the*
> *Year one thousand eight hundred and eight, but a*
> *Tax or duty may be imposed on such Importation,*
> *not exceeding ten dollars for each Person.*

Importation of persons reminds us that at the founding of this nation slavery was legal and human beings were being imported like cattle in some of the states. Since the Constitution was ratified in 1787, this clause prevented Congress from prohibiting the immigration or importation of people for 20 years.

Great Britain had mandated that slavery be kept legal in the colonies. After we separated from the crown and won the war for our independence, the new states were divided about whether to keep the practice of slavery legal. Like the three-fifths clause,[166] this 20-year protection against the banning of slavery in the new nation was a compromise between slave holding and abolitionist states. It gave slaveholders time to transition to a more ethical way of business. While Congress passed the Act Prohibiting the Importation of Slaves on March 2, 1810, it was, unfortunately, the politicians and not the Constitution that kept slavery legal in American until the 13th Amendment was ratified on December 6, 1865.

Clause 2 – Habeas Corpus

> *The Privilege of the Writ of Habeas Corpus shall*
> *not be suspended, unless when in Cases of Rebellion*
> *or invasion the public Safety may require it.*

A writ of habeas corpus (literally "produce the body") is a court order for a person or agency holding someone in custody to deliver them to the court and show a valid reason for the detention. Your ability to force the government to show a valid reason for your detention is a valuable protection of your due process rights. This privilege may not

---

[166]   United States Constitution, Article I, Section 2, Clause 3.

be suspended except in cases of rebellion or invasion and must be for the public safety.

Many of you may know that President Lincoln suspended the right of habeas corpus at the beginning of the Civil War. What you may not know is the story around it.

On April 27, 1861, President Lincoln issued a proclamation suspending the right of habeas corpus for anyone held in a military facility by sentence of a military court martial or military commission. The question we should all ask is, was it legal?

First, we must recognize that nowhere in the Constitution is the President given explicit power to suspend habeas corpus, or in fact to enact any policy at all. In addition, the language protecting the right of habeas corpus is in Article I, along with the other powers and limitations on Congress, not the President. However, the language does not specify who can suspend the right of habeas corpus, and the President is the Commander-in-Chief of the military when in time of service.[167] Seeing that America had just started the Civil War, the military was certainly in service, so the President was in command of them; however, it is Congress that sets the rules for the military. In the portion of his proclamation regarding habeas corpus, President Lincoln specifically identifies military imprisonment as the scope for the suspension.

> *that the writ of habeas corpus is suspended in respect to*
> *all persons arrested, or who are now or hereafter during*
> *the rebellion shall be imprisoned in any fort, camp,*
> *arsenal, military prison, or other place of confinement*
> *by any military authority or by the sentence of*
> *any court-martial or military commission.*[168]

The constitutional problem here is not that the Commander-in-Chief ordered military detention locations to suspend habeas corpus,

---

[167]   United States Constitution, Article II, Section 1, Clause 1.

[168]   Records of Rights http://recordsofrights.org/assets/record/000/001/068/1068_original.jpg.

but that it applied to anyone held in those locations regardless of whether they were in the military or not, and did so without a rule established by Congress. A case could be made that if Lincoln had limited the suspension to military personnel captured in the act of rebellion, his order would have stood on better constitutional footing, as long as it was within the rules Congress had established.

The question of the legitimacy of Lincoln's proclamation was challenged quickly. John Merryman of Baltimore was arrested by Union troops on May 25, 1861, and petitioned for a writ of habeas corpus. On May 26th, Chief Justice of the supreme Court Roger B. Taney issued an order to General George Cadwalader, Commander of Fort McHenry, to produce Mr. Merryman for a hearing before him and to explain the legal justification for his detainment. Instead, General Cadwalader sent a response to the judge explaining that he was acting under the orders of President Lincoln to suspend habeas corpus.

As you can imagine, this did not please the chief justice who found General Cadwalader in contempt of court and ordered the U.S. Marshal to seize him and bring him before the justice. However, the U.S. Marshal could not gain entry to Fort McHenry and therefore could not seize General Cadwalader. Chief Justice Taney filed a written opinion with the Circuit Court for the District of Maryland arguing that President Lincoln had no authority to suspend habeas corpus or to order military officers to do so. The controversy continued until Congress passed, and President Lincoln signed, the Habeas Corpus Suspension Act on March 3, 1863.

For two years, we had an arguably illegal presidential order and a conflict between two of our three branches of government. The third branch, the one that represents us, finally stepped in and suspended habeas corpus. However they caved in and rubber stamped the President's actions rather than asserting their legitimate power, invalidating the illegal detentions, reprimanding the President, and instituting the suspension of habeas corpus properly,.

In 2006, Congress passed and President Bush signed *Military Commissions Act of 2006*. This law included the following language:

> No court, justice, or judge shall have jurisdiction to
> hear or consider an application for a writ of habeas
> corpus filed by or on behalf of an alien detained by
> the United States who has been determined by the
> United States to have been properly detained as an
> enemy combatant or is awaiting such determination.[169]

There are a couple of important differences between this suspension of habeas corpus and the one in 1862. Every article I could find about the 2006 suspension of habeas corpus identified it as President Bush doing the suspension. However, unlike President Lincoln, President Bush did not order the suspension of habeas corpus, Congress did. It was Congress who passed the Military Commissions Act of 2006, making this a legislative act not an executive one. While this was a legislative act that suspended habeas corpus, Congress violated the law since no rebellion or invasion was underway in 2006. A case could be made that it was necessary to maintain public safety, but Article I, Section 9, Clause 2 is specific: Habeas corpus cannot be suspended for public safety except in the case of rebellion or invasion.

In short, both the legislative and executive branches have had dubious histories in regards to the protection against detentions outside of the warrant system.

Clause 3 – Ex Post Facto

> *No Bill of Attainder or ex post*
> *facto Law shall be passed.*

Clause three prohibits two types of laws: Bills of attainder and ex post facto laws.

---

[169] S.3930 - Military Commissions Act of 2006.

BILL OF ATTAINDER: a legislative act that
imposes punishment without a trial[170]

A bill of attainder is any legislation that imposes a punishment without a trial. Today, however, we have the IRS, FDA, EPA, and other agencies punishing Americans without a trial. If you dispute these fines and punishments, you are sent to an administrative law court. An administrative law court trial does not include a jury as the decision is made by the presiding judge. Part of what makes an administrative law court different is the fact that all the parties are represented by the government. That means that not only is the attorney for the government paid by the government, but so is the judge and your defense attorney as well. Do you get the feeling the deck is stacked against you? Furthermore, many of the statues which are used to bring you to administrative law courts include language that denies you the ability to appeal the judge's decision? Yet the 5th Amendment is supposed to protect your right to due process of law. (We will talk more about due process in the chapter on the 5th Amendment.)

EX POST FACTO: after the fact: RETROACTIVELY[171]

Ex post facto simply means "after the fact." So, let's say you've been doing business a certain way for years and it's been legal. Congress can pass a law making what you do illegal as long as it cannot be used against you regarding something you did before the law was in place. For example, Congress can pass a law making it illegal for you to file your tax returns by mail, but you cannot be charged for the times you filed your returns by mail before the law was put in effect. It seems simple, but then again, Washington, D.C. always finds ways to skirt the issue when they don't like it.

For example, the numerous laws outlawing certain types or classes of firearms. We discuss the right to keep and bear arms in the chapter

---

[170] Merriam-Webster Dictionary https://merriam-webster.com.
[171] IBID.

on the Second Amendment. Here, however, in our discussion of ex post facto laws, the concern is if Congress passes a law banning possession of a legally acquired item, they cannot (at least not legally) keep you from possessing that object as long as you did it prior to the law being put in place. Both state and federal legislatures do this all the time. We do little about it because we are generally unfamiliar with our rights and authority to control Congress.

Clause 4 – Direct Taxes

No Capitation, or other direct, Tax shall be
laid, unless in Proportion to the Census or
enumeration herein before directed to be taken.

Unfortunately, this clause was superseded by the 16th Amendment which not only allowed taxation on income, but allows the federal government to tax the people's income however they choose rather than based on the population. Why is this change so important? Before the 16th Amendment was ratified in February 1913, the federal government was not legally allowed to tax a person's income and taxes were laid upon the states based on their population. This means that before 1913 the federal government could not tax you directly, but had to apportion taxes to the states. Since the federal government could not tax your income, they did not care how much you made or where and how you spent it. In short, unless you were in the military, the federal government had no reason to invade your life. We discuss this in more detail in the chapter on the 16th Amendment.

Clause 5 – No Interstate Export Tax

No Tax or Duty shall be laid on Articles
exported from any State.

Remember, unlike how they are treated today, each state is sovereign. Just as one nation can place taxes, duties, imposts, or tariffs on the goods from another nation, one state could impose them on another state. Also remember the purpose of this Constitution, as stated in its preamble, is to create a more perfect union and to insure domestic tranquility. To avoid infighting, our Founding Fathers placed this restriction upon the states to avoid trade wars within the Union.

Clause 6 – Free Ports

No Preference shall be given by any Regulation
of Commerce or Revenue to the Ports of one
State over those of another: nor shall Vessels
bound to, or from, one State, be obliged to
enter, clear or pay Duties in another.

Regulations cannot give preference to the ports of one state over another state. When this Constitution was drafted and ratified, the vast majority of commerce traveled by ship or river boat. Imagine a regulation giving the ports of New York lower duties from those in New Jersey, or preferring the ports in Virginia over North Carolina? The ports of all the states were to be treated equally under federal legislation. In addition, ships traveling between the states could not be forced to dock in another state or pay any duty to those states. Imagine a ship traveling from Norfolk, VA to Boston, MA having to stop, be inspected, and possibly even pay a fee in a port of every state they passed. What would be the impact on commerce of said ship having to stop in Delaware, New Jersey, New York, Connecticut, and Rhode Island? Not only in time and paperwork, the advantage in revenues these states would have over those along less traveled routes would be sizable. To keep the Union fair and equal, the states had to agree to let commerce flow equally among the states.

Clause 7 – Appropriations

No Money shall be drawn from the Treasury,
but in Consequence of Appropriations made by

> *Law; and a regular Statement and Account of*
> *Receipts and Expenditures of all public Money*
> *shall be published from time to time.*

The next time you hear someone complain about a President's spending, remind him or her that money can only be spent through appropriation laws created by and passed in Congress. Therefore, the treasury can only spend money that has been appropriated by Congress. Since there is little the federal government can do without spending money, we once again see that our Founding Fathers placed the power of the United States squarely in the hands of those who represent the people and the states.

As I'm writing this, there is yet another call for transparency in federal spending. Transparency is a good thing, which is why the Constitution requires that an accounting of all public money be published from time to time. Sadly, few Americans seem to expend any effort in learning how the United States spends our money, much less hold those who appropriate the funds accountable for what they are spending it on.

Clause 8 – Titles and Emoluments

> *No Title of Nobility shall be granted by the*
> *United States: And no Person holding any Office*
> *of Profit or Trust under them, shall, without the*
> *Consent of the Congress, accept of any present,*
> *Emolument, Office, or Title, of any kind whatever,*
> *from any King, Prince, or foreign State.*

Look at the news, at politics, and at just about any policy discussion, and you'll see Americans being divided into different classes. The poor, the working poor, the middle class, the rich, and the elite, are just a sample of the different classes we divide ourselves into. Yet when America was created, our Founding Fathers specifically set up a nation without classes. The Declaration of Independence states that "all men are created equal". You will see this idea is unique to 18th century politics if you put aside the social stigmas so prevalent today, and realize that the English language uses the terms "man" and "men" to refer to mankind as a whole. If all men are created equal, they are not different classes of people. We have not lived up to this standard, but what disturbs me more is how quickly we devolved into a class society.

> *NOBILITY: The persons collectively who enjoy*
> *rank above commoners; the peerage; as the English*
> *nobility; French, German, Russian nobility*[172]

America is not to have titles of nobility, yet today we see elected, appointed, and bureaucratic officials alike enforcing the use of their titles just as if they were those of nobility. Senator Barbara Boxer from California demanded that Brigadier General Michael Walsh use her title of "Senator" rather than the military standard of "Ma'am" after the first use of her title. Watch any footage of a House of Representative committee meeting and you'll see every member has a sign referring to them as the "honorable" so and so, even while they frequently act in dishonorable ways. These elected officials demand that those who come before them act with due reverence even though they work for the American people and not the other way around. They refer to those who do not recognize their opinions or authority as deplorables, the unwashed masses, or from fly-over country.

Government officials, judges, pundits, and everyday Americans claim the authority to determine how you should live your life and do what they say, but not necessarily what they do. In effect, they claim authority of nobility, if not its title. They act as if they are better than the common folk, an idea anathema to the founders of this nation. If "A rose by any other name would smell as sweet,"[173] then a noble by any other title is just as offensive.

---

[172] Webster's 1828 Dictionary http://webstersdictionary1828.com.

[173] Romeo and Juliet by William Shakespeare.

Just as our Founding Fathers wanted to avoid the entrapments of nobility within the nation, they were even more concerned about foreign influence.

> *Against the insidious wiles of foreign influence (I*
> *conjure you to believe me, fellow-citizens) the jealousy*
> *of a free people ought to be constantly awake, since*
> *history and experience prove that foreign influence is*
> *one of the most baneful foes of republican government...*

> *The great rule of conduct for us in regard to foreign*
> *nations is in extending our commercial relations, to*
> *have with them as little political connection as possible.*
> *So far as we have already formed engagements, let them*
> *be fulfilled with perfect good faith. Here let us stop...*
> *Hence, therefore, it must be unwise in us to implicate*
> *ourselves by artificial ties in the ordinary vicissitudes*
> *of [Europe's] politics, or the ordinary combinations*
> *and collisions of her friendships or enmities.*[174]

George Washington recognized the danger foreign influences can have on a republican form of government. Our founders wished to protect us from undue influences by requiring Congressional approval for anyone in service of the federal government to accept any presents, positions, or titles from foreign nations. This would provide a balance between the need of the nation to avoid foreign influences and our need to respect the generosity and traditions of those nations.

Section 10 – Restrictions on the States

As the states delegated some of their power to this new central government, they also accepted restrictions placed on them.

---

[174]   George Washington's Farewell Address, September 19, 1796.

Clause 1 – Federally Delegated Powers

No State shall enter into any Treaty, Alliance,
or Confederation; grant Letters of Marque and
Reprisal; coin Money; emit Bills of Credit; make
anything but gold and silver Coin a Tender in
Payment of Debts; pass any Bill of Attainder, ex
post facto Law, or Law impairing the Obligation
of Contracts, or grant any Title of Nobility.

The 10th Amendment declares that any power not delegated to the United States remain with the states or the people. This clause restricts the states from executing many of the powers delegated to the United States. For example: States cannot enter into treaties or alliances with foreign nations, neither can they issue letters of marque, or print and coin money. While Congress can coin money, the states can use gold and silver as legal tender. In fact, there are bills in many states to set up gold and silver depositories so states can protect their citizens from the machinations of the Federal Reserve and the federal government. States are also prohibited from issuing bills of attainder, ex post facto laws, and granting titles of nobility.

Let's take a few minutes and look at the prohibition of the state from passing laws that impair the obligations of contracts (the Contracts Clause). What does it mean to impair the obligations of a contract? Most contracts place obligations on the parties involved.

For example, this Constitution is a compact, a contract between sovereign entities. It places obligations on the signatories, the states, and the product of the compact, which is the United States (what we now call the federal government). Say you enter into a contract, which we do all the time; this contract places obligations on both you and with whomever you enter the contract. For example, when you sign up for phone services, Internet service, electrical, water, or sewer service, you are signing a contract. You enter into a contract when you buy a home, a car, you borrow money, or even take a job. These contracts place obligations on you; you have to pay the bill, buy the home, or pay back the loan. They also place obligations on who you contract with; they must provide the goods or services specified, they must allow for the agreed upon terms for payment, etc. In short, the reason we have contracts is to provide a legal method to redress our grievances with those we do business. What would it mean to impair those obligations?

IMPAIR: *To make worse; to diminish*
in quantity, value or excellence.

To weaken; to enfeeble.[175]

I'm sure many of you would jump at the idea of a law that said you didn't have to pay back your student loan or pay your utility bills, but what if the shoe was on the other foot? What if there was a law that the car dealership didn't have to give you the car you bought, only one that was "substantially similar"? Or what if your utilities could be turned off, yet you were still required to pay the bill? Or what if the person you contracted to build a house for you took your money, then moved to a state that did not recognize your contract?

For a contract to be a viable tool to redress grievances between parties, it must be enforced without change. An excellent example of the violation of this clause is the case *Sveen v. Melin*. In this case, when Mark Sveen and Kaye Melin divorced in 2007, the state of Minnesota effectively changed the contract for the life insurance policy Mr. Sveen entered into in 1998 by removing Ms. Melin as primary beneficiary. It was argued before the supreme Court that since the law was not in effect when the contract was signed, this was a violation of the Contracts Clause. While what happened was a violation of the Ex Post Facto Clause, the mere fact that the law changed the obligations of a contract at all means it is a violation of the Contract Clause. Unfortunately, but not surprisingly, our supreme leaders in black robes said that changing

---

[175]   Webster's 1828 Dictionary http://webstersdictionary1828.com.

who gets paid on a contract "does not substantially impair pre-existing contractual arrangements."[176]

If contracts don't mean what they say and what they meant at the time they were signed, then no contract is worth the paper it is written on, including the Constitution itself. If changing who gets paid at the end of a contract does not impair it, then what about the contract that says we are to be secure in our persons, houses, papers, and effects? What about the contract that says you have a right to trial by jury and to confront your accuser? What about the contract that says the federal government is only empowered to do the things specifically delegated to it? By this time you should be aware that the compact between the states is being reinterpreted wholesale. As parties to this compact, it is up to the states to once again enforce the compact, not just on the parties of it, but the product of it as well. This would not be the first time. The states of Kentucky and Virginia proposed resolutions to overturn the Alien & Sedition Acts of 1798/99.

Clause 2 – State Imposts and Duties

> *No State shall, without the Consent of the Congress,*
> *lay any Imposts or Duties on Imports or Exports,*
> *except what may be absolutely necessary for executing*
> *its inspection Laws: and the net Produce of all*
> *Duties and Imposts, laid by any State on Imports*
> *or Exports, shall be for the Use of the Treasury of*
> *the United States; and all such Laws shall be subject*
> *to the Revision and Control of the Congress.*

States can impose duties in shipping, but only with the consent of and under the control of Congress or to cover their costs for inspections. However, whatever proceeds are left over go into the federal treasury. Why? As a union, there is supposed to be free trade among the states. Foreign commerce is the purview of Congress (Article I, Section 8,

---

[176] *Sveen et al. v. Melin* No. 16–1432.

Clause 3), so they get to set the rules. A state can impose duties to cover their inspection costs, but they cannot gain any revenue from it. We don't want different states setting different rules for foreign commerce, so that's why it's in the hands of Congress.

Clause 3 – Peacetime Rules

> *No State shall, without the Consent of Congress,*
> *lay any Duty of Tonnage, keep Troops, or Ships of*
> *War in time of Peace, enter into any Agreement or*
> *Compact with another State, or with a foreign Power,*
> *or engage in War, unless actually invaded, or in*
> *such imminent Danger as will not admit of delay.*

States cannot impose duties of any kind as a matter of commerce without the consent of Congress.

> *DUTY OF TONNATE: A fee that encompasses all taxes*
> *and Customs Duties, regardless of their name or form,*
> *imposed upon a vessel as an instrument of commerce*
> *for entering, remaining in, or exiting from a port.*[177]

As we said with the previous clause, foreign commerce is a power delegated to Congress. Since the treaty-making authority rests with the President and the Senate, states are barred from making any agreement with other states or nations on their own.

Also, states are prohibited from keeping troops or ships of war in time of peace. Neither can they engage in war unless they are invaded or under imminent threat, since war and the military are under the control of Congress. States may have, and in fact most of the Founding Fathers thought they should have, their own militia, but as we've discussed in Section 8, there is a difference between a state militia and a standing

---

[177] The Legal Dictionary https://legal-dictionary.thefreedictionary.com/Duty+of+Tonnage.

army. The Second Amendment clearly states that a well-regulated (functioning) militia is necessary to the security of a free state. How else do you expect a state to combat an invasion until Washington, D.C. gets its act together? Remember, the military did not have bases all over the nation when the Constitution was ratified, and it took days or weeks to move troops around the country. The principle still stands though; if we are to remain a union of free and independent states, the states must able to protect themselves from all hazards, foreign and domestic.

Conclusion

We have here the establishment and regulation of the most powerful branch of the federal government: The legislative. Accountable now only to the people, this branch creates our laws, taxes us, and spends our money and, most importantly, oversees the other branches of government. Davy Crockett told the story[178] of changing his mind after being told off by a constituent because he had violated his oath to support the Constitution. It is time the American people once again take up the responsibility of overseeing those who represent us, not only to do what we want them to do, but to abide by their oath to support the Constitution. We the people of the United States of America are supposed to oversee Congress, not the other way around. We are supposed to tell Congress what to do, not blindly follow what they say. If we wish to remain the land of the free, then we must do our duty and fulfill our responsibilities as citizens of this nation. Otherwise, like sheep to the slaughter, we will continue to watch our rights and liberties taken away, even though we had the power to stop it but were unwilling to exert the effort.

---

[178] BPCR http://www.bpcr.net/documents/Miscellaneous/good%20-%20crockett%20learns%20from%20a%20farmer.htm

Article II – Executive Branch

Congress, as the legislative branch of the federal government, passes the laws, and the President, as the executive branch, executes them. If America were a corporation, then the President would be the Chief Executive Officer.

Section 1 – The Office of President

Over the decades we have begun asking the President to do more, to exercise powers not given to him in the Constitution and, in fact, not given to the federal government at all. Our founders wanted an executive with limited individual power except in times of war, yet now we ask the President to be a king rather than an executive.

Clause 1 – Executive Powers

The executive Power shall be vested in a President of the United States of America. He shall hold his Office during the Term of four Years, and, together with the Vice President, chosen for the same Term, be elected, as follows:

When the Constitution says, "The executive Power shall be vested in a President", it means the power to execute laws is executive power; neither the legislature nor the judicial branches have any executive power. It also means that any agencies, bureaus, or other creations of the federal government that execute the laws of the United States are under the authority of the President. I'm sure we've all heard the terms "checks and balances" or "separation of powers", but both mean that no one person or group has all the power.

Remember that, in the 18th century, the King of England not only had the power to execute law, but he held a lot of sway over Parliament to write law and control the judges who interpreted it. Our Founding Fathers knew that was too much power to place in the hand of one person; in truth, that was too much power to place in any one group's hands. As we learned in Article I, all legislative power is vested in a Congress. Here we see that the power to execute those laws does not reside with those who create them; rather it resides with a President, and by extension, the executive branch.

The President, along with the Vice President, serves a four-year term. That means the length of their term is between the term of a Representative in the House and one in the Senate. It was expected that those serving in the House, as representatives of the people, would turn over rather quickly, having only a two-year term. Meanwhile those in the Senate, who represent the states (more on that in clause 2), would be around longer, hence the six-year term. Their terms are also aligned in such a way that when the President is elected, all the Representatives in the House and one third of the Senators are also being elected.

Next, let's see how this President is to be elected.

Clause 2 – Electing the President

> *Each State shall appoint, in such Manner as*
> *the Legislature thereof may direct, a Number of*
> *Electors, equal to the whole Number of Senators and*
> *Representatives to which the State may be entitled*
> *in the Congress: but no Senator or Representative,*
> *or Person holding an Office of Trust or Profit under*
> *the United States, shall be appointed an Elector.*

The first thing to recognize about this section is that the people are not mentioned in the election of the President. That's because the people do not elect the President, the states do. What I find interesting is how we got to this process.

> *The executive power of the U–S–shall be vested in*
> *a single person. His stile shall be "The President*
> *of the U–S. of America" and his title shall be "His*
> *Excellency". He shall be elected by ballot by the*
> *Legislature. He shall hold his office during the term of*
> *seven years; but shall not be elected a second time.*[179]

From my research of the Constitutional Convention, it appears the first plan was to have the President elected by Congress.

> *Mr. Gouvenerr Morris opposed the election of the*
> *President by the Legislature. He dwelt on the danger of*
> *rendering the Executive uninterested in maintaining the*
> *rights of his Station, as leading to Legislative tyranny*[180]

Many concerns were brought up concerning the loyalties a president elected in this fashion may have, as noted by this quote from Gouvenor Morris. Wouldn't the separation of powers be compromised? What about the impeachment process, since those who chose the president would be asked to remove him? A solution was proposed, also by Gouvenor Morris.

> *To guard against all these evils he moved that*
> *the President "shall be chosen by Electors to be*
> *chosen by the people of the several States"*[181]

This plan apparently had wide-spread support in the convention as both Alexander Hamilton and James Madison would later write.

---

[179] Farrand's Records –MADISON Friday August 24, 1787.
[180] IBID.
[181] IBID.

All these advantages will happily combine in the plan devised by the convention; which is, that the people of each State shall choose a number of persons as electors, equal to the number of senators and representatives of such State in the national government, who shall assemble within the State, and vote for some fit person as President.[182]

I agree entirely with you in thinking that the election of Presidential Electors by districts, is an amendment very proper to be brought forward at the same time with that relating to the eventual choice of President by the H. of Reps. The district mode was mostly, if not exclusively in view when the Constitution was framed & adopted; and was exchanged for the general ticket & the Legislative election, as the only expedient for baffling the policy of the particular States which had set the example.[183]

However, there was a large faction that wanted the President elected by the House of Representatives, which would place additional power in the hands of larger states. Eventually, a compromise was found and the language in the Constitution was set.

Each state has a number of electors (votes) based on their populations, which is a combination of their representation in both houses of Congress. How these electors are chosen is up to the individual state legislatures. Today, the legislatures in each state have chosen to appoint electors based on statewide elections held at the same time they hold elections for House and Senate seats. This is not required by the Constitution, but makes sense due to the time and effort necessary to hold a statewide election.

---

[182] Alexander Hamilton, Federalist #68 https://www.congress.gov/resources/display/content/The+Federalist+Papers#TheFederalistPapers-68

[183] Letter from Madison to Hay 1823.

Most states appoint electors chosen to support the winner of the state's election. This is called a "winner take all" election. A few states appoint electors proportionally to the vote in that state. For example, should candidate A win with 57% of the vote, candidate B 33%, and candidate C 10%, then 57% (or as close as humanly possible) of the electors would be those who have pledged to vote for candidate A, 33% pledged to candidate B, and 10% pledged to candidate C. I use the word "pledged" because the electors have said they would vote for a particular candidate, usually based on party affiliation, although the Constitution does not require it. In fact, that is not how the founders expected the President to be elected.

As Mr. Hamilton stated, the plan was to choose individuals with the skill and character to select the President and let them vote for themselves. Today, however, the influence of the political parties is evidenced by the fact that people now vote for electors who have promised to vote for a particular candidate. While states have different laws regarding how a pledged elector can vote, there is nothing in the Constitution that requires an elector to vote based on his or her state's election; that is an issue for state law.

Some states' legislators have proposed what I can only describe as the most destructive method of appointing electors: Based on the "national popular election." With this method a state would wait until all the state elections are completed, then choose electors pledged to support the candidate who won the most votes across all the states, completely ignoring the will of the people of their own state. Let's say that in your state candidate B won the election, but candidate A won the "popular election". In that case, a state with this method of appointing electors would appoint electors for candidate A in direct opposition to the wishes of the citizens they claim to represent.

Why would I refer to this method of choosing electors as destructive? Because it is all based on the myth that there is a popular election for President. Remember, the states elect the President, not the people. This idea of a popular vote is an invention of sore losers and a media looking to make news. You never hear much complaining about the popular election except when a candidate wins the election, meaning they won a majority of the electors, but their opponent got more of the people's votes. Suddenly, there are calls to repeal the electoral college and complaints that it's an archaic solution to a problem that doesn't exist anymore. Quite the contrary, having the states elect the President helps keep the federal government in check by making sure the President is elected by a majority of the states rather than by corridors of influence and power in our nation. As we study more of Article II, we'll see that a large part of the President's job is to represent the states in foreign affairs, so having the states elect the President makes perfect sense.

It appears that in the minds of those who support the "popular election" method of appointing electors, the United States is a collectivist community where states have no sovereignty, no authority, and their citizens should bow to the will of the nation as a whole. They view the United States as a democracy not a republic. (We'll talk more about our republic in Article IV.) They act like the needs and desires of Texas are the same as New York. Based on what I've heard from those who have publicly supported this, it appears like sour grapes; their candidate didn't win so they want to change how the game is played. We are supposed to be a Union of States governed by laws, not a homogeneous collective governed by the will of a ruling elite. Why have states if they all subvert their sovereignty and individuality to the collective views of others? It reminds me of the Star Trek character known as the Borg, except the Borg took over and absorbed other cultures. In this case, many in America seem willing to give their culture away because they didn't get what they wanted.

Clause 3 – The Actual Vote for President

> *The Electors shall meet in their respective States, and*
> *vote by Ballot for two Persons, of whom one at least*
> *shall not be an Inhabitant of the same state with*
> *themselves. And they shall make a List of all the Persons*
> *voted for, and of the Number of Votes for each; which*

*List they shall sign and certify, and transmit sealed
to the Seat of the Government of the United States,
directed to the President of the Senate. The President
of the Senate shall, in the Presence of the Senate and
House of Representatives, open all the Certificates, and
the Votes shall then be counted. The Person having the
greatest Number of Votes shall be the President, if such
Number be a Majority of the whole Number of Electors
appointed; and if there be more than one who have such
Majority, and have an equal Number of Votes, then the
House of Representatives shall immediately choose by
ballot one of them for President; and if no Person have
a Majority, then from the five highest on the List the
said House shall in like Manner choose the President.
But in choosing the President, the Votes shall be taken
by States, the representation from each state having
one Vote; A quorum for this purpose shall consist of
a Member or Members from two thirds of the States,
and a Majority of all the States shall be necessary to a
Choice. In every Case, after the Choice of the President,
the Person having the greatest Number of Votes of the
Electors shall be the Vice President. But if there should
remain two or more who have equal Votes, the Senate
shall choose from them by Ballot the Vice President.*

Meet in their respective states

All the electors from a state shall meet in their state to vote. As we've
mentioned, the people do not vote for president, the states do. When the
electors vote, they vote for two (2) people, at least one of which cannot
be from their state. Our Founding Fathers understood the fallibility of
man, so they made sure a state's electors couldn't only vote for "their

guy." After the ratification of the 12th Amendment, each elector voted for a candidate for President and another for Vice President.

We'll talk more about why that changed when we discuss the 12th Amendment, but it's important to notice that the Constitution does not require primaries or even that the electors be bound to vote a certain way. It is the law in many states that require an elector's vote to be bound to a certain candidate, and usually only for the first few votes. (That becomes important when we discuss majorities and ties.) After the 2016 elections, there was some discussion, almost to the point of bullying, to try to get electors to vote contrary to the elections that led to their appointment. I keep making the point that ultimately the electors vote for president, not the people.

It's only state law that requires electors to vote a certain way based on state elections, which is important. Since state legislatures are closer to, and therefore more responsive to, the people of their state, you can push legislation to change the way electors are appointed and how long they are bound to those results. I hear a lot of people talk about changing the way the President is elected, often without considering the constitutional implications. If we want to change things, how about we try working within the Constitution and change how our state's electors are chosen?

Majorities and ties

As I said, originally the person who got the most votes would be president and the one with second most would be Vice President. This quickly caused problems when John Adams, our second President and a federalist, was elected president and Thomas Jefferson, an anti-federalist, as Vice President. As you can imagine this caused quite a bit of friction. I'm sure this was a large factor in the ratification in 1804 of the 12th Amendment. Now, two elections are held every four years, one for President and another for Vice President.

What happens in the case of a tie, or when no candidate gets a majority of votes? In the case of the President, the House of Representatives votes for President, while the Senate votes for the Vice President. Even then, though, each state only gets one vote, so while the representatives of the people and the states cast the vote, it is still a state vote.

Primaries and parties

During the 2016 election, there were reports, articles, and discussions about the primary process and how it was handled by the parties. I even heard some recommend that Congress get involved to "protect the election process". One small issue: Primaries are not in the Constitution. Though that does not make them unconstitutional, Congress has absolutely no role in the election unless no one gets a majority.

Article 2 Section 1 says that the electors are appointed in a manner determined by the state legislatures. It is the states, through their legislature, that define the primary process and execute it. States determine what the process is, when voting will happen, and who can vote in their primaries.

Speaking of primaries, how many people realize that political parties are not part of the government? They are private entities, organizations created by private citizens. What does this have to do with primaries? Why do you pay, through your tax dollars, for the elections of a private organization? We aren't expected to pay for the elections to the board of Walmart, Starbucks, or any other private organization, why do we pay for the private elections of the Republican and Democratic parties? Why do these private groups hold so much influence on our political process? Because as a nation we have become captured by the spirit of party.

Most people I've encountered think our current system, of two powerful parties controlling the election process through primaries and a "pick one of two" election, is normal. I've even heard it said that was what our Founding Fathers wanted. What did our Founding Fathers say about that?

Let me ... warn you in the most solemn manner
against the baneful effects of the spirit of party.

*The alternate domination of one faction over
another, sharpened by the spirit of revenge,
natural to party dissension, which in different ages
and countries has perpetrated the most horrid
enormities, is itself a frightful despotism.*[184]

*There is nothing which I dread so much as a
division of the republic into two great parties,
each arranged under its leader, and concerting
measures in opposition to each other. This, in
my humble apprehension, is to be dreaded as the
greatest political evil under our Constitution.*[185]

*The happiness of society depends so much on preventing
party spirit from infecting the common intercourse
of life, that nothing should be spared to harmonize
and amalgamate the two parties in social circles.*[186]

*Nothing could be more ill-judged than that
intolerant spirit which has, at all times,
characterized political parties.*[187]

This list of quotes shows that our Founding Fathers at best distrusted political parties and at worst despised them. Yet today, it seems all political discourse revolves around parties and the need for their support. This devotion to party has transformed our election system from a search for the best people to create and execute our laws to the need for our party to win at all cost. Just look at recent news regarding scandals among our political elite. What is dismissed when done by a member of

---

[184] George Washington, Farewell Address.
[185] John Adams, Letter to Jonathan Jackson (October 2, 1780).
[186] Thomas Jefferson, To William C. Claiborne, July 1801.
[187] Alexander Hamilton, Federalist #1 https://www.congress.gov/resources/display/content/The+Federalist+Papers#TheFederalistPapers-1.

one party is excoriated when it's a member of the opposition. Even the concept of an "opposition party" should be anathema to our republic. Instead, state and national capitals alike are driven by party agenda, entrapped by party loyalty, and drowning in internal party politics.

Constitutional elections

Think about this for a moment: The electors are to choose one person for President and another for Vice President. But you are not given that choice; you must choose a ticket with both President and Vice President. Is this Constitutional? Yes, but it misses the spirit of how we are to choose our executives. The state legislatures choose how to select electors for these two votes, and they have chosen to present a party ticket rather than individuals as options, or better, just names of electors. Once again, we see party politics replace state interest in the presidential election process.

Why the electoral college matters

Every so often I'll hear another call to abolish the electoral college; it's called antiquated and undemocratic. Some even call it racist, but I haven't seen any reasonable evidence that was ever the case. So why does the electoral college matter?

First, we must understand what the electoral college is:

> COLLEGE: *In a general sense, a collection, assemblage*
> *or society of men, invested with certain powers*
> *and rights, performing certain duties, or engaged*
> *in some common employment, or pursuit.*[188]

The electoral college is simply the collection of electors who will vote for the President. Remember, it is the states and not the people who vote for the President and Vice President. Why is this collection of people so important to our republic? Because this republic is a union

---

[188] Webster's 1828 Dictionary http://webstersdictionary1828.com.

of sovereign states. Just as we select people to represent us in the house, and the states select representatives for them in the Senate, they also pick someone to represent them in foreign affairs. As we learn more about the rest of the article, we'll see that a lot of the executive powers vested in the President have to do with our engagement with foreign governments, either through diplomacy or through military engagement. By abolishing the Electoral College, or weakening it into uselessness, we change the face of our chief executive. Rather than the representative of the union of states as the position was designed, the Presidency would effectively become a democratically elected king. Some in American seem to think this would be a very good thing, though democracy in America was something our Founding Fathers feared very much. (We'll discuss democracies in the chapter on Article IV.)

Clause 4 – The Real Election Day

> *The Congress may determine the Time of*
> *choosing the Electors, and the Day on which*
> *they shall give their Votes; which Day shall be*
> *the same throughout the United States.*

Once again, while the states choose the electors, Congress chooses the time of elections. Notice, the President isn't elected on what we call election day; that is the day the people vote to select their representatives, senators, and determine the electors. Congress chooses the day when the electors get together in each state to actually vote for President and Vice President. For example, in 2016 "Election Day" was November 8th. However, the day of the actual vote for President and Vice President was December 19th.

Clause 5 – Qualification for the President

> *No Person except a natural born Citizen, or a*
> *Citizen of the United States, at the time of the*
> *Adoption of this Constitution, shall be eligible to*

> *the Office of President; neither shall any Person be*
> *eligible to that Office who shall not have attained*
> *to the Age of thirty five Years, and been fourteen*
> *Years a Resident within the United States.*

So why does our Constitution restrict the Presidency to natural born citizens?

> *Against the insidious wiles of foreign influence (I*
> *conjure you to believe me, fellow-citizens) the jealousy*
> *of a free people ought to be constantly awake, since*
> *history and experience prove that foreign influence is*
> *one of the most baneful foes of republican government...*

> *The great rule of conduct for us in regard*
> *to foreign nations is in extending our*
> *commercial relations, to have with them as*
> *little political connection as possible.*[189]

Remember, in the 18th century, European nations would arrange marriages between their sovereigns to make alliances and prevent wars, a practice which continued into the 20th century. As you may imagine, someone who is born in another country is likely to have a different view of policy, politics, and rights, than someone born here. It would be natural for them to be greatly influenced by their country of birth. George Washington expressed this concern in his farewell address, calling foreign influence a "baneful foe" of a republic. Therefore, since the role of President is in large part (as we will see) that of a representative of the states to other nations, our Founding Fathers did not want such a person to have a political preference for another nation's ways over those of the United States. By insuring the President was born a citizen of this nation and most likely raised in this nation, they hoped their preferences would be toward the liberties this nation was founded on. While this

---

[189]   George Washington's Farewell Address.

has not always been the case, that appears to be the reasoning behind this clause of the Constitution.

There has been debate lately about the definition of a natural born citizen. Whether addressing the qualifications of Barack Obama or Ted Cruz, we need to understand what this term meant to our Founding Fathers and those who ratified the Constitution in the states.

Some people claim the definition of the term "natural born citizen" can come from the work of Emmerich de Vattel, specifically his book *The Law of Nations*. While there is evidence from the journal of the constitutional debates that Vattel's work was read by members of the Constitutional Convention, I have found no evidence that it was used as the standard definition for the term "natural born". Since the term "natural born" was a part of British common law, a fact noted by Blackstone and other legal scholars used by the Founding Fathers, that is the one I believe is the we should use today. Add to that the definition of "natural" in Noah Webster's 1828 dictionary, "A native; an original inhabitant"[190] and it seems quite clear that a natural born citizen is anyone who is a citizen at birth. And since Congress has the sole authority to establish uniform rules for naturalization[191], they establish the requirement for someone to be a natural citizen at birth.

Our Founding Fathers did include an exception for those who were citizens of the United States when the Constitution was ratified. When the nation was just starting, there were no natural born citizens of the United States, so they needed a way to have a President with the same preference toward liberty they would expect from a natural born citizen. The exception was made for someone who was a citizen of one of the states at the time of the adoption of the Constitution. Since you don't see many 250+ year old citizens running for the Presidency, that's not really an issue today.

Of the three age requirements to serve in the federal government, the one for President is the oldest. While members of the House and

---

[190] Webster's 1828 Dictionary http://webstersdictionary1828.com.
[191] United States Constitution, Article I, Section 8, Clause 4.

Senate work as a team, the President often works alone. The President needs Senate consent for most of his powers, but it is the President who is the point man for negotiations with other nations, so our Founding Fathers wanted to make sure anyone serving in that office had sufficient life experience to perform their duties with honor and circumspection.

Clause 6 – Presidential Succession

> *In Case of the Removal of the President from*
> *Office, or of his Death, Resignation, or Inability to*
> *discharge the Powers and Duties of the said Office,*
> *the Same shall devolve on the Vice President, and*
> *the Congress may by Law provide for the Case of*
> *Removal, Death, Resignation or Inability, both*
> *of the President and Vice President, declaring*
> *what Officer shall then act as President, and such*
> *Officer shall act accordingly, until the Disability*
> *be removed, or a President shall be elected.*

John Nance Garner, 32nd Vice President of the United States, said "the vice presidency is not worth a bucket of warm spit." The Vice President is the president of the Senate, but other than breaking ties there isn't much he or she has to do. The biggest constitutional role of the Vice President is to take over for the President if he is unable to discharge the office.

If the President dies or resigns, it's easy to see we need somebody to do the job. What else defines "inability to discharge the powers and duties" of the Presidency? It wasn't defined, until the 25th Amendment set up a method to determine if the President was unable to discharge his duties and a method for him to regain them as well. Nine times the Vice President has assumed the office of President; eight because the President died (John Tyler, Millard Fillmore, Andrew Johnson, Chester Arthur, Theodore Roosevelt, Calvin Coolidge, Harry Truman, and Lyndon Johnson) and once because the President resigned (Gerald Ford).

But what happens if both the President and the Vice President can't do the job? Then it's up to Congress to determine the order of succession. The Presidential Succession Act of 1947 set the order of Presidential succession. After the Vice President, first the Speaker of the House, then the President pro-tempore of the Senate are the line of succession, after they resign those offices. If neither of them can fulfill the office of President, then the highest officer who can legally hold the office of President will be among the Secretary of State, Secretary of the Treasury, Secretary of War, Attorney General, Postmaster General, Secretary of the Navy, Secretary of the Interior, Secretary of Agriculture, Secretary of Commerce, and Secretary of Labor, assumes the office.

As part of the continuity of the government plan, whenever the President, Vice President, and others in the line of succession are to-gether, one person in that line who can hold the office of President must be at a physically distant and secure location should something kill or disable the others in the line of succession. This person is known a the "designated survivor".

Clause 7 – Presidential Pay

> *The President shall, at stated Times, receive for his Services, a Compensation, which shall neither be increased nor diminished during the Period for which he shall have been elected, and he shall not receive within that Period any other Emolument from the United States, or any of them.*

That the President gets paid is not a big surprise, but who determines how much the President gets paid? Who in the federal government can authorize the spending of money? That's right, Congress spends the money, so they determine, by legislation, what the President gets paid. Once a President takes office, his or her pay cannot be changed while in office. Also, the President cannot be paid anything else either from the United States or the states themselves. While the "Emoluments Clause" in Article I, Section 9, Clause 8 prevents any officer in the federal government from any sort of pay from a foreign nation, the "Presidential Emoluments Clause" further restricts him from additional pay, over and above his pay as President, either from the federal government or one of the states.

Notice, the Constitution does not say the President cannot earn money outside of his salary as President. Senior federal officials often place their assets in a blind trust to avoid conflict of interest, but there is nothing in the Constitution, and I could find no federal law, that required this step. However, with political discourse as it is today, I'm not surprised at the efforts of those in government to avoid the appearance of evil, if not the actual evil itself.

Clause 8 – Presidential Oath

> *Before he enter on the Execution of his Office, he shall take the following Oath or Affirmation: -- "I do solemnly swear (or affirm) that I will faithfully execute the Office of President of the United States, and will to the best of my Ability, preserve, protect and defend the Constitution of the United States."*

While all political officers take an oath or affirmation, only the President has constitutionally specified language. The fact that a President can affirm what they will do is another nod to religious liberty. Some religions and denominations do not allow their adherents to swear oaths, yet this simple but powerful oath is used as the basis for most oaths for political offices in the nation and was codified into law with 5 U.S. Code § 3331.

What must the President swear to do? He or she must faithfully execute the office of President, which means all that the office entails and nothing that the office was not delegated to do. As we'll see, the

President can do things like appoint ambassadors and judges of other federal officers, with the advice and consent of the Senate. However, if a President were to sign a treaty without the consent of the Senate, then he or she would not be faithfully executing their office. When the President tries to enact laws via executive order, that person is not faithfully executing the office. The President is also to preserve, protect, and defend the Constitution and do so to the best of his or her ability. Now the President cannot preserve the Constitution by violating it, and he or she cannot protect the Constitution with "a pen and a phone". And they cannot defend the Constitution by taking on the responsibilities of Congress or turning over their responsibilities to the supreme Court.

Section 2 – Presidential Powers

While Article I, Section 8 lists the power delegated to Congress, this section lists the powers delegated to the President.

Clause 1 – Commander in Chief

The President shall be Commander in Chief of the Army and Navy of the United States, and of the Militia of the several States, when called into the actual Service of the United States; he may require the Opinion, in writing, of the principal Officer in each of the executive Departments, upon any Subject relating to the Duties of their respective Offices, and he shall have Power to grant Reprieves and Pardons for Offenses against the United States, except in Cases of Impeachment.

Commander in Chief

One of the best-known powers of the President is that of Commander-in-Chief of the military. The Constitution only lists the Army and the Navy, but that's because they were the only military in the 18th century. When the Coast Guard and Air Force were formed, they were added to the Armed Forces of the United States and placed under the military chain of command. What most people don't know is that the President is only the Commander-in-Chief of the military when they are called into actual service. The case could be made that the active duty military is in actual service, but not the reserves, the National Guard, or the militia. Remember the Founding Fathers wanted to avoid a standing army, and they wanted a small professional military supported by large state militias, all of which were to be under the control of Congress.

> *To make Rules for the Government and*
> *Regulation of the land and naval Forces;*[192]

This arrangement has a problem though, when situations are moving fast like in times of war or imminent invasion: Congress cannot respond fast enough. Enter the Commander-in-Chief, who can respond to events within the rules and regulations for the military created by Congress.

Departmental Reports

Since all executive power is vested in the President, all the executive departments exist under the President. Therefore, it makes sense for the President to request the opinions of the heads of those departments on anything related to their duties. Notice, the department heads give their 'opinion' to the President, but as Harry S. Truman said, "The buck stops here." 'The buck' for all executive departments stops with the President himself. The skills a President must have to be effective are different from those of the legislative or judicial branches, because the President must run a huge operation. The executive branch of the United States has over two million (2,000,000) employees and a budget of approximately $4 Trillion dollars ($4,000,000,000,000). That's about the same as the combined revenue of the top 15 companies on the Fortune 500 list in 2018, and eight times the size of the largest company on the list,

---

[192]   United States Constitution, Article I, Section 8, Clause 14.

making the U.S. Government the single largest enterprise in the nation, by far. As the title of "Chief Executive" denotes, the President spends most of his time, or at least he should, running the equivalent of giant corporation.

Reprieves and Pardons

The President has the authority to issue reprieves and pardons.

Reprieve: The temporary suspension of the
execution of sentence of death on a criminal.
Respit; interval of ease or relief.

Pardon: Forgiveness; Remission of a penalty. An
amnesty is a general pardon. Forgiveness received.[193]

The President can issue a reprieve, a temporary suspension on a sentence, specifically a death sentence, or a pardon, which is not only forgiveness, but the removal of the penalty. This power is limited to federal crimes since the President can only issue reprieves and pardons for offenses against the United States. The one restriction that is mentioned is that a President cannot issue a reprieve or pardon for an impeachment. While other convictions and sentences are issued by the judicial branch, an impeachment comes from the legislative branch. That means the executive can modify the sentence of the judicial branch, but he cannot modify one from the legislative branch, making this another example that the three branches of government are not equal.

Do you notice what is not included? Commuting sentences. According to the U.S. Department. of Justice, "Under the Constitution, the President has the authority to commute sentences for federal criminal convictions."[194] However, a quick look at this clause shows that the power to commute sentences is not given to the President. You could

---

[193] Webster's 1828 Dictionary http://webstersdictionary1828.com.

[194] United States Department of Judgement https://www.justice.gov/pardon/commutation-instructions.

say it falls under the power to issue reprieves, but, by definition, those would be temporary. This is yet another example of the federal government ignoring the supreme law of the land when it suits their purposes.

Clause 2 – Treaties and Appointments

> *He shall have Power, by and with the Advice and*
> *Consent of the Senate, to make Treaties, provided two*
> *thirds of the Senators present concur; and he shall*
> *nominate, and by and with the Advice and Consent of*
> *the Senate, shall appoint Ambassadors, other public*
> *Ministers and Consuls, Judges of the Supreme Court,*
> *and all other Officers of the United States, whose*
> *Appointments are not herein otherwise provided for,*
> *and which shall be established by Law: but the Congress*
> *may by Law vest the Appointment of such inferior*
> *Officers, as they think proper, in the President alone,*
> *in the Courts of Law, or in the Heads of Departments.*

There is a lot of confusion in this nation about Presidential powers, especially those listed here. This clause lists the powers the President has only with the advice and consent of the Senate. Why the Senate and not the entire Congress? Because a large part of the role of the President is to act on behalf of the states, which are represented in the Senate. That means a major role of a President is to represent the states, which is why so many of his powers require the advice and consent of the Senate. Today we focus most federal powers on the President, but if we look at the powers which he can only exercise with the Senate, we'll see that is not the role of the office.

One thing that people often get wrong is the idea that the President nominates and the Senate confirms or, in the case of treaties, the President negotiates and the Senate ratifies. While that is the way things are done today, the Constitution says the President makes treaties and appoints people to various positions with the advice and consent of the

Senate. These are not "footballs" to be handed off from one branch to another; they are meant to be working together. Keep that in mind as we look at these powers.

Treaties

> *Treaty: An agreement, league or contract between*
> *two or more nations or sovereigns, formally*
> *signed by commissioners properly authorized,*
> *and solemnly ratified by the several sovereigns*
> *or the supreme power of each state.*[195]

Like any other nation, the states initially had the power to enter into treaties, or as the Declaration of Independence said, "have full Power to levy War, conclude Peace, contract Alliances, establish Commerce." Since the United States is a union of independent states, they delegated their treaty making powers to the central government, specifically to the President and their representatives in the Senate. The President makes treaties with the advice and consent of the Senate, meaning the Senate needs to be involved in the negotiations so they can give their advice. Today everyone expects the President to negotiate the treaty then hand it over to the Senate for their consent, but does that qualify as advice? Isn't that just another example of the states handing over their advice role to the executive branch and the President becoming more like a king rather than an executive?

Appointing Ambassadors, Judges, and Officers

Since one of the jobs of the President is to represent the states in foreign affairs, it makes sense the he should be involved in selecting ambassadors. Also, since the President is the head of the executive branch, he should help choose those who lead the departments in that branch. Judges are a little different. If they neither serve in foreign affairs nor are part of the executive branch, why are they appointed by the President?

---

[195]   Webster's 1828 Dictionary http://webstersdictionary1828.com.

The judiciary is the weakest of the three branches of government be-cause they are overseen by the other two branches. The Constitution created the supreme Court, but Congress determines its size and creates and oversees the inferior courts. And as we see here, along with the Senate, the President determines who can serve as judges.

Clause 3 – Recess Appointments

> *The President shall have Power to fill up all*
> *Vacancies that may happen during the Recess*
> *of the Senate, by granting Commissions which*
> *shall expire at the End of their next Session.*

With today's social media and 24-hour news cycles, we often forget that both 18th century America and the federal government moved at a much slower pace. Congressmen did not spend most of their time in Washington; in fact, the Constitution required them only to meet at least once a year. Since it took many congressmen days to travel to the capital, what was the government to do if there was a sudden vacancy? The answer was: Give the President the power to make temporary ap-pointments when the Senate is in recess.

Recess: A withdrawing from public business or notice[196]

Remember, since the Senate represents the states, many of the President's powers can only be exercised with the advice and consent of the Senate. So, who better to deal with a vacancy than the person with the job of representing the states? Those who represented the states were not fools when they drafted this part of the Constitution; the President's power is strictly limited to a vacancy during a Senate recess and the duration lasts only until the end of their next session. Notice that the commission for a recess appointment ends at the end of the Senate's

---

[196] Webster's 1828 Dictionary http://webstersdictionary1828.com.

next session, not the end of that Congress. (A Congress ends with the seating of the newly elected members of the House of Representatives.)

> *SESSION: The time, space or term during which*
> *a court, council, legislature and the like, meet for*
> *daily business; or the space of time between the*
> *first meeting and the prorogation of adjournment.*
> *... The Supreme Court of the United States has one*
> *anual session. The legislatures of most of the states*
> *have one annual session only; some have more. The*
> *congress of the United States has one only.*[197]

A recess appointment can last as little as one day or as long as two years.

While this clause seems straight forward, leave it to Washington to make a mess out of even this. In the 2014, supreme Court case National Labor Relations Board V. Noel Canning et al., Mr. Canning claimed that three of the five members of the NLRB were invalidly appointed. On December 17, 2011, the Senate passed a resolution stating they would hold pro forma sessions every Tuesday and Friday until January 20, 2012. While no business was performed during these pro forma sessions, they were required, since the Constitution forbids a house of Congress to adjourn for more than three days, and therefore go into recess without the consent of the other.

> *Neither House, during the Session of Congress,*
> *shall, without the Consent of the other, adjourn for*
> *more than three days, nor to any other Place than*
> *that in which the two Houses shall be sitting.* [198]

The controversy started when President Obama appointed three members to the board on January 3rd and 6th of 2012, claiming that the

---

[197] Webster's 1828 Dictionary http://webstersdictionary1828.com.
[198] United States Constitution, Article I, Section 5, Clause 4.

Senate was in recess even though the Senate had said it was not. The supreme Court delivered a rare 9-0 decision that the appointments were in fact invalid since the Senate was in session. In another twist, while the court got the decision correct, I believe their justification was invalid. The court's opinion was the Senate was in session because it said it was in session and that a recess of three days was insufficient to trigger the Recess Appointments clause.

While I agree that three days is not sufficient to trigger the Recess Appointments clause, the wording of the Constitution gives us a much better standard. Since the Senate cannot adjourn for more than three days without the consent of the House of Representatives, I believe the Recess Appointments clause can only be used when both houses agree that the Senate is not in session and therefore in recess. Any other standard would make the determination of recess arbitrary, even to the point of allowing the President to make recess appointments over the weekend.

Section 3 – Further Presidential Duties

He shall from time to time give to the Congress information of the State of the Union, and recommend to their Consideration such Measures as he shall judge necessary and expedient; he may, on extraordinary Occasions, convene both Houses, or either of them, and in Case of Disagreement between them, with Respect to the Time of Adjournment, he may adjourn them to such Time as he shall think proper; he shall receive Ambassadors and other public Ministers; he shall take Care that the Laws be faithfully executed, and shall Commission all the Officers of the United States.

Section 3 lists other duties of the President. Some may seem mundane and others are handled with great pomp and circumstance, but unlike the powers in Section 2, Clause 2, these the President can exercise on his own.

State of the Union

Every year we go through the motions of the State of the Union Address. While the President is required, from time to time, to inform Congress of the state of the union and the measures the President thinks they should consider, The State of the Union address has become a political three-ring circus designed more to motivate voters than inform Congress. When more emphasis is placed on who stands and applauds, what guests were invited, or what the First Lady wears, the State of the Union Address has become a theatrical presentation rather than a governing one.

Joint Sessions

When I think of joint sessions of Congress, my mind turns to December 8, 1941. After the extraordinary event of the bombing of Pearl Harbor, Hawaii, President Franklin D. Roosevelt requested Congress to declare war against the empire of Japan. While these joint sessions are often called for much less serious reasons, this is the one time the President can tell the Congress to do something. While the President cannot force attendance, he does have the power to convene either or both houses, but only in extraordinary circumstances.

Adjournment Tie Breaker

Being men and women with important responsibilities, you would never expect the members of the House and Senate to be so petty as to be unable to come to an agreement on whether, or how long, to adjourn. Foreseeing this possibility, the Constitution gives the President the power to settle disagreements between the houses of Congress about when and how long they will adjourn. So far, I don't believe this power has ever been used, but with the growing polarization and almost extinct statesmanship exhibited by those in Congress, I believe it is only a matter of time before it happens.

Receive Ambassadors & Officials

Imagine you're a diplomat from a foreign country here to handle a situation, and you had to go before the Senate to state your case. Besides the difficulty of dealing with 100 different Senators with different agendas, the glacial pace at which the Senate is designed to move means you'd probably never get an audience. Our Founding Fathers saw this as an issue of direct negotiation with a group, so they delegated the power of receiving foreign officials to the President. Since there is little the President can do in foreign affairs without the consent of the Senate, this is more a ceremonial act than true negotiations. In actuality, this is just another example of how much of the President's real job is to represent the states in foreign affairs.

Faithfully Executing Laws

Although we often focus on the President's duty to execute federal law, the power to do so only comes near the end of Article II. Like so many clauses in the Constitution, the details here are often lost, yet truly matter.

> *Faithfully: With strict observance of promises,*
> *vows, covenants or duties; without failure*
> *of performance; honestly; exactly*[199]

For the President to faithfully execute the laws of the United States, he must do so with strict observance of the laws and duties, he must execute the laws exactly, he or she must not fail to perform this duty. That means, contrary to popular belief, once a bill is signed into law, the President does not have the Constitutional authority to ignore it, bend

---

[199] Webster's 1828 Dictionary http://webstersdictionary1828.com.

it, or reinterpret it based on what he believes, and neither does he have the power to effectively create law.

The only leeway a President has in enforcing the laws of the United States is his oath of office to "preserve, protect and defend the Constitution of the United States." This means if he believes a law to be unconstitutional, he is duty bound to support the Constitution above a law not made in pursuance to it. If the President had the power to determine for himself if or how he would execute the laws of the United States, he would cease to be a constitutional president and become a dictator. Yet follow the news today and you see everyone from politicians, pundits, news casters, judges, to everyday people, telling the President what laws he should not enforce and what he should do without the benefit of law.

This again shows how our general ignorance of the Constitution and the way our federal government was designed to run leads us farther and farther from the land of the free and the brave toward the home of the dictator and tyrant.

Commission Officers

When an officer is appointed to a post, it is the responsibility of the President to commission him or her.

Commission: Charge; order; mandate; authority given.[200]

More than a simple ceremony, the commissioning of an officer of the United States is not only the granting of authority, but a solemn charge and a mandate that they do so properly. That is why the oath sworn by both military and civilian officers includes the charge to faithfully execute the office and to support the Constitution of the United States. This reinforces that everyone in federal service is subject to, and expected to, defend the Constitution directly.

---

[200] Webster's 1828 Dictionary http://webstersdictionary1828.com.

Section 4 - Impeachment

> *The President, Vice President and all civil Officers*
> *of the United States, shall be removed from Office*
> *on Impeachment for, and Conviction of, Treason,*
> *Bribery, or other high Crimes and Misdemeanors.*

We've all heard talk of impeaching a President. In our history, only two Presidents have ever been impeached, Andrew Johnson in 1868 and William Jefferson (Bill) Clinton in 1998, neither of whom were convicted. Andrew Johnson was impeached for removing from office Secretary of War Edwin M. Stanton in violation of the Tenure of Office Act.[201] Bill Clinton was impeach for committing perjury before a grand jury in 1998.

We discussed the power of impeachment in Article I, Section 2, Clause 5 and Section 3, Clause 6, but here I want to focus on what reasons, exactly, a President, Vice President, or civil officer can be impeached.

Treason

Article III, Section 3, Clause 1 of the Constitution gives a definition of treason.

> *Treason against the United States, shall consist*
> *only in levying War against them, or in adhering to*
> *their Enemies, giving them Aid and Comfort.*[202]

A President or Vice President can be impeached for levying war against the United States, or joining with their enemies by giving aid and comfort to them. This seems straight forward. If Franklin D. Roosevelt had assisted the Nazis or the Japanese Empire before they surrendered in

---

[201] National Park Service https://www.nps.gov/articles/why-was-andrew-johnson-impeached.htm.

[202] United States Constitution, Article III, Section 3, Clause 1.

World War II, we certainly would not have wanted him as Commander-in-Chief and removal would have made sense. However, simply disagreeing with the foreign affairs position of a President does not rise to treason. When those who called for the impeachment of President Obama for the Iran Nuclear Deal (which was unconstitutional), or for President Trump for withdrawing from that deal, they could not claim what either had done was treason. While Iran may be an enemy of the United States, with no declaration of war what we have is a policy disagreement, not treason.

Bribery

Bribery: The act or practice of giving or taking rewards for corrupt practices[203]

Bribery is not only rampant in the federal government, it is how it effectively operates now. Politicians take campaign contributions in exchange for an expectation of access and influence should the candidate win. Companies and organizations spend billions of dollars in an attempt to guide legislation or regulation. In effect, the entire federal government is a giant pay to play endeavor where money provides influence and power to help direct both law and policy.

Some may say this is how the game is played, but this corruption of the republic has not only led to the federal takeover of state authority, but the continued infringement on our rights, and the bankrupting of this nation. Americans acceptance of, or even dependence on this corruption, has led to our fall from the freest nation in the world to number eight according to the 2018 Index of Economic Freedom from the Heritage Foundation[204] and number six in the 2016 Economic Freedom Ranking from the Fraser Institute.[205] Yet even though we know bribery

---

[203] Webster's 1828 Dictionary http://webstersdictionary1828.com.

[204] The Heritage Foundation https://www.heritage.org/index/ranking.

[205] Fraser Institute https://www.fraserinstitute.org/economic-freedom/map?geozone=world&page=map&year=2016.

is commonplace in our nation's capital, we've never seen a President or Vice President impeached on bribery charges. As we'll see next, I believe part of the reason is a misunderstanding of what a President or Vice President needs to do to be impeached.

High Crimes and Misdemeanors

Of those often misused and misunderstood phrases in the Constitution, "high crimes and misdemeanors" must be near the top of the list. This is often used to say someone cannot be impeached except for some infamous crime.

> *Legal Definition of high crime: a crime of*
> *infamous nature contrary to public morality*
> *but not technically constituting a felony[206]*

But is that what our Founding Fathers meant by the phrase?

> *Crime: An act which violates a law, divine or human;*
> *an act which violates a rule of moral duty; an offense*
> *against the laws of right, prescribed by God or man, or*
> *against any rule of duty plainly implied in those laws.*

> *Misdemeanor: In law, an offense of a less atrocious*
> *nature than a crime. Crimes and misdemeanors*
> *are mere synonymous terms; but in common usage,*
> *the word crime is made to denote offenses of a*
> *deeper and more atrocious dye, while small faults*
> *and omissions of less consequence are comprised*
> *under the gentler name of misdemeanors.[207]*

---

[206] Merriam-Webster Legal Dictionary https://www.merriam-webster.com/legal/high%20crime.

[207] Webster's 1828 Dictionary http://webstersdictionary1828.com.

A crime is a violation of law while a misdemeanor is a lesser offense and given a gentler name. But what is a high crime or misdemeanor?

High: Exalted in nature or dignity.

Elevated in rank, condition or office.[208]

A high crime is not only one that is infamous or exalted, but one committed at an elevated rank. You may think I'm playing with words to come up with this definition, but remember the Merriam-Webster Legal dictionary definition of high crime I used above? Well, here's the rest of the definition:

specifically: an offense that the U.S. Senate deems to constitute an adequate ground for removal of the president, vice president, or any civil officer as a person unfit to hold public office and deserving of impeachment[209]

Those at Merriam-Webster were close, in that the Senate tries the impeachment, though it is the House of Representatives that actually impeaches an officer. As you can plainly see, even the modern definition of high crime includes anything that Congress determines makes a person unfit to hold public office, which is the only punishment that can be applied to a conviction of impeachment.

Who Decides

Who decides if the President or Vice President has committed treason, bribery, or other high crimes and misdemeanors? The answer is twofold: First, the House of Representatives must determine if, in their opinion, some officer of the federal government has acted in a way that

---

[208]   Webster's 1828 Dictionary http://webstersdictionary1828.com.

[209]   Merriam-Webster Legal Dictionary https://www.merriam-webster.com/legal/high%20crime.

disqualifies them for public office. Second, the Senate must try the case from the House to determine guilt or innocence. It is important to notice here it is the representatives and only the representatives of the people, who determine if there is cause to impeach someone. If the House wants to impeach the President for jay-walking they are perfectly within their Constitutional authority to determine if that charge is worthy of removal from office. However, it is up to the Senate to try the case and determine not only if the person is guilty, but if the charge is valid. Like any jury in a criminal trial, the Senate is the trier of both fact and law in this case, which is why we've had two impeachments in our history, but neither have led to a conviction.

This power, once again vested solely in the representatives of the people and the states, is extremely important, since conviction of impeachment not only involves the removal from office, but also the disqualification from holding future offices in the federal government.

Conclusion

What we see in this article of the Constitution is that our Founding Fathers did not want a king (i.e., a single person with power) over the nation and its people. For as Lord Acton said:

> *"Power tends to corrupt and absolute power corrupts*
> *absolutely. Great men are almost always bad men,*
> *even when they exercise influence and not authority;*
> *still more when you superadd the tendency of*
> *the certainty of corruption by authority."*[210]

Instead, they wanted a single person who could command the military in time of war, represent the states in foreign affairs, and handle the ceremonial duties of receiving foreign dignitaries. Today, both the Congress and the people have not only let the President exercise enormous power outside his constitutional limits, but we continue to ask him

---

[210] The Acton Institute https://acton.org/research/lord-acton-quote-archive.

to do more, and act more, like a king than a constitutional president. Putting the power to remove a sitting President in the representatives of the people and the states demonstrates that the office of President was never meant to wield so much power on its own. Until we elect constitutionally minded congressmen, we will have little hope of finding a constitutionally minded Presidential candidate.

Article III – Judicial Branch

nd now we come to the third and weakest branch of the federal government. Unfortunately, today it gets treated as the most powerful, with both Congress and the President deferring to its decisions, and its opinions still being treated as law. How can this be, especially from a branch of government with neither force nor will?

> Whoever attentively considers the different departments of power must perceive, that, in a government in which they are separated from each other, the judiciary, from the nature of its functions, will always be the least dangerous to the political rights of the Constitution; because it will be least in a capacity to annoy or injure them. The Executive not only dispenses the honors, but holds the sword of the community. The legislature not only commands the purse, but prescribes the rules by which the duties and rights of every citizen are to be regulated. The judiciary, on the contrary, has no influence over either the sword or the purse; no direction either of the strength or of the wealth of the society; and can take no active resolution whatever. It may truly be said to have neither FORCE nor WILL, but merely judgment; and must ultimately depend upon the aid of the executive arm even for the efficacy of its judgments.[211]

---

[211] Alexander Hamilton, Federalist #78 https://www.congress.gov/resources/display/content/The+Federalist+Papers#TheFederalistPapers-78.

As we'll see, the courts hold no power over the laws or wealth of this nation or its military. Yet by not knowing our Constitution, both we and our representatives have bowed to their judgment, leading to an oligarchy of nine high-priests who dictate to us that they have the power to determine what the Constitution says. They change law and we, in our ignorance, have submitted to it. The supreme Court is like the one-eyed man in the land of the blind; it may be weak, but we have made ourselves weaker. We need to open our eyes to the truth and restrain this tyrannical branch of government, putting it back in its rightful role of providing judgment while leaving law-making and its enforcement to their rightful branches.

Section 1 – The Courts

> *The judicial Power of the United States, shall be vested in one Supreme Court, and in such inferior Courts as the Congress may from time to time ordain and establish. The Judges, both of the supreme and inferior Courts, shall hold their Offices during good Behaviour, and shall, at Stated Times, receive for their Services, a Compensation, which shall not be diminished during their Continuance in Office.*

What is this judicial power that is vested in the courts? To understand that, we need to look at the root of this phrase:

> *JUDICATURE: The power of distributing justice by legal trial and determination. A court of judicature is a court invested with powers to administer justice between man and man.*
>
> *A court of justice; a judicatory.*
>
> *JUDICIAL: Pertaining to courts of justice; as judicial power.*

Practiced in the distribution of justice;
as judicial proceedings.

Proceeding from a court of justice; as
a judicial determination.[212]

Judicial power is the authority to hold courts of justice, which are courts designed to determine the just outcome in a case between two entities. As you read the definitions above, notice how often they refer to the goal of this judicial power being the determination and administration of justice.

> JUSTICE: *The virtue which consists in giving to every*
> *one what is his due; practical conformity to the laws*
> *and to principles of rectitude in the dealings of men*
> *with each other; honesty; integrity in commerce*
> *or mutual intercourse. justice is distributive or*
> *commutative. Distributive justice belongs to*
> *magistrates or rulers, and consists in distributing to*
> *every man that right or equity which the laws and the*
> *principles of equity require; or in deciding controversies*
> *according to the laws and to principles of equity.*
> *Commutative justice consists in fair dealing in trade*
> *and mutual intercourse between man and man.[213]*

If judicial power is the determination and administration of justice, the giving to everyone his due, and conforming to the laws and principles of rectitude, then its role is to try the facts of any case before it, determine the truth, and the rightness of the actions of those involved compared to the law and the moral practices of society, and then use their judgment to administer justice.

---

[212] Webster's 1828 Dictionary http://webstersdictionary1828.com.
[213] Webster's 1828 Dictionary http://webstersdictionary1828.com.

*RECTITUDE: In morality, rightness of principle or
practice; uprightness of mind; exact conformity to
truth, or to the rules prescribed for moral conduct,
either by divine or human laws. rectitude of mind
is the disposition to act in conformity to any known
standard of right, truth or justice; rectitude of conduct
is the actual conformity to such standard.*[214]

Since the courts have no power to enforce their judgment, their
ability to administer justice is limited to the issuing of their opinions
and requesting the other branches enforce it. Why do the courts have
no power to enforce their opinions? For the same reason one branch of
government writes the laws and another executes them. This check on
the power of the judiciary prevents them from becoming an oligarchy
(power of government in the hands of a few; an aristocracy), but only
if it is used. By deferring to every opinion of the courts, regardless of
whether it is Constitutional or within the scope of the court's authority,
our elected officials are effectively placing all their authority into the
hands of the judges.

Placing too much power into one branch of government leads to the
tyranny we see quite plainly today. Read or listen to any discussion of
supreme Court cases and you're likely to hear the phase "settled law"
or "law of the land" attached to one of their opinions. The problem is,
according to the Constitution, nothing the court can do settles or establishes law; only Congress can do that. Congress writes the law and,
therefore, both establishes and settles what it means. The next time you
hear someone say that *Roe v. Wade* or *Obergefell v. Hodges* are the law
of the land, remind them that they are not; they are the opinions of the
supreme Court just like *Dred Scott v. Sanford* (slaves are property) and
Korematsu v. United States (Japanese internment during WWII).

The court was wrong in the past, it is frequently wrong today, and
will almost certainly be wrong in the future. If we allow our elected

---

[214] IBID.

representatives to forfeit their law-making authority to the whim of the courts and to destroy the separation of powers that have protected this nation and its people for so long, then who will stop this out-of-control judiciary? What is to keep those on the courts from ruling our rights and liberties are "unconstitutional" and void? What is to prevent them from declaring the Constitution unconstitutional? Think this would never happen? Some supreme Court justices have already publicly stated that they would not look to the Constitution as a model today, that the Constitution should be looked at as flexible based on the circumstances, and that government has the power to infringe on your rights if it has a compelling interest. With justices like this, how safe do you think your rights and liberties are? And if those we elect to represent us won't keep them in their place, who will?

What Courts

The Constitution establishes the judiciary consisting of one supreme Court and as many other inferior (lower) courts as Congress believes necessary. You may have noticed that, in this book, I do not capitalize the "s" in supreme Court, and thought that an interesting typo to repeat so often. Except it is not a typo; it is the proper term for this court. You see, the word "supreme" is not part of the court's name but an adjective describing the court. Meaning, there are many federal courts, one of which is supreme; the remaining are inferior.

Notice that Congress is put in charge of establishing inferior courts. That means that those courts are responsible to Congress, not the supreme Court, as most people think. Another responsibility our elected representatives have ignored is that of overseeing the courts. Congress determines what federal courts there are, what they look like, and even what cases they are allowed to hear. The only exception to this power is the fact that we must have a supreme Court, it has to have a Chief Justice (required to try an impeachment of the President), and it must have the jurisdiction listed in Section 2. So, the next time you hear of some out of control judge or ridiculous ruling, thank your representative for not doing his or her duty to oversee the judiciary.

Judicial Term

Another often repeated myth about the federal government is the idea that judges have lifetime appointments. Instead, the Constitution clearly states that judges serve for the duration of their good behavior. Who determines what good behavior is for a federal judge? The members of the House of Representatives.

> *The House of Representatives ... shall have the sole Power of Impeachment.*[215]

While Article II, Section 4 gives reasons for officers of the United States to be removed by impeachment, the reason to remove a judge is implied by their ability to hold office only during good behavior. Today it seems there is little, if any, manner in which a judge can behave that Congress will deem as bad behavior; it is yet another way our elected representatives are failing in their duty to support the Constitution.

Judicial Pay

Who determines what a judge gets paid? The same people who determine what Congressmen, the Presidents, and other federal employees get paid: Congress. The only limitation in the Constitution is that a judge's pay cannot be decreased as long as they hold their office.

Section 2 – Jurisdiction

If you've watched a police show or crime drama, you have undoubtedly heard the term "jurisdiction". If we are to understand the role of the judiciary, we must understand its jurisdiction.

---

[215]   United States Constitution, Article I, Section 2, Clause 5.

> *JURISDICTION: The legal power of authority of doing justice in cases of complaint; the power of executing the laws and distributing justice. Thus we speak of certain suits or actions, or the cognizance of certain crimes being within the jurisdiction of a court, that is, within the limits of their authority or commission.*
>
> *The power or right of exercising authority.*[216]

In other words, the jurisdiction of a person, entity, or group is the area where they have the legal authority to execute laws or, as in the case of the courts, distribute justice. With that in mind, let's look at the jurisdiction of the federal courts.

Clause 1 – Primary Jurisdiction

> *The judicial Power shall extend to all Cases, in Law and Equity, arising under this Constitution, the Laws of the United States, and Treaties made, or which shall be made, under their Authority;--to all Cases affecting Ambassadors, other public Ministers and Consuls;--to all Cases of admiralty and maritime Jurisdiction;--to Controversies to which the United States shall be a Party;--to Controversies between two or more States;--between a State and Citizens of another State;--between Citizens of different States;--between Citizens of the same State claiming Lands under Grants of different States, and between a State, or the Citizens thereof, and foreign States, Citizens or Subjects.*

---

[216] Webster's 1828 Dictionary http://webstersdictionary1828.com.

Supreme Law of the Land

In Article VI, we'll see that the Constitution, as well as the laws and treaties made pursuant to and under its authority, are the supreme law of the land. This clause delegates jurisdiction over cases related to the supreme law of the land to the judicial branch of the federal government. That means that if you bring a case based on the U.S. Constitution, federal law, or treaties, it is, pardon the pun, a federal case.

Public Officials

Likewise, cases affecting officers who serve in the federal government are also automatically federal cases.

Maritime Law

Just as Congress has been delegated the power to define and set punishments for crimes committed on the high seas, the federal courts have been delegated the jurisdiction to try cases related to those crimes.

States

The Constitution also lists several situations in and among the states which are also within the federal court's jurisdiction. Specifically, this means any case where the federal government (the United States) is a party to the case, between two or more states or citizens of different states, and those cases that involve foreign countries or their citizens. While the language seems a confusing, it all stems from the fact that, under our Constitution, you are not only a citizen of the United States, but of the state in which you reside. If you have a case involving another state or a citizen of another state, whether that state be in the union or a foreign nation, the federal courts have jurisdiction. That means that, if you lived in Ohio and sued the state of Tennessee or a citizen of the state of Georgia, then you could not pursue your case in state court; it is a federal case. The other side of this jurisdiction is the fact it did not include cases that are within a single state. If you brought a case regarding the law or constitution of the state in which you resided, it could not go to federal court unless it involved the U.S. Constitution directly.

This was changed with the passage of Amendment XI, which removed from the jurisdiction of the federal courts any cases where a citizen of one state sued another state.[217]

It seems many people today think anything they want is a right somehow protected by the Constitution. Unfortunately the federal courts seem frequently willing to reinforce such a misunderstanding, making just about anything a federal case. Does that sound like the basis for a Constitutional republic and the rule of law?

Clause 2 – Original & Appellate Jurisdiction

> *In all Cases affecting Ambassadors, other public Ministers and Consuls, and those in which a State shall be Party, the Supreme Court shall have original Jurisdiction. In all the other Cases before mentioned, the Supreme Court shall have appellate Jurisdiction, both as to Law and Fact, with such Exceptions, and under such Regulations as the Congress shall make.*

Within a judicial system there are two types of jurisdiction: Original and appellate. Original jurisdiction means the case goes directly to, or originates in, the court in question. That means cases affecting an ambassador, minister (an appointed business agent[218]), consul (an appointed foreign agent[219]), or where a state itself is a party (complainant or defendant), the case goes directly to the supreme Court. Appellate jurisdiction means the case cannot be heard in that court first, but a decision of a lower court can be appealed to it. All other cases within the jurisdiction of clause 1, since the supreme Court has appellate jurisdiction,

---

[217] United States Constitution Amendment XI.

[218] Webster's 1828 Dictionary http://webstersdictionary1828.com.

[219] Webster's 1828 Dictionary http://webstersdictionary1828.com.

must go to an inferior federal court first, but can then be appealed to the supreme Court.

Judicial Review

There are a couple of important points in this clause that are often overlooked. First, the supreme Court has jurisdiction "both as to Law and Fact".[220] That means, when a case is appealed to the supreme Court they look not only at the facts of the case (did what was alleged to have happened actually happen), but at the law as well.

The idea of judicial review in America goes all the way back to the supreme Court case *Marbury v. Madison*. While often cited as the court's authority to "strike down" a law, what Chief Justice Marshall said in his opinion is "that a law repugnant to the Constitution is void, and that courts, as well as other departments, are bound by that instrument (the Constitution)."[221]

In other words, the courts and all departments of the United States government are bound to support the Constitution over federal law. If a law is found to be repugnant to the Constitution, then it is considered void, but does the opinion of a single court or a single judge have the authority to strike down a law? They may, in their opinion, determine that the application of a law within the scope of the case before them, since they have jurisdiction of both law and fact in the case, is unconstitutional, but that does not change "the law of the land". Only Congress has the authority to do that. All the judge can do is decide the case in front of him or her, not change the laws of the nation. If their opinion has merit, meaning they provide evidence of the error or unconstitutional impact in the law, then it is up to Congress to review the judge's opinion and change the law accordingly.

Why is this distinction so important? Because the entire design of the Constitution is to prevent the accumulation of power in any one person or branch of government. To give a single branch, and in many

---

[220]   United States Constitution, Article III, Section 2, Clause 2.
[221]   5 U.S. 137 - *Marbury v. Madison*.

cases a single judge, the authority to overrule unilaterally the work of the representatives of both the people and the states is itself repugnant to the Constitution. Judges and courts issue opinions, not rules and certainly not laws. As with any human endeavor, the opinions of judges and courts are often wrong, they match neither the facts of the case nor the laws as written, including the Constitution. The idea that any one person or court can change the plain meaning of any law, including the Constitution, because they claim to find some intention or implication that no one else has found is not only repugnant to the Constitution, but to the very idea of self-government and the rule of law this nation was founded on.

What good are laws if a single judge who doesn't like one can claim to find some intention of the Founding Fathers, with no documentation or evidence to prove it, and therefore claim it null and void? How can the opinion of a single court become law, when the Constitution they swore to uphold says only Congress can create law?

Regulated by Congress

We're often told that the federal government is made up of three co-equal branches, but this clause is another in a long line that prove this to be wrong. Congress can set exceptions and make regulations about the cases the supreme Court, and in fact all federal courts, can hear. Congress can determine that cases relating to immigration, the military, even campaign finance laws, are exceptions to the jurisdiction of the courts. They can even set regulation by which the courts can try cases, such as what level of scrutiny they must use to decide if a right has been infringed. If this is the case, what is to prevent Congress from exempting itself from judicial review? The people of the United States of America. It is our responsibility as citizens to oversee Congress. Since we have no such power directly over the courts, they are regulated and held accountable to the representatives of the people and the states. This is the separation of powers that protects our liberties.

Clause 3 – Trial by Jury

> *The Trial of all Crimes, except in Cases of*
> *Impeachment, shall be by Jury; and such Trial shall*
> *be held in the State where the said Crimes shall*
> *have been committed; but when not committed*
> *within any State, the Trial shall be at such Place or*
> *Places as the Congress may by Law have directed.*

Trial by jury is one of the most fundamental freedoms of our legal system. Being deprived of a trial by jury is one of the grievances listed in the Declaration of Independence. The idea that anyone charged with a crime must have a trial by jury means that their ultimate fate is in the hands of ordinary citizens, or at least it's supposed to be. We talked in more detail about juries in the chapter on Amendment V but the idea is so foundational to our legal system it's worth reviewing a few things here.

> *JURY: A number of freeholders, selected in the*
> *manner prescribed by law, empaneled and sworn*
> *to inquire into and try any matter of fact, and to*
> *declare the truth on the evidence given them in*
> *the case. Grand juries consist usually of twenty*
> *four freeholders at least, and are summoned to*
> *try matters alleged in indictments. Petty juries,*
> *consisting usually of twelve men, attend courts to*
> *try matters of fact in civil causes, and to decide*
> *both the law and the fact in criminal prosecutions.*
> *The decision of a petty jury is called a verdict.*[222]

The definition of jury starts with a group of free people who are sworn to inquire and try a matter of fact. Notice that with both the grand jury and the petty jury in civil cases, their role is only to decide

---

[222] Webster's 1828 Dictionary http://webstersdictionary1828.com.

the facts of the case, the truth of the evidence and claims. However, juries in criminal prosecutions determine both the facts and the law of the case. In a criminal case, the jury must determine not only if the facts of the case meet the requirements of the law, but whether the law itself is justified in this case. Notice that a jury cannot overturn a law, but only determine if the law should be applied in the case before them. This is frequently referred to as "jury nullification", which is a bit of a misnomer. A better description would be "jury review", which, like judicial review, is the power to decide both the law and the facts of the case.

We often hear that we are tried by a "jury of our peers," though, as I said earlier, it seems more like we are tried by a jury of 12 people who couldn't get out of jury duty. Jury duty is one of the most important responsibilities a citizen has, probably second only to voting for constitutional candidates. While it is the government that investigates and tries a case, it is a jury of everyday citizens who determine not only the guilt or innocence of the defendant, but whether the law itself is appropriate in the case. That is why our Constitution puts the final decision of both fact and law in the hands of the people. Remember that the next time you receive that jury summons in the mail.

The requirement that a jury trial take place in the state where the crime was committed is another protection against a grievance found in the Declaration. British officers would often take alleged criminals to foreign ports for their trial, making it very difficult to mount an effective defense. That is why, in America, the trial must happen in the state where the crime happened. The one exception is if the crime did not happen in a state, such as in a territory or on a ship at sea, in which case Congress by law determines where such a trial must take place.

Section 3 - Treason

Treason is a serious offense, and today the charge seems to be one thrown around willy-nilly by people from across the political spectrum. Thankfully, our Founding Fathers put a definition of treason in the

Constitution. And maybe one day the people and politicians of this nation will read it before accusing their opponents of it.

Clause 1 – Definition of Treason

> *Treason against the United States, shall consist*
> *only in levying War against them, or in adhering*
> *to their Enemies, giving them Aid and Comfort.*
> *No Person shall be convicted of Treason unless*
> *on the Testimony of two Witnesses to the same*
> *overt Act, or on Confession in open Court.*

What is Treason

To commit treason, someone must levy war against the United States or give aid and comfort to her enemies.

> *WAR: A contest between nations or states*[223]

If war is a contest between nations, how can an individual levy war against the United States? While war itself is between nations, the actors in war are people. That means that those during World War II who spied and committed sabotage against the United States were committing treason. Both Nazi and Japanese sympathizers in the United States and the resistance in France were committing treason. In fact, since the British crown did not recognize our Declaration of Independence, those who fought for the states in the Revolutionary War were committing treason themselves. Perhaps that is why the Declaration ends with these words:

> *And for the support of this Declaration, with*
> *a firm reliance on the protection of divine*

---

[223] Webster's 1828 Dictionary http://webstersdictionary1828.com.

> *Providence, we mutually pledge to each other our*
> *Lives, our Fortunes and our sacred Honor.*[224]

The 56 men who put their name to that document knew they were committing treason and would surely be severely punished if they were captured or the new states lost. As Benjamin Franklin put it:

> *"We must, indeed, all hang together, or most*
> *assuredly we shall all hang separately."*

The other way a person may commit treason is by giving aid and comfort to an enemy of the United States. During most wars, there are stories about men and women who tend to the wounded of their enemy. Our Judeo-Christian heritage allows for this, since the wounded are no longer able to engage in combat. But while the concept of aid and comfort springs readily to mind, what about the answer to the question: Who is my enemy?

> *ENEMY: A foe; an adversary. A private enemy is*
> *one who hates another and wishes him injury, or*
> *attempts to do him injury to gratify his own malice*
> *or ill will. A public enemy or foe, is one who belongs*
> *to a nation or party, at war with another.*[225]

We may have private enemies, but helping them is not treason. For someone to be a public enemy, they must belong to a nation or party at war with the United States. While there is certainly hatred, malice, and ill will between the political parties, until the Republican party declares war on the Democratic party, or vice-versa, they cannot be public enemies and what they do cannot be called treason for legal or constitutional purposes.

---

[224] Declaration of Independence.

[225] Webster's 1828 Dictionary http://webstersdictionary1828.com.

Proof of Treason

There are only two ways a person can be legitimately convicted of treason: By the testimony of at least two witness to the same act, or by confession in open court. While confession in open court seems straight forward, why the need for at least two witnesses as the only other way to convict someone of treason? The answer again is in our Judeo-Christian heritage.

> *At the mouth of two witnesses, or three witnesses, shall he that is worthy of death be put to death; but at the mouth of one witness he shall not be put to death.*[226]

The punishment for treason can be quite severe, up to and including death. Before sentencing someone to the ultimate penalty, it is important that the proof be more than just beyond a reasonable doubt. For that reason, the Constitution requires multiple witnesses to specific acts of treason before someone can be convicted.

Clause 2 – Punishment for Treason

> *The Congress shall have Power to declare the Punishment of Treason, but no Attainder of Treason shall work Corruption of Blood, or Forfeiture except during the Life of the Person attainted.*

Only Congress has the authority to determine the punishment for treason. As with so many of the powers delegated to the United States, this one comes with limitations, but what is this "attainder of treason" and "corruption of blood"?

> *ATTAINDER: Literally a staining, corruption, or rendering impure; a corruption of blood. Hence,*

---

[226] Deuteronomy 17:6 - King James Version.

*The judgment of death, or sentence of a competent
tribunal upon a person convicted of treason or
felony, which judgment attaints, taints or corrupts
his blood, so that he can no longer inherit lands. The
consequences of this judgment are, forfeiture of lands,
tenements and hereditaments, loss of reputation, and
disqualification to be a witness in any court of law.*[227]

*CORRUPTION OF BLOOD: English criminal.
law. The incapacity to inherit, or pass an
inheritance, in consequence of an attainder
to which the party has been subject*

*When this consequence flows from an attainder,
the party is stripped of all honors and dignities
he possessed, and becomes ignoble.*[228]

Literally a staining of one's life and reputation, an attainder is a judgment of death or forfeiture of rights including owning land and the ability to be a witness in a court of law. If we read this sentence carefully and pay attention to the commas, we'll see that Congress cannot declare a punishment for treason that extends beyond the lifetime of the attained. That means the convicted can be stripped of rights and property, but their family cannot. While the convicted may lose his land, this punishment cannot be extended to their family.

Conclusion

The general ignorance of the role and powers of the judicial branch extend not only to the people in general, but to the lawyers, judges, and justices of the branch itself. I have been told that law schools no longer teach the Constitution, but instead teach Constitutional Law, i.e., what

---

[227] Webster's 1828 Dictionary http://webstersdictionary1828.com.

[228] The Free Legal Dictionary https://legal-dictionary.thefreedictionary.com.

the lawyers and judges say the Constitution says. To that I must ask: How can we have a government of laws and not men if the men who determine what is just do not know what the supreme law of the land says?

If we are to remain free, then those we elect to represent us must once again be required to take up the mantle of overseeing the judicial branch. They must review not only how federal judges act, but how they rule, to determine if their behavior is good. Abusing parties before them, infringing on their rights, and placing their fingers on the scales of justice are not the only bad behavior of judges; issuing opinions, warrants, and court orders that violate the Constitution are also behaviors that must be punished, and severely. After decades of neglect, our federal courts are out of control, taking upon themselves not only the authority to determine what is constitutional and the meaning of law, but of dictating to the other branches what they must do. Unless we reign in these forces of tyranny, we will slide farther and farther away from being the land of the free.

Article IV – The States

Now that the central government (what we call the federal government) has been established, it's time for the states to set up some rules for themselves. Since the Constitution is a compact between the states, it makes sense they document what part they will play under this new contract.

Section 1 – Full Faith and Credit

> *Full Faith and Credit shall be given in each State to the public Acts, Records, and judicial Proceedings of every other State. And the Congress may by general Laws prescribe the Manner in which such Acts, Records, and Proceedings shall be proved, and the Effect thereof.*

Today we think little about the fact that when you get a driver's license in Missouri, it is valid in all 50 states. That holds true until one state decides to give licenses to those in the country illegally. Now states who disagree with giving drivers licenses to illegal residents are stuck, because they must give "full faith and credit" to the public acts of every other state. What does that phrase mean?

The idea behind the Full Faith and Credit clause was simple: The public and legal proceedings of one state should not be invalidated by crossing into another. One state is not allowed to ignore the public and legal proceedings from another. Your driver's license, marriage license, speeding tickets, and court cases (both civil and criminal), don't magically disappear as soon as you cross a state border. Oddly enough though, today your weapon license does.

Congress can, by passing laws, determine how your records are made available to other states and the effect they have. There has been a discussion lately about "National Reciprocity." Reciprocity is the legal recognition of one state's acts in another state, effectively "returning the favor" of recognition. Unfortunately, today in America many states issue different forms of weapon licenses which recognize different privileges the bearer has within their state. (We discuss the legality of weapon licenses in the chapter on the 2nd Amendment.)

However, many states do not recognize licenses from certain other states, and some recognize none. This makes for a hodgepodge mess for anyone wishing to travel to another state with a weapon. These reciprocity agreements between states differ drastically and sometimes change, making it extremely difficult for someone to obey the law and can often result in a felony arrest while simply traveling across the nation. Yet according to the Full Faith and Credit Clause, every state needs not only to recognize the public acts of every other state, but to honor them as well, by giving them credit. Only Congress can determine what the effects of interstate recognition of those acts are, because the phrase "shall be given" means the states do not have a choice; if they do not honor the public acts of another state, they are violating the law.

Yet since the courts have long since made the Constitution subject to their will and preferences, I know of no court that has held that until Congress says otherwise, each state must honor ALL licenses from other states and not just the ones they like. Some say this would invalidate state gun laws, but that is not true. Honoring another state's weapon's license does not mean the holder can violate the law, just as your out-of-state driver license doesn't shield you from traffic laws that don't exist in your state of residence.

In 2017, the House of Representatives passed legislation attempting to solve this problem using their power to determine the effects of interstate public records. The Concealed Carry Reciprocity Act of 2017 was an attempt to require all states to honor the concealed carry license of other states, as is their obligation under the Full Faith and Credit Clause. It did not, however, pass the Senate. Regardless of your feelings about firearms and the carrying of them in public, if the states are allowed to ignore their obligation under the Full Faith and Credit clause for one type of license, what's to stop them from doing so for another? Today it may be someone else's license, but tomorrow it may be yours. If you want to protect your rights and privileges, you must protect others' as well.

Section 2 – Duties of the States

Just as a contract can require you to do certain things, a compact can require that states perform certain duties. This section lists some of them:

Clause 1 – Citizens

> *The Citizens of each State shall be*
> *entitled to all Privileges and Immunities*
> *of Citizens in the several States.*

Though we don't often think of it this way, you are not just a citizen of the United States, but of the state in which you reside as well. The Privileges and Immunities Clause means that any right or privilege granted to citizens of the states as a whole must be granted to citizens in each state. For example, while a citizen of the United States has the privilege of driving while properly licensed (an alienable right), one state cannot remove that privilege because it is granted to citizens of the union (the several states).

Clause 2 – Extradition

> *A Person charged in any State with Treason,*
> *Felony, or other Crime, who shall flee from*
> *Justice, and be found in another State, shall on*
> *Demand of the executive Authority of the State*

from which he fled, be delivered up, to be removed
to the State having Jurisdiction of the Crime.

Remember, the Declaration of Independence declared that we, the united states, were free and independent. If you committed a crime in Maryland, why not escape justice by fleeing to Virginia? The Extradition Clause means the executive authority, the governor of the state where you are charged with a crime, can request that the state where you are found deliver you back to them. This is called extradition or rendition.

Notice that you must be charged with a crime for this clause to be enacted. If you are suspected of a crime or a witness the authorities wish to interview and you flee to another state, that state is not required to extradite you and in fact cannot, since there is no probable cause to issue a warrant to detain you (See the chapter on Amendment IV).

Clause 3 – Long arm of Servitude

No Person held to Service or Labor in one State,
under the Laws thereof, escaping into another,
shall, in Consequence of any Law or regulation
therein, be discharged from such service or Labor,
but shall be delivered up on Claim of the Party
to whom such Service or Labor may be due

It is a sad truth, and one we should not sweep under the rug, that when this nation was founded slavery was a fact of life. While many states moved to outlaw slavery shortly after winning the war for independence, the fact is that slavery remained legal in several states. As part of the compromise that got us our Constitution, the legal requirement was that those held in service, as in slaves who escaped to a free state, had to be returned to those who had claim upon them. Thankfully, this was repealed with the ratification of the 13th Amendment in 1865.

Neither slavery nor involuntary servitude, except as
a punishment for crime whereof the party shall have

been duly convicted, shall exist within the United
States, or any place subject to their jurisdiction.[229]

Section 3 – New States

The Founding Fathers expected new states would want to join the union. With unclaimed territories far beyond what they knew existed, it's no surprise that as the land was settled its inhabitants would want the rights and privileges afforded citizens of the union and therefore would wish to join the compact with the other states.

Clause 1 – New States

New States may be admitted by the Congress into this
Union; but no new States shall be formed or erected
within the Jurisdiction of any other State; nor any State
be formed by the Junction of two or more States, or
Parts of States, without the Consent of the Legislatures
of the States concerned as well as of the Congress.

It is Congress that admits new states into the union. Since Congress is made up of representatives of both the people and the states of the United States, this makes sense. Not only did Congress get to admit the states, they got to determine how they are admitted, by using what is called an "Enabling Act." These enabling acts frequently included language that requires the people of the proposed state to renounce any and all rights and title to unappropriated public lands until the United States extinguishes the title. In short, to enter the Union, a territory had to hand over all its unclaimed public land to the federal government until they decided to give it back. Because of this language, the federal government now owns over one-fourth of all the land in America, including most of the land in the western states of Nevada, Utah, Idaho, Alaska, and Oregon, and they show no sign of releasing it back to the states.

---

[229]   United States Constitution, Amendment XIII Section 1.

In order for a state to be formed from land of another state, not only did Congress have to approve, but the existing state legislature of the states involved had to approve as well. This brings up the interesting history of West Virginia. When Virginia voted to secede from the union in 1861, many delegates from the western part of the state were against it. When their efforts to defeat the secession ordinance failed, they met in Wheeling and formed The Reorganized Government of Virginia. This government sent people to fill the seats for Virginia in the House of Representatives and the Senate. By allowing them to take their seats, Congress effectively recognized as legitimate this new government, even though it was not elected by the people of the state of Virginia.

In reality, Congress allowed a group of rebels to form a coup government and subvert the legitimately elected representatives of the people of Virginia. When this new government approved the creation of a state called "Kanawha" (later renamed "West Virginia") out of the western territory of Virginia, Congress determined that the legitimate legislature of Virginia had voted to approve it, thereby satisfying this clause in the Constitution.

Clause 2 – Territories

> *The Congress shall have Power to dispose of and*
> *make all needful Rules and Regulations respecting*
> *the Territory or other Property belonging to the*
> *United States; and nothing in this Constitution*
> *shall be so construed as to Prejudice any Claims*
> *of the United States, or of any particular State.*

Congress has the authority to make the rules and regulations regarding territories or property owned by the United States. As mentioned previously, the federal government of the United States now owns more the 25% of the land mass of the nation, which means Congress has a lot of property under its jurisdiction. Sadly, nothing in this Constitution was meant to restrict (to prejudice) the claims the United States has on these vast tracts of land.

Section 4 – Republican form of Government

> *The United States shall guarantee to every State*
> *in this Union a Republican Form of Government,*
> *and shall protect each of them against Invasion;*
> *and on Application of the Legislature, or of*
> *the Executive (when the Legislature cannot*
> *be convened) against domestic Violence.*

Republic vs. Democracy

If there's one thing that makes me shiver every time I hear it, it's when someone refers to this nation as a democracy. Nowhere in the founding documents is this nation ever referred to as a democracy. Our Founding Fathers worked very hard to make sure that it wasn't a democracy. Why all this effort to prevent us from being something that is not only almost universally assumed, but lauded? It was because our Founding Fathers had seen what happens to democracies and what they do to their people.

> *Remember Democracy never lasts long. It soon*
> *wastes exhausts and murders itself. There never*
> *was a Democracy Yet, that did not commit suicide.*
> *It is in vain to Say that Democracy is less vain,*
> *less proud, less selfish, less ambitious or less*
> *avaricious than Aristocracy or Monarchy. It is not*
> *true in Fact and no where appears in history.*
>
> *– John Adams*[230]

---

[230] From John Adams to John Taylor, 17 December 1814.

*It has been observed that a pure democracy if it were
practicable would be the most perfect government.
Experience has proved that no position is more
false than this. The ancient democracies in which
the people themselves deliberated never possessed
one good feature of government. Their very
character was tyranny; their figure deformity.*

– Alexander Hamilton[231]

*Democracies have ever been spectacles of turbulence
and contention; have ever been found incompatible
with personal security or the rights of property;
and have in general been as short in their lives
as they have been violent in their deaths*

– James Madison[232]

In a democracy, the majority of people rule and their expressed
desire supersedes laws, protections, and even rights themselves. Look
at most American university and college campuses today and you'll see
democracy in action. Whatever group can make enough noise, bully
enough people, and threaten the administration into submission, gets
what they want and the rights of the other students be damned.

Increasingly, I hear people calling for a more democratic government; they want the President elected democratically and they want the
Senate and even the House elections to be nationally democratic. They
want to suppress speech they don't like, press they don't like, assemblies
they don't like, and if you are not in the right group, they want your right
to petition the government ignored as well. They think your freedom

---

[231] Alexander Hamilton, on Democracy, Speech in New York, urging ratification of the United States Constitution (June 21, 1788).

[232] James Madison, Federalist Papers #10 https://www.congress.gov/resources/display/content/The+Federalist+Papers#TheFederalistPapers-10.

from unreasonable search and seizure, to carry firearms, and even to defend yourself, should bow to their desire to feel safe. While I doubt they have thought it through, what they want is tyranny itself, as long as they are the tyrants and others submit to their will. Somehow, they never seem to realize that if they can strip someone of rights they don't like now, then someone else can strip them of their rights later.

So no, America is not a democracy. We are a republic, and the Constitution requires that every state be a republic as well. And in our republic, everyone, even those we choose to lead our nation, are subservient to the rule of law, with the Constitution supreme over all.

REPUBLIC: A commonwealth; a state in which the exercise of the sovereign power is lodged in representatives elected by the people.

The next time you hear someone refer to our nation as a democracy or discuss the need to protect democracy in America, remind them that the very right of free speech or free press they are exercising is protected not because we are a democracy, but because we are a republic.

Common Defense

In Article I, Section 8, Clause 1, Congress is authorized to collect taxes to provide for the common defense. We discuss what that means in that chapter, but here we see that the United States, today known as the federal government, is required to protect the individual states from invasion. The language "shall protect each of them against Invasion" means the federal government doesn't have a choice; they must rise to the defense of each state from invasion. And should the state request it, they must defend them against domestic violence as well. While it should be noted that it's the state legislature that must request assistance in quelling domestic violence, the executive can only do so when the legislature cannot convene.

The domestic violence clause brings up an interesting situation. The state militia, whether organized (National Guard) or unorganized, can be called up by the governor at any time, but the Posse Comitatus Act means the Army and Navy cannot be used to enforce the law. So where would the United States get the manpower to quell domestic violence?

> *Whoever, except in cases and under circumstances*
> *expressly authorized by the Constitution or Act of*
> *Congress, willfully uses any part of the Army or*
> *the Air Force as a posse comitatus or otherwise to*
> *execute the laws shall be fined under this title or*
> *imprisoned not more than two years, or both.*[233]

You see, since the Constitution specifies that the United States must assist a state requesting help to quell domestic violence, it does not violate the Posse Comitatus Act.

Conclusion

As with any contract, the parties involved (in this case the states), have duties and obligations they must meet. As the product of this compact the United States, meaning the federal government, has not only duties and obligations, but restrictions placed on it. By knowing what the duties, obligations, and limitations the Constitution places on the United States, the individual states, and the peoples of those states, we will be better able to fulfill our duties as citizens of these great United States.

---

[233]   18 U.S. Code § 1385 - Use of Army and Air Force as posse comitatus.

Article V - Amendments

The Congress, whenever two thirds of both Houses shall deem it necessary, shall propose Amendments to this Constitution, or, on the Application of the Legislatures of two thirds of the several States, shall call a Convention for proposing Amendments, which, in either Case, shall be valid to all Intents and Purposes, as Part of this Constitution, when ratified by the Legislatures of three fourths of the several States, or by Conventions in three fourths thereof, as the one or the other Mode of Ratification may be proposed by the Congress; Provided that no Amendment which may be made prior to the Year One thousand eight hundred and eight shall in any Manner affect the first and fourth Clauses in the Ninth Section of the first Article; and that no State, without its Consent, shall be deprived of its equal Suffrage in the Senate.

We often hear people refer to the Constitution as a "living document." While there is a kernel of truth to this statement, the way it is used is not only blatantly wrong, but destructive to the concept of the rule of law and unalienable rights. The idea that the Constitution may need to be changed wasn't a surprise to our Founding Fathers, and they included a process to update it from the beginning. However, the process is intentionally slow, allowing the people time to discuss the proposed changes and determine if it is appropriate to change the supreme law of the land.

Most importantly, the parties of the compact that is the Constitution, the states and their citizens get to decide what changes are made. Sadly, many who are either unwilling to go through the process or who have tried and failed to convince their fellow citizens of the rightness of their cause, simply say the understanding of the Constitution must change rather than changing the document itself. Imagine if your car loan, mortgage, insurance, housing, employment, or any other contract could be reinterpreted without being approved by the parties that entered said contact? Imagine living in a land where the law doesn't mean what it says on paper, but what some prosecutor or judge interprets it to be, even if that is in direct contradiction to the language that was approved? That would not be freedom and liberty, it would be chaos and tyranny.

Unfortunately, this is the way the supreme law of the land is treated today. Those who subscribe to the "living document" theory simply ignore the process for amending the Constitution in favor of this tyrannical process whereby one group, usually the supreme Court, simply dictates a new understanding in one of their opinions. Erroneously called "rulings", these opinions are now treated as the "law of the land" even though no law was created and in fact many laws were violated in this process.

In short, when you hear someone call the Constitution a "living document", what they are calling for is the overthrow of our entire republic, with its legal and political systems, in an effort to get their way. To put it bluntly, the use of the "living document" theory to implement policy or law is nothing short of a coup d'état (the overthrow of an existing government by a small group). Is that how you want your nation governed?

Proposing Amendments

There are two ways for amendments to the Constitution to be proposed: Via Congress or by a Convention of the States. Notice, this is to propose amendments, not to amend the Constitution. And please remember the Constitution is a compact between the states, so only the states can amend the Constitution through the ratification of the proposed amendment.

Congress

The only way amendments to the Constitution have been proposed so far is through Congress. And in order for Congress to propose an amendment to the Constitution, both houses must vote on the same language and approve it by a two-thirds majority in order for it to go to the states for ratification.

Convention of the States

There has been talk lately of convening a convention of the states to propose new amendments to the Constitution. Sadly, either through ignorance or malice, I've seen this process badly distorted or maligned. This is NOT necessarily a Constitutional Convention like we had in 1787, this is a convention of the states. This difference may seem subtle, but it is very important.

Like the proposed Convention of the states, the Constitutional Convention was called in an effort to make the Articles of Confederation a workable constitution to run the union. After the delegates deemed it unworkable, to amend the Articles they proposed a whole new document which was ratified by all thirteen states. Rather than writing a new document, the only purpose of the requested convention would be to propose amendments to the existing Constitution. What prevents this convention from simply writing a new document? Like the original Constitutional Convention, the delegates would have to get permission from their states to do so, and it would have no force of law until ratified by the states.

Today citizens and politicians alike seem to have little knowledge and even less care for following the rules of the Constitution. Once two thirds of the state legislatures apply for a convention, it is the job of Congress to call the convention. Again, our general ignorance of the

Constitution can easily lead to Congress applying undue and illegal influence on the convention or its delegates. Congress' only role is to call the convention and specify a time and place. Yet how often have we seen Congress stick its fingers where they don't belong? The rules and limitations of any such convention must be made and approved by the delegates to the convention, just as it was in 1787. Therefore, regardless of which method is used to propose amendments, they go through the same process of ratification.

Part of the Constitution

Before we get to ratification, there's a very important point in the middle of this article: Every amendment to the Constitution is part of the Constitution. That means it becomes the supreme law of the land, just as the original articles did. Today, there is something called the "Selective Incorporation Doctrine":

> *The doctrine of selective incorporation, or simply the incorporation doctrine, makes the first ten amendments to the Constitution—known as the Bill of Rights—binding on the states.*[234]

Here at The Constitution Study, we look not to the opinion or even the doctrine of others, but at the language of the Constitution itself. As we'll learn in the chapter on Article VI, the "Supremacy Clause" already binds all the states to the entire Constitution.

> *This Constitution, and the Laws of the United States which shall be made in Pursuance thereof; and all Treaties made, or which shall be made, under the Authority of the United States, shall be the supreme Law of the Land; and the Judges in every State shall*

---

[234] The Free Legal Dictionary https://legal-dictionary.thefreedictionary.com/ Incorporation+Doctrine.

> *be bound thereby, any Thing in the Constitution or*
> *Laws of any State to the Contrary notwithstanding.*[235]

If you read the Legal Dictionary article further, it states that "In the 1833 case Barron ex rel. Tiernon v. Mayor of Baltimore, 32 U.S. (7 Pet.) 243, 8 L. Ed. 672, the Supreme Court expressly limited application of the Bill of Rights to the federal government." There are two problems with that: First, nothing in the Constitution gives the judicial branch the authority to determine the scope of any part of the Constitution, and Second, Article VI clearly states the judges in every state are bound to the Constitution as the supreme law of the land. In this instance, the supreme Court has once again violated their oath to uphold the Constitution, and a flawed opinion of the supreme Court is treated as law. Meanwhile, Congress is not upholding their oath, thereby effectively nullifying the Constitution. This is why we encourage everyone to read and study it for themselves.

Ratification

Once an amendment is proposed, Congress has one more job to do: To propose if ratification will be done by state legislature or by state convention. Whether through your representatives in the state legislature or the delegates they choose for a convention, as parties of the compact, it is up to the states to ratify changes to it.

Timeframe for Slavery

As I have stated before, slavery was a fact in colonial America and it was not going to disappear with the ratification of the Constitution. Part of the compromise to get the slave states to ratify the Constitution was a 20-year ban on any amendment that changed the Constitution's rules about importation of slaves or taxation of people. This would allow time for the slave-holding states to prepare for the abolishment of slavery. While Congress did pass the *Act Prohibiting the Importation*

---

[235] United States Constitution, Article VI, Clause 2.

of Slaves on March 2, 1810, it was, unfortunately, the politicians and not the Constitution that kept slavery legal in American until the 13th Amendment was ratified on December 6, 1865.

State Suffrage

An almost forgotten segment of this article is the fact that states cannot be deprived of equal suffrage (the right to vote) in the Senate without their consent. This was important because states' legislatures, who originally chose their state's Senators, were not known for their efficiency, thus leading to a situation where one or both of their senate seats were not filled. Since this was a condition of their own making, it was understood they had consented to the situation. However, while a senator could be removed from office by the Senate, the seat could not be removed from the state, neither can any state be given additional senators, thus keeping the Senate a democratic body of the states.

Conclusion

While Article V is short, it includes some very important powers. Recognizing the need for the states to amend the compact between them, a power which has been exercised 27 times, is part of the reason the United States of America is the oldest government of any nation under a single Constitution. Rather than fearing the document, as some appear to do, we should educate ourselves on all the powers delegated by it and its methods of controlling the federal government. While this amendment's power has been used to give power to the federal government, it can be just as readily used to restore it to the states and to the people.

Article VI – Supremacy

Article VI is best known for the Supremacy Clause in clause 2. While this is an important part of the Constitution and we will spend some time on it, there are other important rules we must cover as well.

Clause 1 – Debts

> *All Debts contracted and Engagements entered*
> *into, before the Adoption of this Constitution,*
> *shall be as valid against the United States under*
> *this Constitution, as under the Confederation.*

War costs a lot of money, and the states had incurred a lot of debt in their war for independence. The Constitution had the new United States assume the debts of the union incurred under the Articles of Confederation, just as that confederation had assume the debts authorized by Congress before the forming of the union,. So why did the Constitution say that the United States assumes the debt from the United States? Because we have had two governments called the United States since we won our independence.

For this to make sense, you need to understand that the term "United States" is not an abbreviation of "United States of America." While the latter refers to the union of states, what we now call this nation, the former refers to her central government. After we declared independence, the states joined together in a confederacy with a central government called "the United States". The Articles of Confederation that formed this government gave it very little power and no ability to perform its mandated purpose, which is why, after the war was won, the states tried to fix it. Ultimately, they began again and created a new central government also called "the United States". Since the old United States would be effectively dissolved upon the ratification of the new Constitution, it was only right and proper that the new government assume the debts of the old.

Clause 2 – Supremacy Clause

This Constitution, and the Laws of the United States which shall be made in Pursuance thereof; and all Treaties made, or which shall be made, under the Authority of the United States, shall be the supreme Law of the Land; and the Judges in every State shall be bound thereby, anything in the Constitution or Laws of any State to the Contrary notwithstanding.

Frequently forgotten, yet often misquoted and misrepresented when it is remembered, the Supremacy Clause not only establishes the hierarchy of laws for the new union, but insures a unified legal structure to protect the rights of its people. One myth about the Constitution is that this clause means any federal law is supreme in the land, but that's not what the Supremacy Clause says. Let's look at the hierarchy the Constitution establishes.

The Constitution, Laws, and Treaties

At the top of the legal system is the Constitution itself; no person, law, policy, or treaty can supersede it. We've all been told that federal law is supreme over state law, but what you have not been told is that's only true if it's "made in pursuance" of the Constitution. That means that any law, regulation, or opinion cannot undo or supersede what the Constitution says.

*There is no position which depends on clearer
principles, than that every act of a delegated authority,
contrary to the tenor of the commission under which
it is exercised, is void. No legislative act, therefore,
contrary to the Constitution, can be valid. To deny
this, would be to affirm, that the deputy is greater
than his principal; that the servant is above his
master; that the representatives of the people are
superior to the people themselves; that men acting
by virtue of powers, may do not only what their
powers do not authorize, but what they forbid.*[236]

This idea, that the rules set in place for the new government are supreme, is so important to our republic and the rule of law to a self-governing nation our Founding Fathers not only placed it within the Constitution but said to deny this legal hierarchy would put the servant, the United States, above its master, the people themselves. Now think of your life today: Who is the master and who is the servant? This is not a trivial question. As a quote often attributed to Thomas Jefferson put it:

*"When governments fear the people,
there is liberty. When the people fear the
government, there is tyranny.*[237]

Our fear of the IRS, FBI, CIA, EPA, DHS, TSA, and a myriad of other three-letter federal agencies, comes from an out-of-control federal government, which long ago tossed aside the Constitution and the rule of law to exercise power and tyranny over the people of the United States of America. Just as Hamilton said, because legislative acts are made

---

[236] Alexander Hamilton, Federalist Papers #78 https://www.congress.gov/resources/display/content/The+Federalist+Papers#TheFederalistPapers-78.

[237] Often attributed to Thomas Jefferson, though there is some dispute since no written record exists, to my knowledge.

contrary to the Constitution, the servants of the people, both elected and appointed, are now superior to the people themselves.

What good is the rule of law if nobody follows it? And how can we call ourselves the land of the free, when our freedoms are dictated by tyrants in Washington and our state capitals? If you want to know when the United States started breaking the law and became a criminal enterprise, the answer is: When the people stopped holding their representatives accountable to submit to the Constitution itself.

Just as laws must be made pursuant to the Constitution, so must treaties be made only within the authority delegated to the United States. There are numerous treaties we are told we should sign on to, that are in direct contradiction to the Constitution. The U.N. Arms Trade Treaty would violate our Second Amendment by infringing on our rights to keep and bear arms. The Convention on the Rights of the Child and Universal Declaration of Human Rights, while sounding nice, both declare "rights" of things that are not delegated to the United States. Things like dictating the education and raising of children, the availability of healthcare, and the rules about fostering and adopting children are not powers delegated to the United States. These treaties also include protections against blasphemy and hate speech, which are both in direct contradiction to our First Amendment. Adopting these treaties would effectively overturn our Constitution by federal dictate, which is why the Supremacy Clause limits legal application of them to within the scope of the powers delegated to the United States.

State Judges

In the chapter on Article V, we discussed the Selective Incorporation Doctrine and the erroneous idea that parts of the Constitution don't apply to the states.

The doctrine of selective incorporation, or simply the incorporation doctrine, makes the first ten

> *amendments to the Constitution—known as*
> *the Bill of Rights—binding on the states.*[238]

This doctrine came from an 1833 supreme Court opinion in the case *Barron v. Mayor & City Council of Baltimore*, where Chief Justice Marshall, in his opinion stated:

> *We are of opinion that the provision in the Fifth*
> *Amendment to the Constitution declaring that*
> *private property shall not be taken for public*
> *use without just compensation is intended solely*
> *as a limitation on the exercise of power by the*
> *[p251] Government of the United States, and is*
> *not applicable to the legislation of the States.*[239]

This opinion was extended to the entire Bill of Rights, yet the court completely ignores the Supremacy Clause, which clearly states that every judge in every state is bound to the United States Constitution. The court also ignored Article V, which says that every amendment to the Constitution which is ratified by the states is part of the Constitution.

> *[Amendments] shall be valid to all Intents and*
> *Purposes, as Part of this Constitution, when ratified*
> *by the Legislatures of three fourths of the several*
> *States, or by Conventions in three fourths thereof*[240]

Therefore, the first ten amendments, what we call the Bill of Rights, are just as much a part of the Constitution as this clause and every judge in every state is bound to it regardless of state law or the individual state's Constitution. Sadly, the supreme Court decided not to be bound

---

[238]   The Free Legal Dictionary https://legal-dictionary.thefreedictionary.com.

[239]   *Barron v. Mayor & City Council of Baltimore* - https://www.law.cornell.edu/supremecourt/text/32/243.

[240]   United States Constitution Article V.

to the language of the Constitution, and our legal system's genuflecting subservience to precedent means that for a little under 200 years our state governments have been violating our rights with the protection of this illegal opinion. The selective incorporation doctrine is just another abuse of the federal government upon the people of this nation, which makes me ask: How can any justice, who has sworn an oath to uphold the Constitution, determine which of your rights will be protected and which will not?

Clause 3 – Oaths

> *The Senators and Representatives before mentioned,*
> *and the Members of the several State Legislatures, and*
> *all executive and judicial Officers, both of the United*
> *States and of the several States, shall be bound by Oath*
> *or Affirmation, to support this Constitution; but no*
> *religious Test shall ever be required as a Qualification*
> *to any Office or public Trust under the United States.*

Every government officer, members of the state and federal legislatures, all executive officers, and judges, are required to bind themselves, either by oath or affirmation, to support the Constitution. This means that the oath or affirmation your state representatives, governors, and judges take must include language to support the U.S. Constitution, just as their federal counterparts do. That also means, when a federal legislator, judge, or officer acts outside of the Constitution, they have violated their oath. It also means that when your state legislator, judge, or officer either acts outside of or fails to oversee and control the federal government, they, too, have violated their oath of office. The next time someone running for a state or federal office asks for your vote, ask him or her to show you they have fulfilled their oath or, if you know of times they've violated that oath, ask them to explain themselves. Until we require those we hire to represent us to fulfill their oaths, we will continue down the road of lawlessness and tyranny.

By the way, why does this say that these people are bound by oath or affirmation? It's another nod to religious liberty, since some religious organization do not allow their adherents to swear oaths. That is also why no religious test can be required to hold office. The truth is, we don't care what your religious beliefs are as long as you uphold your promise to support the Constitution.

Conclusion

What have we learned in this chapter? The new United States honored the promise of the government formed by the Articles of Confederation to pay their debts. We also see that all office holders, at both the state and federal level, are required as part of that position to support the Constitution of the United States of America. Our part, as citizens of this union, is to hold those people accountable to that oath.

Most importantly, we've learned that there is a power above the state, above the President, above the supreme Court, and even above Congress, and that is the Constitution. Our failure to know and understand this supreme law of the land has led to a massive federal government with gigantic bureaucracies, debts, and power. It has led to weak and feeble states, now dependent on and subservient to the federal government rather than to their own citizens. And we have no one to blame but ourselves. It is past time we take up the mantle our Founding Fathers passed to us and once again put the fear of the people into the hearts of all our governments. I pray we do so at the ballot box, for otherwise the alternative is dark indeed.

Article VII – Ratification

*The Ratification of the Conventions of nine States,
shall be sufficient for the Establishment of this
Constitution between the States so ratifying the Same.*

Article VII is quick and easy. Just as it takes three-fourths of the states to ratify an amendment, it took nine of 13 (three-fourths) of the states to ratify, by state convention, the new Constitution.

Delaware was the first state to ratify on December 7, 1787, New Hampshire the ninth on June 21, 1788, and Rhode Island the thirteenth and last on May 29, 1790.

Conclusion

The delegates to the Constitutional Convention, along with the writers of what became known as the Federalist Papers, Alexander Hamilton, James Madison, and John Jay, labored to forge an unanimous decision for this new form of government. It's not perfect, since men are not perfect, but it has proven through history to be the best form of government man has yet devised. While there are many who might disagree, I can find no evidence, in all recorded history, of a system that has survived so long, allowed so much freedom and prosperity, and allowed itself to be corrected without being replaced.

Since the torch of liberty has been passed to us, the real question is: Will we protect it from all attack, will we run our race with honor, and pass the torch to our children better, brighter, and shining its light farther than when we received it? The choice is ours. As President James A. Garfield said:

> *Now more than ever the people are responsible*
> *for the character of their Congress. If that body*
> *be ignorant, reckless, and corrupt, it is because*
> *the people tolerate ignorance, recklessness, and*
> *corruption. If it be intelligent, brave, and pure, it*
> *is because the people demand these high qualities*
> *to represent them in the national legislature. . .*
> *. If the next centennial does not find us a great*
> *nation . . . it will be because those who represent the*
> *enterprise, the culture, and the morality of the nation*
> *do not aid in controlling the political forces.*[241]

It is not hyperbole to say that the very future of our nation, our rights, and our freedoms, along with those of our children and grandchildren, are in our hands. As Daniel Webster said:

> *I apprehend no danger to our country from a foreign*
> *foe... Our destruction, should it come at all, will*
> *be from another quarter. From the inattention of*
> *the people to the concerns of their government,*
> *from their carelessness and negligence, I must*
> *confess that I do apprehend some danger.*[242]

Will you demand intelligence, bravery, and purity from Congress? Or will you tolerate ignorance, recklessness, and corruption? Will you attend to the concerns of your government, or will you let carelessness and negligence be the model of this nation? Will you uphold the torch of liberty or will you let it go out in your hands?

---

[241] James A. Garfield – Centennial celebration.
[242] Great Quotes http://www.great-quotes.com/quote/46184.

Amendment XI – State Sovereignty

*The Judicial power of the United States shall
not be construed to extend to any suit in law or
equity, commenced or prosecuted against one of
the United States by Citizens of another State, or
by Citizens or Subjects of any Foreign State.*

A rticle III, Section 2, Clause 1, which listed the jurisdiction of federal courts, included cases where a state was being taken to court by a citizen of another state or nation. This amendment removed some of this delegated power from the judicial branch. If you live in Kentucky and sue the state of West Virginia, it's not a federal case and must be brought in state court. The federal courts can only get involved if the case involves the U.S. Constitution, federal law, or treaty. So why this change in the jurisdiction of federal courts? I'll tell you it surprised me while I was researching it.

Background

This all started in 1792 when the estate of a South Carolina man, Alexander Chisholm, sued the state of Georgia for not paying for supplies sold to the state during the Revolutionary War (*Chisholm v. Georgia*, 2 U.S. 419). The case was filed at the supreme Court because the defendant was a state and Article III, Section 2, Clause 1 clearly says that cases where a state is a party fall under the judicial power of the United States, and Clause 2 places primary jurisdiction with the supreme Court.

> *The judicial Power shall extend to all Cases, in Law*
> *and Equity, arising under this Constitution, ... —*
> *between a State and Citizens of another State,*[243]

> *In all Cases affecting Ambassadors, other*
> *public Ministers and Consuls, and those in*
> *which a State shall be Party, the Supreme*
> *Court shall have original Jurisdiction.*[244]

Georgia, being a sovereign state, did not believe the supreme Court had jurisdiction in this case or that the federal government had sovereignty over the states. The decision of the court was that the Constitution, a compact to which Georgia was a signatory, specified that cases of law and equity between a state and a citizen of another state was within the judicial power of the Supreme Court.

One thing I find very interesting is how this decision is referred to by other legal texts. Justice Iredell wrote the opinion, but most of the discussion I found revolved around the concurring opinion of Justice Wilson. I find this interesting because the opinion of Justice Iredell focused on the Constitution and the federal Judicial Act codifying the supreme Court's jurisdiction in these matters, but Justice Wilson came up with a much broader and far-reaching reasoning for his position, one which referred to neither the text nor the meaning of Article III, Section 2. According to Justice Wilson, since states are merely groups of people, and since people are subject to laws and higher courts, states must be as well. In what I can only describe as a long, arduous, and confusing diatribe for the basis of his opinion, Justice Wilson, without any rational reference to the actual words of the Constitution that I could find, put forth the opinion:

> *The fact, uncontrovertibly established in one*
> *instance, proves the principle in all other instances*

---

[243]   United States Constitution, Article III, Section 2, Clause 1.
[244]   United States Constitution, Article III, Section 2, Clause 2.

> *to which the facts will be found to apply. We*
> *may then infer that the people of the United*
> *states intended to bind the several states by the*
> *legislative power of the national government.*[245]

While completely ignoring the many restrictions put on the United States by the Constitution, as well as the Tenth Amendment's expressed assertion which had been ratified just two years prior, that any power not specifically delegated to the United States remains with the states, Justice Wilson suggests the entire power structure of the union be inverted from its original intent. While this is only a concurring opinion, it has been used by those who wish to invest power into the federal government as proof that the states are not truly sovereign, but colonies of the national government.

Why an Amendment?

As you may have guessed, the states were not happy about the supreme Court allowing this suit to go forward. The states claimed that, as sovereign entities, they had immunity from such suits, even though they had clearly delegated the authority to have such cases heard at the supreme Court. After the decision in *Chisholm v. Georgia*, it took only two days for a senator to propose a bill to amend the Constitution. Remember, senators were still chosen by state legislatures at that time. The proposed amendment quickly made its way through Congress, approved on March 4, 1794, and was ratified less than a year later, on February 7, 1795, by 13 of the 15 states.

Since then, just as lawyers have used an illogical and tortured opinion to infer that states are subject to the federal government, there are those who expand on what the 11th Amendment says to include:

---

[245] Opinion of Justice Wilson in supreme Court case Chisholm v. Georgia, 2 U.S. 419.

> • *Lawsuits may be brought before federal courts against subdivisions of states, such as cities, counties, and municipalities;*

> • *Any state may consent to having a lawsuit against it brought before a federal court;*

> • *Congress has the ability to "abrogate" or remove any state's immunity from lawsuits in federal court upon satisfactorily showing that its intent in doing so is "unmistakably clear."*

> • *If federal law is violated by a state, the federal court can specifically name state officials and direct them to comply with the law (although the state cannot be sued in federal court).*[246]

Note, none of this is in the actual language of the amendment.

Conclusion

To me, the history of this amendment shows three issues of human nature. First, even though the states delegated some of their powers to the United States, when put into actual practice some will balk and claim they didn't delegate the powers they clearly delegated. Second, when given the chance, people tend to torture the clear text in order to get the outcome they want. And lastly, lawyers, politicians, and judges are human. They will all make mistakes and are prone to the same temptations as we are. That is why it is so important that we read and understand the plain language of the Constitution for ourselves. To do otherwise is to leave our fate and our freedoms in the hands of whoever can convince others that the law says exactly what it doesn't, something lawyers, judges, and politicians do very well.

---

[246] Totally History http://totallyhistory.com/11th-amendment-to-the-constitution/.

Amendment XII

The Electors shall meet in their respective states and vote by ballot for President and Vice President, one of whom, at least, shall not be an inhabitant of the same state with themselves; they shall name in their ballots the person voted for as President, and in distinct ballots the person voted for as Vice President, and they shall make distinct lists of all persons voted for as President, and of all persons voted for as Vice President, and of the number of votes for each, which lists they shall sign and certify, and transmit sealed to the seat of the government of the United States, directed to the President of the Senate;--The President of the Senate shall, in the presence of the Senate and House of Representatives, open all the certificates and the votes shall then be counted;--the person having the greatest number of votes for President, shall be the President, if such number be a majority of the whole number of Electors appointed; and if no person have such majority, then from the persons having the highest numbers not exceeding three on the list of those voted for as President, the House of Representatives shall choose immediately, by ballot, the President. But in choosing the President, the votes shall be taken by states, the representation from each state having one vote; a quorum for this purpose shall consist of a member or members from two-thirds of the states,

*and a majority of all the states shall be necessary to a
choice. And if the House of Representatives shall not
choose a President whenever the right of choice shall
devolve upon them, before the fourth day of March next
following, then the Vice President shall act as President,
as in the case of the death or other constitutional
disability of the President[11]. The person having the
greatest number of votes as Vice President, shall be
the Vice President, if such number be a majority of the
whole number of Electors appointed, and if no person
have a majority, then from the two highest numbers on
the list, the Senate shall choose the Vice President; a
quorum for the purpose shall consist of two-thirds of the
whole number of Senators, and a majority of the whole
number shall be necessary to a choice. But no person
constitutionally ineligible to the office of President shall
be eligible to that of Vice President of the United States.*

Amendment 12 effectively changes the way the President and Vice President are elected from Article II, Section 1, Clause 3. By comparing the language here in Amendment 12 to Article II, Section 1, Clause 3, we see there are only two changes to the process of electing a President, but one of them is fairly major.

Separate Elections

By far the most significant change made by this amendment is how we choose the Vice President. As we discussed in the chapter on Article II, the electors originally placed two names on their ballot and the person who got the largest number of votes was President and the second largest was Vice President. This quickly caused problems when John Adams, our second President and a federalist, had Thomas Jefferson, an anti-federalist, as his Vice President. While the executive power is vested in the President, the Vice President is President of the Senate, which could have made for some touchy situations. Recognizing the potential for serious consequences should a President and Vice President be at odds, Congress proposed what became the 12th Amendment.

Now the electors place one name on their ballot for President and another for Vice President, making them separate elections. However, think about the last time you voted in a Presidential election: Did you have a choice to vote for different electors for President and Vice President? No, you were shown different tickets with electors who would vote for the President and Vice President of the same party. In fact, the way our elections are run today, the only person with a choice for Vice President is the candidate for President. This is because the political parties control the state elections, limit the choices of the people, and give themselves tremendous influence upon the office of President.

How We Currently Choose A President

Hopefully, we are all familiar with the current process for Presidential elections. It starts with political parties choosing their candidates for President. The process these parties have chosen usually involves a series of statewide elections called primaries or caucuses, followed by a convention where the actual candidate is chosen. The rules about who can vote, how the delegates are allocated, and how they vote are all controlled by the political party. Isn't it interesting how this mirrors the Presidential process with statewide elections to choose delegates (electors) for an actual vote? Of course, there is something else to notice: None of this is required by the Constitution.

Once the parties have chosen their candidates, the American people are given a choice: Do we want to choose electors for candidate A or B? Sure, there are a few others on the ballot, and technically you can write in an elector's name, but you will be told again and again that to choose anyone other than A or B is a waste of your vote. Once the people of the states have made their choice, the electors are sent to their state capital to vote for President and Vice President, and with rare exception, these electors have no choice at all. Every state I've checked has laws that require the electors to follow the results of their state's election, usually for the first few ballots. Only in the case of no candidate winning the majority of electors do the electors actually get a choice of who to vote for.

The first thing we need to remember, if we are to understand our current voting process, is that political parties are private organizations. They are not public entities and they are not an official part of the election process; they are simply a tradition we have adopted over the years, one many of our Founding Fathers feared would take hold in this nation.

> *The alternate domination of one faction over*
> *another, sharpened by the spirit of revenge,*
> *natural to party dissension, which in different ages*
> *and countries has perpetrated the most horrid*
> *enormities, is itself a frightful despotism.* [247]

This spirit of party has turned politics into a team sport, one where the need to win surpasses all others. And like many sports, the participants will often push or even break the rules in their effort to win. Like the great rivalries among ancient nations, the two largest political parties (the Democratic and Republican parties) fight every two years to control as much of the political landscape as they can. In their own version of a scorched earth policy, they lie, cheat, and spend vast amounts of money in order to destroy those on the other team while sanctifying their own. Meanwhile, all of us are caught in the middle.

Before you blame our Founding Fathers, remember the Constitution doesn't require any of this. Instead, it is a construct of our state legislatures and their devotion to political parties. It's the states who put on primaries and the parties within the states that determine how they work. And it's the state legislature that determines what party tickets will go on the ballot and how their electors will be chosen. Also, don't forget it's the state legislators that appropriate money to pay for these

---

[247] George Washington, Farewell Address.

primaries, which means you're paying for the internal election of a private organization. So if you don't like the way you vote for electors, blame your state's legislature. Better yet, start talking to them about changing it.

If the House Cannot Choose

It seems that as long as politics has existed, there has been political gridlock. So, what happens if none of the Presidential candidates gets a majority of the vote from the electors? The decision goes to the House of Representatives. And what if the House of Representatives does not give a majority of votes to a single candidate? The 12th Amendment added that if the House has not come to a decision by March 4th, the Vice President will act as President. However, you may have noticed there is no similar time requirement should the Senate have to vote for the Vice President. The reason is quite simple: When the House votes for President, there can be up to three candidates they can vote for, but if the Senate has to choose the Vice President, they must choose from only the top two vote candidates. To my knowledge this has never happened, though there is still a chance the states in the Senate may be tied; in that case, the sitting Vice President, as President of the Senate, would choose.

Conclusion

Most Americans seem to know how Presidential elections are currently run, but very few know how we select our President. While this is a rather wordy amendment to propose a relatively simple change to the Presidential election process, the control the political parties exercise today would have horrified those who wrote it.

This is an excellent example of following the letter of the law while ignoring its spirit. Our founders wanted the states to have a choice in the election of President and Vice President, while the states wanted to give their citizens a voice in how their electors were chosen. It is unfortunate that today the process is effectively controlled by the two main parties, and the people's input on the process is limited and contrived.

As American citizens, and especially those who read and study our Constitution, we should be working closely with our state elected representative to push back against the "National Popular Vote" initiative (discussed in Article II) and to get rid of the "winner take all" method of appointing electors. While the idea may seem strange to most Americans today, it's the method preferred by many of the delegates to the Constitutional Convention.

Amendment XIII

The 13th Amendment is the first of three amendments to the Constitution ratified shortly after the Civil War, designed to deal with slavery, racism, and civil rights violations. Called the Reconstruction Amendments for the time in American history when they were created and occasionally referred to as the Civil Rights Amendments for their goal, these amendments have often been the center of controversy, attributable as much from their misunderstanding as to the tumultuous time of their creation. Let us take a calm and reasoned look not only at these amendments, but at the changes they have made to our nation and our society as a whole.

Section 1

> *Neither slavery nor involuntary servitude, except as*
> *a punishment for crime whereof the party shall have*
> *been duly convicted, shall exist within the United*
> *States, or any place subject to their jurisdiction.*

Rarely have I seen so much packed into so few words. This single sentence, once it was ratified by Georgia on December 6, 1865, completed the work started 90 years before when the colonies passed anti-slavery laws that were vetoed by King George III. Slavery was law in the British Empire in the 18th century, and as British colonies, Americans were subject to those laws. It was not only legal to keep slaves, but it was illegal to free them. When some colonial legislatures tried to limit or abolish slavery, their laws were overturned. While the anti-slavery laws are not called out by name, one of the reasons given in the Declaration of Independence for leaving the British Empire was that "[The king] has refused his Assent to Laws, the most wholesome and necessary for the public good." That is one of the reasons some of our Founding Fathers, who were opposed to slavery, still actually owned slaves.

When independence was declared, the states joined together under the Articles of Confederation. Since this document did not deal with slavery, the states proceeded as they had before as colonies, with some restricting slavery, others promoting it, and many doing nothing. Once the war was won, and it was decided the shortcomings of the Articles had to be dealt with, the Constitutional Convention started drafting a new document. Some of the state delegates were anti-slavery while others were for it. While this was due in large part to tradition, a lot was economic. The question before the convention was how could they keep 13 independent states with differing attitudes and agendas on many issues (i.e., not just slavery), united into a single union?

The answer was compromise, and part of the compromise that allowed the union to form was Article IV, Section 2, Clause 3:

> *No Person held to Service or Labour in one State,*
> *under the Laws thereof, escaping into another,*
> *shall, in Consequence of any Law or Regulation*
> *therein, be discharged from such Service or Labour,*
> *but shall be delivered up on Claim of the Party to*
> *whom such Service or Labour may be due.*[248]

This clause meant that any slave who escaped to another state must be returned, even if the state where they'd escaped had outlawed slavery. While the term used is "person held to service or labor", we all know it was slavery. After the Civil War, Congress passed a proposed amendment to the Constitution on January 31, 1865, which was ratified by the states on December 6. We've all heard of Lincoln's "Emancipation

---

[248]   United States Constitution Article IV, Section 2, Clause 3.

Proclamation", but it wasn't until the ratification of the 13th Amendment that slavery became truly illegal in the United States of America.

Section 2

> *Congress shall have power to enforce this*
> *article by appropriate legislation.*

Anyone who has had to deal with legal documents is familiar with "boiler plate" language. We'll find that many of the remaining amendments included a section that says Congress has the power to create legislation appropriate to the amendment. This seems an example of the lawyers getting involved in the process and creating redundant text, since Congress already had the power to enact laws for executing the powers vested in the United States by the Constitution:

> *To make all Laws which shall be necessary and*
> *proper for carrying into Execution the foregoing*
> *Powers, and all other Powers vested by this*
> *Constitution in the Government of the United*
> *States, or in any Department or Officer thereof.[249]*

Conclusion

I'm sure many in 1865 thought the 13th Amendment laid to rest the issue of slavery in America. However, while laws and constitutions may change, they do not change the human heart. Though the 13th Amendment kicked off a renaissance for some in what was then called the negro community, many of those who once "owned" these men and women were not prepared to meet them as equals. The bitterness, animosity, and racism on both sides continues today. While the situation is tremendously better in the 21st century than it was in the 19th, men's focus on the pain and suffering has led many to ignore the gains we have

---

[249] United States Constitution Article I, Section 8, Clause 18.

made. In the meantime, I, like the Rev. Dr. Martin Luther King, Jr., also have a dream, a dream that my daughter will live in a nation where its people learn from their history rather than repeat it. A land where the mistakes of the past are recognized, rather than swept under that rug or used as an excuse for misbehavior. A land where skin, sex, or party doesn't matter, and character does.

> *I have a dream that my four little children*
> *will one day live in a nation where they will*
> *not be judged by the color of their skin but*
> *by the content of their character.*[250]

---

[250] National Archives https://www.archives.gov/files/press/exhibits/dream-speech.pdf.

Amendment XIV

T he 13th Amendment outlawed slavery in the United States, but there was still a lot of work to be done. The 14th Amendment deals with states reluctant to recognize the rights of newly freed slaves, removes a compromise made during the Constitutional Convention, and a few other "housekeeping" items.

Section 1 – Citizenship

All persons born or naturalized in the United States, and subject to the jurisdiction thereof, are citizens of the United States and of the State wherein they reside. No State shall make or enforce any law which shall abridge the privileges or immunities of citizens of the United States; nor shall any State deprive any person of life, liberty, or property, without due process of law; nor deny to any person within its jurisdiction the equal protection of the laws.

As we discussed in the 13th Amendment, many people who had once owned slaves were reticent to treat them as equals. Some southern states passed laws infringing on the rights of newly freed slaves. These "Black Codes" restricted those former slaves from voting, serving on juries, working in certain occupations, their ability to marry, and more. While the slaves had been freed, in many of the former Confederate States they were not treated as citizens. Enter the 14th Amendment.

By ensuring that the newly freed slaves (at least the ones who were born in America) were citizens, they received the protection of Article IV, Section 2, removing any question that these Black Codes were constitutional.

> *The Citizens of each State shall be*
> *entitled to all Privileges and Immunities*
> *of Citizens in the several States.*[251]

Overlooked in this amendment is the diminution of states' sovereignty over the standards of citizenship. Most people today simply assume that citizenship is a federal issue; however, the Constitution only gives the United States Congress the authority to set the rules for naturalization.

> *To establish an uniform Rule of Naturalization,*
> *and uniform Laws on the subject of Bankruptcies*
> *throughout the United States;*[252]

It's important to remember that the states are free, independent, and therefore sovereign. Part of being sovereign is the ability to determine who is a citizen, which is different from setting the rules for how an alien becomes a citizen.

> *NATURALIZATION: The act of investing an alien with*
> *the rights and privileges of a native subject or citizen.*[253]

Originally, states determined the standards for citizenship even though they were required to follow Congress' rules for naturalizing aliens. With the 14th Amendment, the states turned over the determination of citizenship to the United States.

---

[251] United States Constitution, Article IV, Section 2.

[252] United States Constitution, Article I, Section 8, Clause 4.

[253] Webster's 1828 Dictionary http://webstersdictionary1828.com.

Birthright Citizenship

Contrary to what you've been told, probably by the majority of people who have commented on this subject, the 14th Amendment does not grant citizenship to anyone who is born in the United States. It comes with the caveat that they must also be subject to the jurisdiction of the United States as well. What does it mean to be subject to the jurisdiction of the United States?

> SUBJECT: *Being under the power and dominion of another; as, Jamaica is subject to Great Britain.*

> JURISDICTION: *Power of governing or legislating. The legislature of one state can exercise no jurisdiction in another.*[254]

To be subject to a jurisdiction means to be under the power and dominion of a governing body. While a person who is living in the United States is subject to our laws, is that what Congress meant by this language? Not according to the man who authored the amendment to the bill that eventually became the 14th Amendment, Senator Jacob Merritt Howard of Michigan. He suggested we change the language of the proposed amendment to include "and subject to the jurisdiction thereof."

> *This amendment which I have offered is simply declaratory of what I regard as the law of the land already, that every person born within the limits of the United States, and subject to their jurisdiction, is by virtue of natural law and national law a citizen of the United States. This will not, of course, include persons born in the United States who are foreigners, aliens, who belong to the families of ambassadors or foreign*

---

[254] Webster's 1828 Dictionary http://webstersdictionary1828.com.

> *ministers accredited to the Government of the United*
> *States, but will include every other class of persons."*[255]

This idea of being "subject to the jurisdiction thereof" meant those who are not citizens of another nation was summed up quite nicely by Senator Reverdy Johnson of Maryland. I only wish they had used his language rather than Senator Howard's.

> *Now all this amendment provides is, that all persons*
> *born in the United States and not subject to some*
> *foreign Power — for that, no doubt, is the meaning of*
> *the committee who have brought the matter before —*
> *shall be considered as citizens of the United States.*[256]

Since it is well-established legal precedent that when ambiguity exists in the law, one must determine, as best as possible, the intent of those writing the law. There is no possible way to interpret the language of Senator Howard, who wrote the language in question, to mean anything other than those who are born in the United States and are not subjects (or citizens) of another nation, something Senator Johnson confirmed in no uncertain terms. However, it appears that the research and understanding of this language is beyond the comprehension of many pundits, politicians, and justices in this nation.

For decades, it has been claimed by many that the simple act of being born within the borders of the United States granted you the privileges of citizenship. However, no such language can be found in either the Constitution or federal law. The only case I could find regarding the question of citizenship for those born to foreigners is the 1898 supreme Court case United States v. Wong Kim Ark. In this case, the court decided that the child of a Chinese couple with permanent residency in the United States but "subject to the Emperor of China" was a citizen. In the opinion of the court, permanent residency status means the resident

---

[255] Congressional Globe p. 2890.
[256] Congressional Globe p. 2893.

is subject to the jurisdiction of the United States. By history, precedent, and sound jurisprudence, that is a weak position at best.

As we've already discussed, the understanding of the text when it was ratified was that "subject to the jurisdiction thereof" excluded both foreigners (those born in another country[257]) and aliens (citizens of other countries[258]). So, if both the Constitution and federal law say that only persons who are subject to the United States at birth are citizens, why does the government grant citizenship to those who are not subject to them? Good question. Unfortunately, the answer is we don't follow the law anymore, or at least not when it's inconvenient for certain political figures and their supporters.

Due Process and Equal Protection

The 14th Amendment reiterates the language of the 5th Amendment guaranteeing the protection of due process.

> *nor be deprived of life, liberty, or property,*
> *without due process of law;[259]*

It also introduces the "Equal Protection Clause". You would think that the idea of everyone being treated equally under the law would be obvious. In fact, it was so obvious that our Founding Fathers never put the language in the Constitution, although the idea that we are all created equal is in the Declaration of Independence. While it is human nature to want to treat others differently, it took politicians to do so with the law.

As we mentioned earlier, Black Codes severely restricted the freedoms of black people in the former Confederate states. People of color were singled out and treated differently and they were not given the

---

[257] Webster's 1828 Dictionary http://webstersdictionary1828.com.

[258] IBID.

[259] United States Constitution, Amendment V.

same protections under the law as white people. Unfortunately, this did not stop with the ratification of the 14th Amendment.

Starting in the 1870s, as legislatures in the southern states returned to the control of the Democratic Party, laws were passed making voter registration and voting more restrictive for black citizens as well as many poor white citizens. Since being registered to vote was a requirement to serve on a jury or run for local office, the suppression of black voter registration also decreased their political power in these states. The creation of separate public schools and libraries led to the black versions being underfunded when compared to the white. In 1896, in the supreme Court case *Plessy v. Ferguson*, Plessy stated that, among other things, the Louisiana law requiring separate railroad accommodations for blacks, and white and color (mixed race), violated the 14th Amendment. Often described as the court validating "separate but equal" as constitutional, the details of the decision show that:

> *[W]e cannot say that a law which authorizes or even requires the separation of the two races in public conveyances is unreasonable, or more obnoxious to the fourteenth amendment than the acts of congress requiring separate schools for colored children in the District of Columbia, the constitutionality of which does not seem to have been questioned, or the corresponding acts of state legislatures.*[260]

If we are to do this case justice, we must remember that segregation was common in the late 19th century, not just in law, but in society. The eugenics movement, started by Sir Francis Galton in the 1880s, believed in improving the genetic quality of the human race. This was used in the late 19th and early 20th centuries in an attempt to improve the native populations at the expense of what was thought to be the lower races.

---

[260] Transcription of the Judgment of the Supreme Court of the United States in *Plessy v. Ferguson*.

This led not only to laws against such things as interracial marriage, but to social stigmas as well.

As evil as we see segregation today, it was a societal norm in 1896, which surely informed the Plessy court. The court looked at what Congress had done with the Washington, D.C. schools, and since no one had brought a constitutional challenge to it or similar state laws, then it must be constitutional. So much for the vaunted theory of "Judicial Review."

The question we need to look at today is: What should equal protection of the laws look like? Does a law, that says every child must be provided with an education, protect all equally if they are forced to segregate to different schools, and especially those of differing quality? Should it matter if the segregation is based on race, income, or zip code? Does giving favorable criteria for public college entrance to certain groups above another qualify as equal protection? Do we receive equal protection under the law when those creating those laws exempt themselves from them? Does the creation of "protected classes" insure equal protection or violate it? Is it equal protection to protect the free speech rights of some but not others, based on their race or membership in a particular group or party? Does equal protection mean the requirement is for an equal outcome or merely an equal opportunity? Is there equal protection of the law when some are allowed to riot and vandalize while government officials watch and do nothing? If the answer to any of these questions is no, then we need to ask ourselves what we can do about it.

It is human nature to want protection for ourselves but not think about the same protection for others. If we want equal protection, then we must demand that others receive the same protections we want for ourselves. It is distressing that today this seems to be a step too far for many Americans.

Section 2 – Voting Rights

Representatives shall be apportioned among the several
States according to their respective numbers, counting

*the whole number of persons in each State, excluding
Indians not taxed. But when the right to vote at any
election for the choice of electors for President and
Vice President of the United States, Representatives in
Congress, the Executive and Judicial officers of a State,
or the members of the Legislature thereof, is denied to
any of the male inhabitants of such State, being twenty-
one years of age, and citizens of the United States, or in
any way abridged, except for participation in rebellion,
or other crime, the basis of representation therein shall
be reduced in the proportion which the number of
such male citizens shall bear to the whole number of
male citizens twenty-one years of age in such State.*

Article I, Section 2, Clause 3, known as the "Three-Fifths Clause," is often vilified for treating blacks as "three-fifths of a human being" even though it did nothing of the sort. It was a way to restrict the influence of slave holding states in Congress. Now that slavery was illegal in the United States of America, it was time to repeal that clause. Now the representation in the House of Representatives and apportionment of taxes would be done by counting everyone in the state except Indians, who were not taxed. Since Native Americans who are citizens of their tribe are not subject to taxation, they are also not entitled to representation.

Unfortunately, there was still a problem. What should we do with those states that were still restricting access to elections? The answer was, if the people can't vote, the state does not get credit for them in representation. If the right to vote in elections for state or federal offices is denied or abridged in any way, then that state's representation is reduced by the number of those not allowed to vote. There was, however, an exception for those who for rebellion or other crimes, have forfeited their right to vote.

Voting Rights For Felons

There is a discussion today about the lifetime removal of voting rights of those convicted of felonious crimes. While this is a state issue, it is important to note that the Constitution does not require the removal of voting rights for felons, not even for treason or impeachment. Like many discussions of rights today, the facts are often lost in the rhetoric. From a Constitutional standpoint there are two questions that should be answered. First, can the state revoke a person's voting rights, and second, does the automatic revocation of those rights constitute a cruel or unusual punishment?

Let's start with the power to revoke. Voting rights are alienable rights, meaning that since the government gives you the right to vote, they also have the authority to determine who can vote, when, and how. In other words, the government gives and the government takes away. Since voting is always a state power, it's the states and not the federal government who determines who is allowed to vote. That's why the language of the 14th Amendment does not say the states must let certain people vote, but only gives the consequences if they deny the vote for reasons other than criminal conviction. If you think the revocation of voting rights is being abused, you need to work through your state legislature and not the federal government.

As for the question of the revocation of voting rights constituting cruel and unusual punishment and therefore violate the Constitution's 8th Amendment, I would say the punishment is harsh, but that does not necessarily make it cruel. Neither does the severity of the punishment make it unusual. However, I personally believe it is both overused and often misrepresented. I've heard many people say it's unfair to permanently remove voting rights because it continues punishment after the person has served his or her sentence or "paid their debt to society". Even so, punishments that extend beyond incarceration are not automatically wrong. Sentencing for crimes can include multiple punishments with different durations. The fact that state law mandates the revocation of voting rights for anyone convicted of a felony does not mean the person is still being punished for a debt they've already paid, it's instead part of their debt. However, I do believe that for non-violent or infamous felonies, the lifetime revocation of voting rights is a punishment that does not fit the crime. If you agree, then it's up to the people of the states to push their representatives in the state legislature to make the punishments for these crimes more just.

Age and Sex

Here, two very interesting things were added to the Constitution: The use of age and sex to determine voting rights. This is the first time in the Constitution that the sex of citizens is used to determine if their voting rights were being violated. While male and female citizens are counted for representation and apportionment, this is the first time that a right denied only to one sex, males, is considered an infringement of a right. Women voting was nothing new, although cultural customs of the time made it less frequent than it is today. For example, the New Jersey constitution of 1776 granted the right to vote to all inhabitants who were 21 years of age and owned property worth at least 50 English pounds.

While the act of women voting was rare in the states, with the ratification of the 14th Amendment in 1865 we see the United States considering only men when determining if the right to vote has been denied. It's also interesting to note that the reduction of representation is only based on the number of males who are denied the right to vote. If 10% of a state's eligible population is a certain ethic minority, that means roughly half of that population, 5% in total, would be both male and counted toward the decrease in that state's representation.

The 14th Amendment also adds an age requirement for the consideration of voting rights. It had been, and continued until the 26th Amendment was ratified in 1971, up to the states to determine the age at which voting rights were endowed. While the 26th Amendment established a national voting age, the 14th Amendment merely set a standard for determining if voting rights were being denied, and if punitive action was required.

Section 3 – Punishment for Treason

> *No person shall be a Senator or Representative in Congress, or elector of President and Vice President, or hold any office, civil or military, under the United States, or under any State, who, having previously taken an oath, as a member of Congress, or as an officer of the United States, or as a member of any State legislature, or as an executive or judicial officer of any State, to support the Constitution of the United States, shall have engaged in insurrection or rebellion against the same, or given aid or comfort to the enemies thereof. But Congress may by a vote of two-thirds of each House, remove such disability.*

Section 3 says that anyone who had sworn an oath to support the Constitution and then commits treason, defined in Article III, Section 3 as levying war against the United States or giving aid and comfort to her enemies, could no longer hold any elected or appointed office in either the United States or any of the states. Only a two-thirds vote of Congress could remove such a punishment.

Why was this language included? It was a punishment to the elected and military officials who joined the Confederate States, which was an act of rebellion against the United States. There is some logic to the idea not to have those who denounced their oath to support the Constitution put in a place where they might betray it again. But was this meant to protect the country or to exact revenge? Only those who proposed it know.

Section 4 – Public Debt

> *The validity of the public debt of the United States, authorized by law, including debts incurred for payment of pensions and bounties for services in suppressing insurrection or rebellion, shall not be questioned. But neither the United States nor any*

State shall assume or pay any debt or obligation
incurred in aid of insurrection or rebellion against
the United States, or any claim for the loss or
emancipation of any slave; but all such debts,
obligations and claims shall be held illegal and void.

War is expensive to all sides involved. Section 4 not only confirms that the debts the United States incurred during the Civil War, including pensions and bounties, would be honored by the union, but that the debts incurred by the Confederate States would not. In fact, not only would the United States not honor any Confederate debt, but no other state would either. In addition, nobody could legally claim a loss due to the emancipation of a slave. Those claims were illegal and void.

Section 5 – Authorize Legislation

The Congress shall have power to enforce, by
appropriate legislation, the provisions of this article.

Once again, the lawyers add unnecessary language stating that Congress can pass legislation, which they are already authorized to do under Article I, Section 8, Clause 18.

Conclusion

As the nation continued to work through the issues that arose from outlawing slavery and freeing the slaves, we see steps taken to protect their rights as citizens and their right to vote. Unfortunately, we also see the federal government assuming more control over the states. While I am sure most of it had to deal with righting the wrongs they saw in slavery and racism, as frequently happens the unintended consequences, both directly and indirectly attributable to these actions, are often detrimental to liberty. Whether it's the question of determining citizenship, voting eligibility, or state debt, we see the ever encroaching hand of the United States on the free and independent states of America.

Amendment XV – Voting Rights

The last of the Reconstruction Amendments deals with a previously mentioned issue still going on in the former Confederate States: The denial of voting rights.

Section 1

The right of citizens of the United States to vote
shall not be denied or abridged by the United
States or by any State on account of race,
color, or previous condition of servitude.

Ratified in 1870, the simple language here clearly states that the right to vote for any citizen shall not be abridged because of race, color, or previous servitude (slavery).

ABRIDGED, Made shorter; epitomized; reduced
to a smaller compass; lessened; deprived.[261]

In the 19th century, just as today, many people twist, manipulate, or rationalize just about any position regardless of what the plain text of the law says. Though the 15th Amendment clearly states that the right to vote shall not be denied or abridged (restricted) based on race or color, that is exactly what happened for almost 100 years. Poll taxes, literacy, and other tests, including blatant intimidation and threats of violence, were used to deny blacks in southern states their right to vote. And

---

[261]   Webster's 1828 Dictionary http://webstersdictionary1828.com.

Congress did nothing until the Voting Rights Act of 1965. As with so much legislation, the stated intent, "To enforce the fifteenth amendment to the Constitution of the United States"[262] was not enough; they had to add "and for other purposes."[263] Those other purposes had the effect of centralizing even more power in the federal government.

While the Voting Rights Act did a lot to fulfill its purpose of enforcing the 15th Amendment, it did so by placing the federal government in charge of voter registration and polling place access in any state, county, or local election, if the Attorney General of the United States "institutes a proceeding ... to enforce the guarantees of the fifteenth amendment".[264]

Once the Attorney General institutes proceeding, the courts are required to authorize federal examiners from the United States Civil Service Commission to oversee the voter registration process and voting access for as long as the court determines is appropriate.[265] The determination of the Attorney General cannot be reviewed in any court.[266] Any changes to voting procedures from the time the Attorney General institutes proceedings until five years after the court issues its final judgment must be approved by the court before it can be put in place.[267]

If you disagree with a name that is put on the voting rolls by one of the federal examiners, you cannot take it to court. It must be heard by a hearing officer appointed by the same Civil Service Commission that appointed the examiner in the first place.[268]

There doesn't even have to be an actual violation of the 15th Amendment, if there are "reasonable grounds to believe that any person is about to engage in any practice prohibited by" sections of the law, the Attorney General can institute "an action for preventative relief,

---

[262] Voting Rights Act (1965).

[263] IBID.

[264] Voting Rights Act (1965) Sec. 3(a).

[265] IBID.

[266] Voting Rights Act (1965) Sec. 4(b)(2).

[267] Voting Rights Act (1965) Sec. 3(c) & Sec. 5.

[268] Voting Rights Act (1965) Sec. 8(a).

including application for a temporary or permanent injunction, restraining order, or other order."[269]

In other words, rather than simply establishing a method for reporting, investigating, and prosecuting violations of the 15th Amendment, Congress determined that the federal government had to meddle with certain states' election processes in an attempt to protect the election process as a whole, and in doing so has frequently delayed reforms needed to insure the integrity of the election process. Put simply, Congress avoided a simple fix in favor of creating a complicated mess.

Section 2 - Authorize Legislation

The Congress shall have power to enforce
this article by appropriate legislation.

Once again the lawyers add unnecessary language stating that Congress can pass legislation, which they are already authorized to do under Article I, Section 8, Clause 18.

Conclusion

The 15th Amendment was a simple solution to an enduring problem in America: The denial of the right to vote for certain American citizens. As frequently happens, after waiting 95 years, Congress stepped in and made a bad situation worse and continues to do so today.

These reconstruction amendments were created, I believe, with the best of intentions, and their stated goals are laudable. However, as we drift father and farther away from the actual language of the Constitution and the original intent of the Founding Fathers, the Constitution and the laws of the land are being twisted and used to infringe on the rights we inherited through the blood, sweat, and tears of previous generations. That is why it's so important for us to read and study our Constitution, to hold our elected representatives to their oaths of office, and to teach those after us how to be free.

---

[269] Voting Rights Act (1965) Sec. 11(d).

Amendment XVI

The Congress shall have power to lay and collect
taxes on incomes, from whatever source derived,
without apportionment among the several States,
and without regard to any census or enumeration.

Beware the Ides of April

Every April 15th, Americans far and wide complain about paying taxes. We can thank the 16th amendment for the fact that the federal government can collect income taxes, but the damage this amendment has done to the republic is far greater than the pain we feel every year and is almost never talked about.

Before the 16th Amendment

Representatives and direct Taxes shall be apportioned
among the several States which may be included within
this Union, according to their respective Numbers, [270]

All Bills for raising Revenue shall originate in the
House of Representatives; but the Senate may propose
or concur with Amendments as on other Bills.[271]

The Congress shall have Power To lay and collect Taxes,
Duties, Imposts and Excises, to pay the Debts and

---

[270] United States Constitution, Article I Section 2.
[271] United States Constitution, Article I Section 7.

> *provide for the common Defence and general Welfare*
> *of the United States; but all Duties, Imposts and Excises*
> *shall be uniform throughout the United States;*[272]

Before the 16th amendment direct taxes were apportioned to the states based on their respective populations. In other words, people didn't pay taxes directly to the federal government. Instead, Congress, starting with the House of Representatives (Article I, Section 7), laid direct tax burdens on the states. It was then up to the states to gather the monies necessary to pay those taxes however they chose. That means you paid state taxes of one form or another, part of which they sent to the federal government.

These direct taxes were apportioned to the states based on their population, not their income. In other words, each person bore an equal burden of the cost of the federal government. Whether you think it was fair for John D. Rockefeller to have the same federal tax burden as John Q. Farmer isn't the point; it was up to the states to determine what each individual owed. Since the state governments are much closer to the people, they are much more responsive to their situations and needs. Also, since each citizen got the same (albeit much smaller) benefit from the federal government, apportioning the costs equally does make sense. Lastly, since the federal government taxed the states rather than the people, unless you were in the military, you had very little direct contact with the federal government.

The income tax didn't start with the 16th amendment; it started in 1862 to fund the Civil War. Since it was a consistent revenue stream, the income tax was sold to the people with a warning that it was necessary, the promise that it would be limited by a person's income, and was scheduled to expire in 1870.

Then, in 1894, Republican Senator John Sherman argued that the income tax should become permanent and that the consumption taxes of the day were not "fair" and that the burden of this tax should be

---

[272]   United States Constitution, Article I Section 8.

borne by the wealthy rather than by everyone. Senator Sherman believed they could not "single out a tax like this, the only tax that bears upon property as against consumption, the only tax that bears upon sixty thousand people rather than upon thirty or forty million."[273]

Does this sound familiar? We still hear the call to tax the rich to pay for government wars and programs, but is that what our founders had in mind? The Revenue Act or Wilson-Gorman Tariff of 1894 instituted a 2% tax on all income over $4,000 (approximately $88,000 in 2010 dollars). The supreme Court in 1895 found this tax to be unconstitutional in the case Pollock v. Farmers' Loan & Trust Company. In this opinion, the supreme Court stated these taxes were direct taxes and were unapportioned to the states by population; therefore they violated Article I Section 2.

> *Third. The tax imposed by sections 27 to 37, inclusive,*
> *of the act of 1894, so far as it falls on the income*
> *of real estate, and of personal property, being a*
> *direct tax, within the meaning of the constitution,*
> *and therefore unconstitutional and void, because*
> *not apportioned according to representation, all*
> *those sections, constituting one entire scheme*
> *of taxation, are necessarily invalid.*[274]

If the income tax in the Wilson-Gorman Tariff is unconstitutional, does that mean the 1862 income tax was as well? The Revenue Act of 1862 instituted a direct tax based on income rather than apportioned to the states. This is just another example of how the supreme Court is NOT infallible when it comes to constitutionality and how it is up to We the People to hold our elected representatives to their oaths.

---

[273] The Civil War Income Tax and the Republican Party, 1861-1872 By Christopher Michael Shepard p.134.

[274] *Pollock v. Farmers' Loan & Trust Company*, 157 U.S. 429 (1895).

In 1906 and 1908, two republicans, President Theodore Roosevelt and Presidential Nominee William Howard Taft, both publicly stated their support for an income tax.

> A *"graduated income tax of the proper type would be a desirable feature of federal taxation, and it is to be hoped that one may be devised which the Supreme Court will declare constitutional."*[275]

Roosevelt believed in a graduated income tax like we have today. He thought it would be a "desirable feature of federal taxation." Notice that Roosevelt didn't say a graduated tax would be better or more constitutional, but desirable for the federal government.

> *"I believe that an income tax, when the protective system of customs and the internal revenue tax shall not furnish enough for governmental needs, can and should be devised which, under the decisions of the Supreme Court, will conform to the Constitution."*[276]

Taft also wanted an income tax, but his reasoning was that it would provide revenue for "governmental needs" when other forms of taxation were insufficient. Notice the change in how federal officials viewed taxes. Rather than seeing taxes as fees collected to perform specific legitimate functions of the federal government, they are seen as funds owed to the government to finance the programs they want. This is the equivalent of an employee telling their boss how big a salary they need to live the way they want, rather than living within the means of their income.

Both Roosevelt and Taft had one serious concern: Could a method of income tax be devised that would, at least in the eyes of the supreme Court, pass constitutional muster? In June 1909, President Taft proposed a 2% income tax on corporations, then on July 12th of that year, the

---

[275] Theodore Roosevelt quoted in Seligman, Income Tax: pp.591-592.

[276] William Howard Taft Republican Presidential Nomination acceptance, 1908.

resolution proposing the 16th amendment was passed in Congress. On February 3, 1913, Delaware became the 36th state to ratify the amendment, making it part of the Constitution.

Foundering Fathers Thoughts on Direct Taxation?

Our Founding Fathers put the restriction on taxation into the Constitution for a reason, but why? The short answer is: Who gets to control the purse strings?

> *This power over the purse may, in fact, be regarded*
> *as the most complete and effectual weapon with*
> *which any constitution can arm the immediate*
> *representatives of the people, for obtaining a*
> *redress of every grievance, and for carrying into*
> *effect every just and salutary measure.*[277]

To understand this power, we need to recognize two truisms.

People have the most influence over the governments closest to them

Have you ever tried to get in touch with your U.S. Representative? How about one of your U.S. Senators? How responsive are they to your calls, emails, or letters? How much influence do you have on how they vote or if they get re-elected? How about your state legislators? It's a lot easier to get a meeting with them, and you hold much more sway over whether they get re-elected. So, the people have the most power over the governments that are most local.

He who pays the piper calls the tune

The person or group who controls the money determines where it goes. Seems simple, I know, but it is foundational to understanding

---

[277] James Madison, Federalist Paper #58 https://www.congress.gov/resources/display/content/The+Federalist+Papers#TheFederalistPapers-58.

the reasoning behind Article I Section 2. Before the 16th amendment, the federal government had to go to the states to get funds like a child having to go to a parent or trustee to get money. They had to justify what they were going to spend that money on and since we didn't have the 17th amendment yet, the Senate was still in the control of the state legislatures. Even though their influence on bills for raising revenue was limited (see Article I, Section 7), this still gave the states input on federal taxes.

What Was the Effect of the 16th Amendment?

Why does the change made by the 16th amendment make such a difference? Well, the 16th amendment had three major impacts on the lives of all Americans:

Bypasses the states

For the first time in our history, the federal government had a direct influence on the American people. Without the states as a buffer, the federal government not only had the power to make up just about any taxes they wanted, but they could go after your bank account directly. How can an individual fight the federal government when they have the power to take everything you have? Don't like a regulation? The government fines you into bankruptcy. Want to start a business not in favor with the current administration? Watch them tax you into oblivion. Federal government decides you need to buy something? We'll get some judge to call it a tax so they can force it down your throat.

What about the states? Since the federal government can now tax the people directly, the states have no power to restrict any unconstitutional behavior. The EPA declares your home to be on a federally protected wetland? What is the state supposed to do? The Department of Education decides to implement new school programs? How can the state defund them? In short, by giving the federal government the power to directly tax their citizens, the states have left their citizens undefended from an ever growing, ever more tyrannical federal government. Like the USS

Enterprise from Star Trek without its shields, we stand defenseless before the might of the federal government we created.

Apportioned by income not by population

Until the 16th amendment, the federal government had absolutely no reason to know or care about your personal finances. The only thing the federal government cared about were the number of heads in your house, so it would know how to divvy up the representatives and tax burden among the states.

Now, think of the time and effort we spend telling the federal government all about what we make and how we spend it. Not just in preparation of April 15th, which is bad enough with its W-2s, 1099s, and 1040 forms, but don't forget we have to keep track of receipts to prove to our overseers where we spent those hard-earned dollars. Think about the amount of time your employer spends calculating and submitting withholdings on all those taxes: Income tax, social security taxes, and Medicare taxes. Don't forget our employers have to report their earnings and expenses so they can be taxed as well. Then, of course, you have the many tax accountants and lawyers we pay to help us figure out how much we owe and where we can save. All thanks to the people in the 42 states who ratified this disastrous amendment.

Limitless Taxation

By allowing the federal government to tax incomes "from whatever source derived", the 16th amendment gave the federal government an unlimited power to tax. Anything they could conceivably call income could now be taxed. And without any limits put on the rate of taxation, they have the constitutional authority to take any and all compensation you receive. They can tax your paycheck, but that's not all. Sell something and that's a capital gain, a form of income, so they can tax it. Inherit the family farm or grandma's jewelry, and that's income, too, so tax it. I'm sure there's a way bartering for something can be called income, so tax that. Make something or invent something, fine, but as soon as you do anything with it that's income you can be taxed on. In effect, the 16th amendment has made our entire lives nothing but a series of taxable events. It is now impossible to live in America without owing taxes to the federal government pretty much every day of your life.

Destroying the Republic

The power of the federal government to directly tax is the power to directly and limitlessly oppress.

> *"But if our Trade may be taxed why not our Lands?*
> *Why not the Produce of our Lands and every thing we*
> *possess or make use of? This we apprehend annihilates*
> *our Charter Right to govern and tax ourselves…are*
> *we not reduced from the Character of free Subjects*
> *to the miserable State of tributary slaves?"*[278]

By giving the federal government the power to directly tax the people, we have let loose a Frankenstein monster of our own making to trample and destroy us and our nation. Think that statement is a bit overblown? Consider the size and scope of the federal government and how it has changed over the 100 years since the 16th amendment was ratified.

Federal spending now tops $3.5 trillion dollars every year. With a national GDP of approximately $18 trillion that means that almost 20% of every dollar spent was first confiscated from someone and then spent by the federal government. Compare that to 1900 when the total federal budget was $8.3 billion.[279] The federal government employs approximately 3 million people and controls over 600 million acres of land. The Federal Register, an annual record of all newly proposed rules, is published along with final rules, executive orders, and other agency notices;

---

[278] Samuel Adams May 15, 1764.

[279] The Growth of Government in America, Foundation for Economic Education, April 1993. https://fee.org/articles/the-growth-of-government-in-america/.

it has grown from 2,620 pages in 1936 to 97,069 in 2016[280], a growth of over 3,600%. That's not the total number of pages of regulations, that's how many new regulations are created every year!

And who is there to stop them? The states have given away their power of the purse and we keep voting in people who feed this monster. Rather than an annual annoyance, the 16th amendment dramatically altered the relationship between the citizens and the federal government. Rather than some distant group charged with foreign policy and national defense, the federal government now lives with us every day, telling us how much money we can make, what types of light bulbs we can use, what type of health insurance we must have, where we can get our milk, how big our cars can be, and on and on and on . . .

Conclusion

In effect, we are no longer a free people. We are serfs, slaves to a federal government who can demand any and all that we have in payment of taxes. Don't believe me? When you are audited, who is afraid, you or the IRS? How many have been fined (taxed) or even gone to jail for accidentally filling out some paperwork wrong, or violating some IRS regulation? If you are not free to live, to acquire food, clothing, and shelter without paying for the privilege, how are we not in "the miserable state of tributary slaves?"

"When government fears the people,
there is liberty. When the people fear the
government, there is tyranny."[281]

---

[280] Pages in the Federal Register (1936 – 2016) https://regulatorystudies.columbian.gwu.edu/reg-stats.

[281] Attributed to Thomas Jefferson.

Amendment XVII

The Senate of the United States shall be composed of two Senators from each State, elected by the people thereof, for six years; and each Senator shall have one vote. The electors in each State shall have the qualifications requisite for electors of the most numerous branch of the State legislatures.

When vacancies happen in the representation of any State in the Senate, the executive authority of such State shall issue writs of election to fill such vacancies: Provided, That the legislature of any State may empower the executive thereof to make temporary appointments until the people fill the vacancies by election as the legislature may direct.

This amendment shall not be so construed as to affect the election or term of any Senator chosen before it becomes valid as part of the Constitution.

What the 17th Amendment Changed

What was changed by the 17th Amendment? It was how Senators are elected, but the changes that it brought to the republic were game changing.

*The Senate of the United States shall be
composed of two Senators from each State,
chosen by the Legislature thereof, for six Years;
and each Senator shall have one Vote.*[282]

Originally senators were chosen by the legislatures of the states they represented. "So what," you say, "shouldn't the people elect those who represent them? Isn't this more democratic?" To understand the change that was made, we need to review how the federal legislature was originally designed and why.

The Legislative Branch

*All legislative Powers herein granted shall be vested
in a Congress of the United States, which shall consist
of a Senate and House of Representatives.*[283]

The very first legally binding statement in the Constitution is that "All legislative (p)owers herein granted shall be vested in a Congress of the United States." The one and only place in our nation where laws can be made is in Congress. Every legitimate federal law, rule, tax, or spending must come from Congress. During the debate over the Constitution though, a large issue arose: How to apportion representation in this congress?

If congressmen were apportioned by population, then large states would have greater influence in congress than small ones. If congressmen were apportioned equally among the states, then the peoples of the smaller states would have a larger influence on congressional proceedings. (This was one of the failings of the Articles of Confederation that caused so many problems during the Revolutionary War.) The Virginia Plan, drafted primarily by James Madison, proposed a solution: Two houses in congress. One house would be apportioned to the states by

---

[282] United States Constitution Article I Section 3.
[283] United States Constitution Article I Section 1.

population (the House of Representatives) and the other equally among the states (the Senate). I'm sure most of you learned this in school, but there is one very important part of what became Article I of our Constitution you probably have not heard.

> *The House of Representatives shall be composed of Members chosen every second Year by the People of the several States,*[284]

> *The Senate of the United States shall be composed of two Senators from each State, chosen by the Legislature thereof*[285]

The members of the House of Representatives were to be chosen by the people while the members of the Senate were to be chosen by the state legislatures. Why two houses and why were their members chosen differently?

The House of Representatives

Remember how the preamble starts with "We the People"? It's the people of the United States who formed the union, therefore their voice needed to be heard in the federal government. The House represents the people, so its members must be chosen by the people. Understanding this helps us understand why the Constitution gives certain powers to the House:

> *All Bills for raising Revenue shall originate in the House of Representatives; but the Senate may propose or concur with Amendments as on other Bills.*[286]

---

[284]   United States Constitution Article I Section 2.
[285]   United States Constitution Article I Section 3.
[286]   United States Constitution Article I Section 7.

> *The House of Representatives... shall have*
> *the sole Power of Impeachment*[287]

The power to tax, and by implication the power to spend, rests solely with the House of Representatives. It's the people's representatives that decide how much shall be collected and where it shall be spent. Sure, the Senate may concur or offer amendments, but only the people's representatives can tax and spend. The House of Representatives also has sole power of impeachment. Only the people's representatives can charge any federal official with a crime worthy of being removed from office:

> *The President, Vice President and all civil Officers*
> *of the United States, shall be removed from Office*
> *on Impeachment for, and Conviction of, Treason,*
> *Bribery, or other high Crimes and Misdemeanors.*[288]

> *Judgment in Cases of Impeachment shall not*
> *extend further than to removal from Office, and*
> *disqualification to hold and enjoy any Office of*
> *honor, Trust or Profit under the United States*[289]

The Senate

On the other hand, since the Senate's members were chosen by the state legislatures, they therefore represented the states themselves. Remember, it was the individual states that declared themselves independent and had the right and authority to act as other nations. It was only right to make sure they were also represented in this new union. By recognizing the role the states had, we can better understand the authority their representatives in the Senate were given.

---

[287] United States Constitution Article I Section 2.
[288] United States Constitution Article II Section 4.
[289] United States Constitution Article I Section 3.

> *The Senate shall have the sole Power*
> *to try all Impeachments.* [290]

> *[The President] shall have Power, by and with the*
> *Advice and Consent of the Senate, to make Treaties*[291]

> *and [the President] shall nominate, and by and*
> *with the Advice and Consent of the Senate, shall*
> *appoint Ambassadors, other public Ministers*
> *and Consuls, Judges of the Supreme Court, and*
> *all other Officers of the United States*[292]

Though the House of Representatives may have the power to charge a federal official, it's the states, through their representatives in the Senate, who were given the power to try those officials. It was also the states, not the people, whose advice and consent was needed to make treaties, and it was the states, not the people, whose advice and consent was needed to appoint judges and other public officials.

Originally, there was a logical division of power and responsibility in Congress. The people, through their representatives, handled the money and could charge officials with misconduct, and the states, through their representatives, handled treaties with foreign nations, appointed government officials, and their trials when charged. Yet all this changed with the 17th Amendment.

The "Problem"

In the mid-19th and early 20th centuries, there were two main complaints about Senatorial elections. One was that, since state politicians determined the elections, they were corrupted, and seats in the Senate were "bought and sold" rather than obtained based on merit. Corruption in politics is nothing new, and as late at 2009 Illinois Governor Rod

---

[290] United States Constitution Article I Section 3.
[291] United States Constitution Article II Section 2.
[292] IBID.

Blagojevich was convicted for, among other things, the "selling" of a vacant Senate seat.

For this to truly be a problem though, the majority of legislators in a state must agree to the selling of Senate seats since it takes a majority in each state house to vote for the candidate. In fact, between 1857 and 1900 only three (3) Senatorial elections were investigated for corruption. Only one election was voided, and even that was questionable since there was little evidence that William A. Clark bought votes in the Montana legislature. If this was a real problem, it was not with how senators were elected, but with citizens tolerating corruption in their state legislatures.

The other issue was with election deadlocks. Between 1891 and 1905, 46 senatorial elections were deadlocked across 20 states. One Delaware Senate seat sat empty from 1899 to 1903. While those numbers seem excessive, overall most elections proceeded to a vote and the appointment of a senator. The more likely scenario seems to be that politicians like to fight over everything. State legislatures would argue, debate, and generally grandstand, to get the appointment they wanted. (Sound familiar? Have you been watching the last several supreme Court nominations?) And what was the outcome of these deadlocks? The state involved would not be fully represented in the Senate until they worked out their dilemma. In other words, it was a self-punishing and self-regulating problem.

Rather than how the Senate was constituted, the real problem was with state politicians and the fact that the people would not hold their representatives accountable. Rather than looking at the law or a person's qualification, it sometimes became a war of wills between political parties. Again, this was a state matter, not a problem with how Senators were elected.

The Solution

Rather than dealing with corruption and political infighting in the states, politicians proposed to take the decision out of the hands of the people's representatives and give it to them directly. I mean, what could go wrong? We've never had popular elections bought and sold and money has never made a difference, has it? And, of course, popular elections never devolve into bickering and political name calling, do they? Quite the contrary, the 17th Amendment moved the corruption and political divisiveness from a small group in the state capitals to a very large group across each state. So, the 17th Amendment, rather than fixing a problem, instead spread it like a virus across the entire nation.

The push for the direct election of senators seemed to center around two goals.

1) Take the Pressure Off the State Legislatures

By the 1890s, the propaganda war against legislative election of senators was in full swing. Notable people from William Randolph Hurst to Theodore Roosevelt attacked those who opposed direct elections as traitors and accused them of theft, perjury, and bribery. Under this onslaught, one legislative body after another began to fold and call for direct elections. I do not know how much of their decision was based on pressure from the media or the people they represented, but I've found little discussion of the second goal.

2) Centralize Power in Washington.

By taking another power away from the states, the 17th Amendment further centralized power in the federal government. The states that declared they were rightly to "assume among the powers of the earth, the separate and equal station" of other nations, were now giving up their representation in the federal government. Rather than having two different houses populated by different peoples with different goals and agendas, we now effectively have two houses of representatives. The states have no say in what laws will be passed, what taxes levied, or monies spent, and they have no say in who will take public office or what treaties the nation would enter into. In short, by ratifying the 17th Amendment, the states voluntarily gave away their last vestige of sovereignty and independence.

Conclusion

Although seen as a simple procedural update to the Constitution, the 17th Amendment effected a fundamental change in the republic. By giving up their representation in Washington. D.C., the states have demoted themselves to servants of the federal government. Unable to fight and overturn laws that infringe on their authority, the states sit powerless before their federal overlords. Rather than a small step toward liberty and freedom, this amendment has pushed this nation one giant step toward totalitarianism and oligarchy.

Amendment XVIII – Prohibition Amendment

Prohibition. The very word has come to symbolize the failed attempt of government to enforce morality on the people. Yet we can learn a lot today from this amendment, even though it was repealed just under 15 years later.

Section 1 – Prohibition

After one year from the ratification of this article the manufacture, sale, or transportation of intoxicating liquors within, the importation thereof into, or the exportation thereof from the United States and all territory subject to the jurisdiction thereof for beverage purposes is hereby prohibited.

As is so often the case, what started out with the best of intentions turned into a nightmare when wisdom and advice turned into power, control, and tyranny. It started with the Temperance Movement, which can trace its origins to a 1784 tract written by Founding Father Dr. Benjamin Rush, "An Inquiry Into the Effects of Ardent Spirits Upon the Human Body and Mind."[293] In this treatise, Dr. Rush examined the effects of "ardent spirits" (what we today call distilled spirits or hard liquor), on the body, the mind, and a person's property. He also answered

---

[293] An Inquiry into the Effects of Ardent Spirits Upon the Human Body and Mind by Benjamin Rush, M.D.

critics who argued for the regular use of these spirits, cases where they may be used safely, and substitutes for them. Finally, Dr. Rush listed several methods by which someone could "destroy the desire for ardent spirits", categorizing them as "religious, metaphysical, and medical".

What is notable is the fact that none of the methods Dr. Rush suggested for curing chronic drunkenness involved using the legal system. However, it didn't take long for groups to form and attempt to ban the production of whiskey and other hard liquors. Apparently, a group of Connecticut farmers formed just such a group in 1789. These early groups generally allowed for moderate or temperate drinking, which may have led to the term "Temperance Movement."

> *TEMPERANCE: Moderation; particularly,*
> *habitual moderation in regard to the indulgence*
> *of the natural appetites and passions; restrained*
> *or moderate indulgence; as temperance in eating*
> *and drinking; temperance in the indulgence of*
> *joy or mirth. temperance in eating and drinking*
> *is opposed to gluttony and drunkenness,*
> *and in other indulgences, to excess.[294]*

The American Temperance Society was formed in 1826 in Boston, MA, and quickly grew. By 1834, there were an estimated 5,000 temperance organizations with an estimated 1,250,000 members, all of whom took a pledge to abstain from drinking distilled beverages.[295] During the 1830s, there was a split among the different groups between those who used moral persuasion to promote voluntary limits on the amount of alcohol consumed and more radical elements that promoted laws to restrict and even ban it. However, with the Civil War and slavery a much more prominent issue, the influence of temperance societies waned. While there was a resurgence of the Temperance Movement

---

[294] Webster's 1828 Dictionary http://webstersdictionary1828.com.

[295] The evolution of prohibition in the United States of America by Ernest H. Cherrington.

after reconstruction, with some state and local efforts to restrict alcohol consumption, it was only when the Anti Saloon League formed in 1893 that we see the national application of political pressure to force others to bend to their will. This led both to the 18th Amendment and to the Volstead Act.

Section 2 – Joint Power

The Congress and the several States shall
have concurrent power to enforce this
article by appropriate legislation.

While the reconstruction amendments included language that said Congress has the authority to pass legislation to enforce them, this is the first time authority is extended to the state legislatures. The National Prohibition Act, better known as the Volstead Act, was federal legislation to enact the 18th Amendment. The act prohibited intoxicating beverages, regulated the manufacture, sale, and transportation of intoxicating liquor, and promoted the use of alcohol in research and industrial development.[296] Interestingly, the Volstead Act did not ban the consumption of intoxicating liquors, but neither did it really define prohibiting them.

It should not be a surprise to anyone that the prohibition on the manufacture and sale of alcohol quickly led to a black market in illegal booze. From bootleggers to organized crime, the creation and transportation of illegal alcohol not only exploded in the 1920s and '30s, but has become part of our national culture. From Al Capone to growth of the FBI, from NASCAR to gun control legislation, we see today many of the effects of early 20th century attempts to force people to act in a way some group believes is best for them, and we have the scars and chains to prove it.

Organized crime has led to the FBI not only being given more and more power to enforce the ever-growing list of federal crimes, but to insert themselves into state and local law enforcement. It also led to the

---

[296] DocsTeach https://www.docsteach.org/documents/document/volstead-act.

National Firearms Act (NFA), which was passed in an attempt to restrict access to certain firearms in the vain hope of reducing gun crime. Even the National Association for Stock Car Auto Racing (NASCAR), the only non-governmental group in this list, was formed in an attempt to organize the bootleggers who were racing their high-performance cars on the streets and roads. And all because politicians listened to a group of people who not only thought they knew how other people should live, but wanted to force them to do so through law.

One Redeeming Quality

With all the tyranny, hubris, and federal power exercised, it may be hard to see anything good coming from the 18th Amendment, but there was. Often lost in most of the discussion about this amendment is the recognition, by politician and activist alike, of the need to amend the Constitution in order to give the federal government the authority to regulate stuff. All involved recognized that the federal government did not have the authority to prohibit certain types of drinks or the manufacture and use of particular products; that remained with the states. Which means, in order for Washington, D.C. to legally regulate alcohol, the states had to delegate that power to them through an amendment.

Today, Washington regulates just about everything in your life. From alcohol, tobacco, and firearms, to medicine, mattresses, and clothing, pretty much everything you buy comes with some federal regulation. There are tags that cannot be removed, ages which must be verified, and prescriptions which must be filled, and none of it is legal because the Constitution does not give the federal government the authority to regulate such things, other than to make sure that interstate commerce is standardized (made regular). This question has gotten some, if only a small amount, of attention with recent actions by the states to legalize different uses of marijuana.

The federal government still classifies marijuana as a Schedule 1 drug ("Schedule I drugs, substances, or chemicals are defined as drugs with no currently accepted medical use and a high potential for abuse"[297]), though a few states have legalized its use. In fact, the only thing keeping the federal government from swooping in and arresting people are the optics of the situation with which neither politician nor bureaucrat wish to deal. Since nothing in the Constitution delegates the power to regulate "drugs, substances, or chemicals" to the federal government, the 10th Amendment states that such power remains with the states. Regardless of your view on whether marijuana should or should not be legalized, states reminding the federal government of their limited and enumerated powers is a good thing. I only wish it would happen more often and regarding issues of much greater substance.

Section 3 – Ratification Deadline

> *This article shall be inoperative unless it shall have been ratified as an amendment to the Constitution by the legislatures of the several States, as provided in the Constitution, within seven years from the date of the submission hereof to the States by the Congress.*

There are two new features added in this amendment: Time limits and the ratification process. The 18th Amendment is the first instance where the opportunity to ratify the amendment was limited. If the states did not ratify the amendment within seven years it would be invalid. Also, Congress used its authority under Article V, to dictate what method of ratification the states would use: State legislatures.

> *when ratified by the Legislatures of three fourths of the several States, or by Conventions in three fourths thereof, as the one or the other Mode of Ratification may be proposed by the Congress;* [298]

---

[297] United States Drug Enforcement Agency https://www.dea.gov/drug-scheduling.

[298] United States Constitution, Article V.

Conclusion

The 18th Amendment is important not only for the abject failure that it was, but as the harbinger of things to come. While recognizing the limitation the Constitution places on the federal government, the 18th Amendment shows the willingness of many to use the power of government to force their will on others. Previous amendments were used to force change on others, most notably the Reconstruction Amendments, but those were created to protect the rights of people within the nation. This, however, is the first time in our history it was used to force a moral decision and the opinion of a political group on the nation. As we have seen, the only way the government could or, in fact, can effect such a decision on the people is by force. And once force is applied, it is rarely diminished and usually grows.

It should be no surprise that the temperance movement changed its tactics around the same time the progressive movement started in America. Finding power in getting the federal government to force their will on others, comforting themselves with the rightness of their cause, and adopting an "ends justify the means" mentality, the seeds that were planted in the late 19th century have flowered in the late 20th and early 21st.

Now the federal government doesn't even bother with Constitutional limitations. Questions about the limitations of constitutional authorities granted to Congress are greeted with, "Are you serious?"[299] None of the three branches of government bothers with limiting themselves to their enumerated power, so politics becomes little more than a continuous power grab between them and the parties with their donors, leaving people and their rights trampled in the stampede.

More and more, our federal government looks like the one we declared independence from in Great Britain, and we have no one to blame but ourselves. Not just because those in the past let it happen, but

---

[299] Speaker Nancy Pelosi answers question about constitutional authority to enact individual mandate in Affordable Care Act. - https://www.youtube.com/watch?v=08uk99L8oqQ.

because today we will not correct the mistakes of our past. If only we could repeal the effects of the 18th Amendment as easily as we repealed the amendment itself.

Amendment XIX – Right to Vote Based on Sex

We discussed in the chapter on the 14th Amendment, it was the first time sex was considered in determining if voting rights had been abridged. In the 19th Amendment, we see the right to vote explicitly including people of either sex.

Clause 1 – Right to Vote

> *The right of citizens of the United States to vote*
> *shall not be denied or abridged by the United*
> *States or by any State on account of sex.*

Early in our nation's history, states determined a person's eligibility to vote was not based on sex or race, but on the owning of property. The New Jersey constitution of 1776 granted the right to vote to all inhabitants who were 21 years of age and owned property worth at least 50 English pounds. While each state set different standards, they all required the owning of land or other property of a certain value in order to vote. In the society of the time, and in English common law, married women were not considered independent from their husbands. Young women lived with their parents until they were married and any land and property was in the husband's name. That did not mean women couldn't vote, but the women who owned land were primarily widows, so they were the only ones qualified to vote. The few women who were eligible to vote were unable to retain the right once states began eliminating property requirements in the early 19th century.

This led to the suffrage movement which started in America in the 1840s. In the 1870s, women tried to get the legal system to recognize their right to vote. Susan B. Anthony voted in the 1872 election only to be arrested and convicted in a highly publicized trial. In the 1875 case *Minor v. Happersett*, the supreme Court held that while Virginia Minor was a citizen of Missouri and the United States, the question of which citizens were allowed to vote was a state matter since it was not delegated to the federal government by the Constitution nor was voting added as a privilege or immunity under the 14th Amendment.

While the court was correct that voting is a state issue and not the purview of the federal government, this left the women of America on the outside looking in. The solution was to amend the Constitution to ban voting eligibility restrictions based on sex. So, the 19th Amendment did not "grant women the right to vote", as is often said, but protected their right. When states started infringing on their rights simply because of their sex, the people amended the Constitution to protect the right to vote for women in every state. While it took until the 1920s for the Amendment to pass, it is worth noting that Americans of that day were still following the rules in order to do what was right.

Clause 2 – Authorize Legislation

The Congress shall have power to enforce
this article by appropriate legislation.

Once again, the lawyers add unnecessary language stating that Congress can pass legislation which they are already authorized to do under Article I, Section 8, Clause 18:

Congress shall have power to enforce this
article by appropriate legislation.

Conclusion

While often spoken of in glowing terms, today it seems the right to vote is treated only slightly better than the duty to serve on a jury. While roughly 60% of citizens voted in the 2016 elections[300], campaign and exit polls seem to indicate more interest in what party a person is a member of or what socioeconomic group they identify with than their principles or views on constitutional powers of the candidate.

There was a certain logic to property ownership being considered for voter eligibility, since it is those who own things that paid most of the taxes in early America. However, the exclusion of women from voting simply because of their sex certainly does not meet up with the standard from the Declaration of Independence that all men (mankind) are created equal. While common law did not consider a married woman separate from her husband, as our society saw the illogic of that situation, we changed our constitution accordingly.

The 19th Amendment also shows two important things that should be considered when writing an amendment to the Constitution. First, short and clearly worded language leaves little to debate or argue about (just compare the 19th Amendment with the 14th). Second, rather than trying to use government to change society, we should use society to change government. While I'm sure many during that time used "the end justifies the means" explanation towards how to obtain women's suffrage, by following the law and process of the Constitution the gains they made are firm and unchallenged. Compare that to today's attempts to change the law through court decisions rather than legislative or constitutional means. When government dictates to the people, we have tyranny, but when the people tell the government, we have liberty. Not bad for what is essentially a 28-word paragraph.

---

[300] U.S. Census Bureau Reported Voting and Registration, for States: November 2016.

Amendment XX – Terms and Succession

The 20th Amendment adjusts the required meeting date for Congress and uses that date to adjust when the terms of elected federal officials end. It also refines the succession process to include the situation where a President is elected but dies or is unable to fulfill the office before his term begins.

Section 1 – Presidential Term

The terms of the President and Vice President shall end at noon on the 20th day of January, and the terms of Senators and Representatives at noon on the 3d day of January, of the years in which such terms would have ended if this article had not been ratified; and the terms of their successors shall then begin.

Article I, Section 4 requires that Congress meet at least once a year on the first Monday in December, but nothing in the Constitution declared when the term of the President, Vice President, Representative, or Senator ends. In this amendment the time for the end of terms for Presidents and Vice Presidents is set as noon, January 20th, and for Senators and Representatives as noon January 3rd, both in the years when their terms would have otherwise ended. George Washington's first inauguration was April 30th, 1789, so the term of office for every

President and Vice President ever since has ended on that four-year cycle.

Subsequent Presidential inaugurations were held on March 4th, the anniversary when the United States (the federal government) began. This was also the day when the new congress was seated. With the ratification of the 20th Amendment on January 23, 1933, Congress' session now ended on January 3rd and the new Congress was sworn in. Then, on January 20th at the end of a Presidential term, the new President and Vice President are sworn in. In another nod to religious freedom, if the end of a congressional or presidential term lands on a Sunday, by tradition the term is extended to the following Monday.

Section 2 – Congress' Required Meeting

The Congress shall assemble at least once in every year, and such meeting shall begin at noon on the 3d day of January, unless they shall by law appoint a different day.

Congress is required to meet at least once a year. I wish they only met once a year, but that's a discussion for another time. The 20th Amendment changed the date from the first Monday in December to January 3rd, the same date as the start of their new terms.

Section 3 – President Elect Succession

If, at the time fixed for the beginning of the term of the President, the President elect shall have died, the Vice President elect shall become President. If a President shall not have been chosen before the time fixed for the beginning of his term, or if the President elect shall have failed to qualify, then the Vice President elect shall act as President until a President shall have qualified; and the Congress may by law provide for the case wherein neither a President elect nor a Vice President elect

shall have qualified, declaring who shall then act as
President, or the manner in which one who is to act
shall be selected, and such person shall act accordingly
until a President or Vice President shall have qualified.

What happens if the President dies or is unable to take office between the time of his election and his inauguration? If the President dies in office, the Constitution has a plan for that, but what if he dies before taking office? Now it's confirmed: The Vice President elect becomes President. What if neither the President nor the Vice President can take office? Then it's up to Congress to determine the line of succession by law.

Section 4 – Presidential Selection Succession

The Congress may by law provide for the case of the
death of any of the persons from whom the House of
Representatives may choose a President whenever the
right of choice shall have devolved upon them, and for
the case of the death of any of the persons from whom
the Senate may choose a Vice President whenever
the right of choice shall have devolved upon them.

There is a situation where the House must choose the President and another where the Senate must choose the Vice President. What happens if a member of the House of Representatives or a Senator dies before they cast this vote? Once again, it's up to Congress to determine, by law, what will happen.

Section 5 – Effective Date

Sections 1 and 2 shall take effect on the 15th day of
October following the ratification of this article.

Here we see another delayed effective date. I'm not sure why the change would not take effect immediately other than should the amendment be ratified in the time between when we did hold inaugurations and seat new Congresses and when the new amendment specifies.

Section 6 – Limited Time for Ratification

This article shall be inoperative unless it shall have been ratified as an amendment to the Constitution by the legislatures of three-fourths of the several states within seven years from the date of its submission.

Once again, Congress set a time limit for the states to ratify this amendment and selected a method of ratification, as is their authority under Article V.

Conclusion

The 20th Amendment is a perfect example of a "we never thought of that" moment. That is why our Founding Fathers set up a process for amending the Constitution. These simple process amendments aren't exciting and they aren't life changing, but they do dispel the myth of the "living document" theory of the Constitution. If the supreme law of the land could be changed by the courts, or even by Congress, why did they need to make these changes through the process of amending the Constitution? Because it is not a "living document" as the term is used by so many today. The Constitution means what it says and that is the law, not what some judge or politician says it means or some social activist wants it to mean. In other words, the only way to change what the Constitution means is to amend it.

For the last 50 years almost all the things that have changed regarding how the federal government runs and the powers it has, have been done by Congress and the courts, and few of them are legal. We like to use the term "unconstitutional" because it sounds impressive, but it's come to mean next to nothing. If the Constitution is the supreme law of the land, then it needs to be interpreted that way. That means the law is what's written on paper, and if there is any ambiguity about the words or language, we must go back to those who wrote and ratified the language and apply their meaning alone. This basic concept of our legal system has been lost by those we've entrusted with it, i.e., Congress and the courts. Isn't it about time we start requiring they return to the proper application of the law if they wish to keep their jobs? And isn't it far beyond the time we hold our elected officials to their oaths to support the Constitution? Because if the Constitution doesn't mean what it says, it really means nothing at all.

Amendment XXI – Prohibition Repealed

Section 1 – Repealed

The eighteenth article of amendment to the
Constitution of the United States is hereby repealed.

While not the first time a bad idea was changed, this is the first, and so far only time the term "repealed" was used. It was a bad idea, as we discussed in the chapter on the 18th Amendment. Many people think the prohibition of alcohol was the problem, but as we found in our study, the actual problem was one group of people using the force of government to bend others to their will, and it took almost 15 years to rectify that mistake.

Not to rehash the 18th Amendment, but a quick look at society and politics today show we still haven't learned that lesson. Now the government doesn't even bother with a constitutional amendment to assume the power to restrict or prohibit certain substances; sometimes they don't even pass a law. Instead, some agency creates a regulation and everything from heroin to raw milk is banned or regulated, regulations that are enforced by sheer brute force. If you don't comply, the government will first take your money, then your freedom, and in some cases even your life, for failure to comply with their will. As George Santayana said:

> *"Those who cannot learn from history*
> *are doomed to repeat it."*

George Santayana

Americans have shown they have not learned from history. The "drug wars" look an awful lot like the FBI vs. the mob back in the 1920s. Today we let the government regulate every part of our lives, and rather than complain, we ask them to regulate more. Since we learned this lesson once already early in the 20th century, it is my sincere hope we don't soon repeat it.

Section 2 – The Law

> *The transportation or importation into any State,*
> *Territory, or Possession of the United States for*
> *delivery or use therein of intoxicating liquors, in*
> *violation of the laws thereof, is hereby prohibited.*

A funny thing happened on the way to ratification: We suddenly learned that breaking the law was illegal. I'm not kidding; if you read this section again you'll find that doing something in violation of the law is prohibited. Isn't that what the law says in the first place? So does this section mean, "No, really, we're serious! Breaking the law is prohibited!" Buried in this usually ignored section of an amendment rarely thought of is an excellent example of the foolishness that began cropping up in the late 19th and early 20th centuries and has grown to full flower today: The idea that everything should be a federal case.

While the 21st Amendment repealed prohibition at the federal level, that didn't mean the plan was to outlaw it entirely. A state or territory could regulate the transportation, importation, or use of alcohol, if it chose. The authors of this amendment could have used language like "nothing in this amendment should be construed as to prevent the regulation of alcohol by the states or territories of the United States", but that would have been a nice, clean, and hard to misinterpret statement.

353

Instead, this amendment says that violating state laws regulating alcohol is now prohibited by the Constitution. This means that if you violate your state's laws about the transportation, delivery, or use of alcohol, you could not only face state charges, but federal ones as well. Not bad for a single sentence that almost nobody seems to think about.

Section 3 – Time Limit

> *This article shall be inoperative unless it shall have been ratified as an amendment to the Constitution by conventions in the several States, as provided in the Constitution, within seven years from the date of the submission hereof to the States by the Congress.*

Once again, we see Congress exercising their authority to determine how this amendment must be ratified, in this case by state conventions. We also have a time limit for ratification. While this general language is becoming "boilerplate" for amendments, it's important not only to recognize it, but what it can tell us about those who wrote it. It can be assumed that if this amendment could not be ratified within seven years, there was insufficient support for it, and prohibition would continue to be legal under the constitution.

Conclusion

As is often said, "The devil is in the details." We think that the 21st Amendment repealed prohibition, but we don't take the time to think what else it does. Namely what was originally a state issue is taken over by the federal government via constitutional amendment and then placed back into the hands of the states, but with federal strings attached. The Bureau of Prohibition was created in 1920. One might think that with the repeal of prohibition this bureau would cease to exist. But as President Ronald Reagan said, "The closest thing to eternal life on earth is a government program." By keeping state alcohol laws tied to the federal government, the justification for the Bureau of Prohibition still existed. If you've never heard of the Bureau of Prohibition, don't think it no longer exists; today it's called the Bureau of Alcohol, Tobacco, Firearms, and Explosives. Like Reagan said, eternal life on earth.

Amendment XXII – Presidential Term Limits

I hear a lot of talk these days about term limits. People complain about how long congressmen serve and the need to "drain the swamp". We had a similar situation in the 1940s and the solution chosen was term limits, though there are two questions we need to ask ourselves before we decide about term limits now. First, are congressional term limits the same as presidential ones? And second, are they a solution to the problem or only a way to cover up the symptoms?

Section 1 – Term Limits

No person shall be elected to the office of the President more than twice, and no person who has held the office of President, or acted as President, for more than two years of a term to which some other person was elected President shall be elected to the office of the President more than once. But this Article shall not apply to any person holding the office of President when this Article was proposed by the Congress, and shall not prevent any person who may be holding the office of President, or acting as President, during the term within which this Article becomes operative from holding the office of President or acting as President during the remainder of such term.

Many of our presidential forms and traditions come from our first President, George Washington, including serving no more than two terms. After the Revolutionary War, all Washington wanted was to go home to Mt. Vernon and live a simple life. However, his country still needed him: They wanted him to run the Constitutional Convention that proposed radically changing the relationship between the states. Only Washington had the skill, character, and reputation to bring all the states (along with their agendas) together and hammer out a compromise everyone could live with. The Constitution Convention debated how long the term of the President should be. Some wanted the President to be a lifetime appointment while others wanted a fixed term. The compromise was an unlimited number of four-year terms.

Once the Constitution was ratified, Washington's eyes once again turned home, only to find that his country needed him yet again, this time as their first President; he was the only man the states would rally around during this fragile and tumultuous time of instituting the new Constitution. After two terms, Washington said he'd given all that he could to his new nation; it was time for him to retire to Mt. Vernon and live out the rest of his life in whatever peace he could find there. Later, Thomas Jefferson noted:

> *If some termination to the services of the chief*
> *magistrate be not fixed by the Constitution, or*
> *supplied by practice, his office, nominally for years,*
> *will in fact, become for life; and history shows how*
> *easily that degenerates into an inheritance.*[301]

Jefferson's concern was that without a limit on the length of service of the President, it would soon become, as he put it, an inheritance much like the monarchies in Europe. Jefferson noted that this limit could be set either by the Constitution or by practice. The tradition of a President serving no more than two terms was followed for almost 150 years.

---

[301] Letter to the Legislature of Vermont - Jefferson, Thomas (December 10, 1807).

That's not to say some didn't try to serve more than two terms. Ulysses S. Grant considered a third term, but lost the Republican nomination to James Garfield. And Theodore Roosevelt, after serving most of William McKinley's second term and being elected to a full term of his own, declined to seek a third in 1908, only to try again in 1912 and lose to Woodrow Wilson. Wilson would also submit his name for nomination for a third term, but was rejected by the Democratic party.

After serving two terms, Franklin D. Roosevelt told the Democratic convention that he would run only if drafted. Roosevelt won nomination on the first ballot and a decisive victory over Wendell Willkie, becoming the only President to serve more than eight years. Term limits became an issue during Roosevelt's 1944 campaign against Thomas Dewey. As Dewey put it:

> *"four terms, or sixteen years is the most dangerous threat to our freedom ever proposed."*[302]

Though he won the 1944 election, President Roosevelt died just 82 days after his fourth inauguration on April 12, 1945. However, after those mid-term elections in 1944, Republicans took control of both the House of Representatives and the Senate by campaigning on the issue of Presidential term limits. The language that was sent to the states limited the President to two full terms or one full term if the President had filled more than half the term of another President.

Congressional vs. Presidential Term Limits

The first thing we should look at as we consider term limits are the different roles a congressman and a President serve. Members of the House of Representatives are elected by the people to represent them in Congress, and Senators are elected by the people (at least they are now) to represent the states. The President is elected by the states to represent them in executing federal laws and foreign affairs. (For more details

---

[302] *FDR, Dewey, and the Election of 1944.* - Jordan, David M. (2011).

about this, read the section Electing the President in Article II, Section 1, Clause 2.) While the roles of House members and Senators involve creating law and policy, the President's constitutional role is focused on being a single point of contact for other nations to interact with the states; this is why the President appoints ambassadors and makes treaties with the advice and consent of the Senate. You may see this as more of a reason to have congressional term limits than presidential ones, but the reason the nation focused on presidential term limits was the amount of power Congress had diverted to the Presidency over the years.

The Constitution delegates most of the power to Congress. Over the years, that same Congress has created executive agencies and diverted many of the powers of the legislative branch to the executive. I believe this was done in an effort to get credit for "doing something" when they are actually doing nothing but avoiding the blame while their "creations" do what needs to be done. In my opinion, they diverted their power illegally, since they actually have no authority to delegate to someone else the powers delegated to them. This political game of "hot potato" has led to a giant executive branch with millions of employees all headed by a single person, the President.

This centralization of power in a single office is not only dangerous from a liberty standpoint, but foolish, too, since the office of President was never designed to function that way. In fact, many of our Founding Fathers feared a strong executive would quickly turn into a king. As we've seen over the years, this locus of power has led many men to act like kings rather than Presidents. And as Franklin D. Roosevelt showed, there was nothing between us and a lifetime dictator except tradition, is there?

Cure or Snake Oil?

What is often lost in these discussions about term limits is the fact that no one serves in an elected office in the federal government for more than six years without facing an election. Now that the Constitution allows the people to decide who the states send to the Senate and the states allow the people to choose which Presidential candidate the state will vote for, that means those we want to term limit are the very same ones we elected to be there in the first place. The reason F.D.R was elected four times was because the people voted for him four times. Would you say that the Patriots couldn't play in the Super Bowl or the Yankees in the World Series because they have won too many of them? Term limits do not fix the problem, they mask the symptoms.

The reason that Thomas Dewey ran on a platform that included presidential term limits was because previous republican candidates couldn't beat F.D.R. That is the same reason people call for term limits today; they cannot beat the incumbent so they want to change the rules to get them off the table. The problem is not that those serving in elected office are there too long, it's that the people keep voting for them. So, why is it that Congress routinely has an approval rating between 10%-15% and a re-election rate approaching 90%?

I believe the answer is three-fold. First, politics has become a team sport. Campaigns have two main focuses, one of which is "we can't let the other team win because ..." Whether they accuse them of planning to change a policy, modify a benefit, or some other rhetoric, the focus is often "we can't let them win." All too often, people vote for the member of the team they support with little, if any, thought about their promised policies or track record. This leaves the political parties in charge, regardless of the person holding the seat.

Second, politics has become about what you can get the government to give to you. Watch any campaign ad or read any of the material they send you in the mail, and most of it has to do with what you're going to get from the government if you elect this person. It may be Social Security, welfare, healthcare, education, military, tax cuts, or any one of thousands of programs that candidates will offer if you will just vote for them. As Benjamin Franklin said, "When the people find that they can vote themselves money, that will herald the end of the republic." The sad part is that Franklin was correct; running the republic has devolved into the candidates bribing the people with benefits and programs while the people bribe the candidates with money or votes.

Third, and what I believe is the root of the other two, is a constitutionally illiterate electorate. When was the last time you heard someone comment on the constitutionality of a candidate's position or record? Or when have you heard someone accuse a candidate of violating their oath to support the Constitution? Personally, I almost never hear the Constitution used as a reason to vote for or against a candidate. Why is that? Because Americans know so little about the Constitution, they don't recognize an argument based on it to be worth considering? In truth, I don't know if most Americans would recognize a constitutionally sound argument from a candidate.

Protect us from ourselves

We end up with people telling us we cannot be trusted with our own vote, so it needs to be regulated for us. While it's covered with flowery rhetoric and promises of change, what these people are really talking about is saving us from ourselves. Like a snake oil salesman of old, we're promised that things will be different; just take this medicine and it will fix all your problems. Except the real problem is still there: An electorate that is ignorant and apathetic about their rights and liberties and interested only in the bread and circuses those in Washington, D.C. can provide.

Presidential term limits did not fix the problem, since we still have leaders who act more like kings than Presidents and are just as submissive to their party as ever. All term limits have done is turn the Oval Office into the biggest game of musical chairs in history. The party of the man behind the Resolute Desk may change, but does the system? How many Kennedys, Bushes, and Clintons have to run for office before we realize the problem isn't how long a person sits in the chair, but the standards we use to choose who that person is? If presidential term limits have not fixed the problem there, what makes us think it will solve the problem in Congress?

Section 2 – Time Limit

This Article shall be inoperative unless it shall have been ratified as an amendment to the Constitution by the legislatures of three-fourths of the several States within seven years from the date of its submission to the States by the Congress.

This is only more boilerplate language that puts the time limit for ratification at seven years and determines the method of ratification as via the state legislatures.

Conclusion

While the debate about presidential term limits finished with the ratification of the 22nd Amendment in 1951, it continues for Congress. Americans always seem to be looking for the quick fix to their problems and, as Ted Hanover put it in the movie *Holiday Inn*, "Poor girl. Always straying to greener pastures and finding spinach." I have absolutely no problem with keeping those elected to office there for a relatively short time; I only wish the American people had the character to do it themselves. Maybe if we educated ourselves on the Constitution and used that knowledge when we vote, the need for term limits would simply disappear.

Amendment XXIII – Washington, D.C. Electors

As the seat of the federal government, Washington, D.C. is prohibited from being part of any state. While they have a non-voting member of the House of Representatives, they are not a state, so they do not have any senators. And before the 23rd Amendment, they did not have any electors for President either.

Section 1 – Giving D.C. electors for President

The District constituting the seat of Government of the United States shall appoint in such manner as the Congress may direct:

A number of electors of President and Vice President equal to the whole number of Senators and Representatives in Congress to which the District would be entitled if it were a State, but in no event more than the least populous State; they shall be in addition to those appointed by the States, but they shall be considered, for the purposes of the election of President and Vice President, to be electors appointed by a State; and they shall meet in the District and perform such duties as provided by the twelfth article of amendment.

It seems Washington, D.C. has always been a
political football, not that we should be surprised.
It certainly didn't surprise our Founding Fathers,
who made sure the seat of the federal government
would be separate from the states as a truly
federal city under the control of Congress.

To exercise exclusive Legislation in all Cases
whatsoever, over such District (not exceeding ten
Miles square) as may, by Cession of particular
States, and the Acceptance of Congress, become the
Seat of the Government of the United States[303]

It wasn't until 1888, 98 years after the nation's capital was formed,
that a bill was presented in the Senate to grant Washington, D.C. residents electors to vote for President. While this and several other previous attempts failed, in 1959 an amendment to a Senate bill about
filling vacancies in the House of Representatives would have granted
Washington, D.C. both electors for President and representation in the
House. The other language was eventually removed from the bill, including the representation in the House, leaving only what became the
23rd Amendment when it was ratified on March 29, 1961.

This amendment grants Washington, D.C. the same number of electors for President and Vice President as it would have if it were a state,
and put the appointment of those electors under the district's legislative
body, the U.S. Congress. These were to be new electors, adding to the
total number, but they were in all other aspects the same as the other
electors who voted for President. The one limitation was the number of
electors from Washington, D.C. could not exceed the number from the
smallest state, by population, in the union. Why does this matter?

---

[303]   United States Constitution, Article I, Section 8, Clause 17.

Voting for President

As our Founding Fathers had feared, the Presidency has accumulated power and is viewed more like a representative of the people than of the states. Remember, according to Article II the primary job of the President is to execute the laws of the United States. He is also delegated the power to interact with foreign nations, either diplomatically, in partnership with the Senate, or militarily, under the rules and restrictions of Congress. When state legislatures started appointing electors based on state-wide votes, the myth that the President is elected by the people, and therefore represents the people, became part of the American psyche. Washington, D.C. residents felt left out because they did not have electors. The problem is, by living in a federal district, the residents of D.C. are not citizens of a state and, therefore, do not have the privileges of the citizens of a state. With the myth of popular votes for the President growing, this was viewed as a voting rights issue rather than one of state sovereignty, a misunderstanding that continues today.

I discuss this in more detail in the section on Article I, Section 8, Clause 17, but what most people fail to realize is that Washington, D.C. has one purpose: To be the nation's capital, which is a place where the federal government can conduct the business of the United States without interference or influence from any state legislature. That doesn't mean there isn't a case for voting rights for the citizens of the district, but most of the ones I've seen completely ignore the structure of the federal government and have consequences no one seems to be discussing.

Representation in the House

Washington, D.C. is a creation of the Constitution, just like the federal government. Since the states are signatories of the compact that is the U.S. Constitution, they are also sovereign over everything that it creates, including Washington, D.C. itself. That's why it's separate from any state and overseen by Congress rather than its own legislative body. But what about the people who live in the district?

2017 estimates puts the population of Washington, D.C. at about 700,000, or .2% of the nation's population. Since it is not a state, it does not have a claim on representation in the Senate, which represent the states. However, I can see a claim being made for the district having representation in the House of Representatives. The House is supposed to represent the people of the United States of America, and residents of the district are citizens of the union, the same as the citizens of any state. While members of the House have always been chosen by the people, they are only chosen by the people of a particular state, by state run elections the number of which is determined by the population of the state.

*The House of Representatives shall be
composed of Members chosen every second
Year by the People of the several States*[304]

At first glance, there may seem to be an easy answer: Simply amend the Constitution to grant Washington, D.C. residents representation in the House the same way the 23rd Amendment granted the electors for President. Unfortunately, that would create a couple of problems.

If residents of a federal district are granted representation in the House, what about those who live in federal territories or other federally controlled land? Would that mean the U.S. Virgin Islands and Guam would get representation as well? And what about Puerto Rico? They have voted several times to remain a distinct and separate territory, with their own laws and government under the protection of the United States and our Constitution. So, if we did grant Washington, D.C. representation in the House, how do you resolve the issues that would come from such a change?

For example, if no candidate for President wins a majority of electors, the House of Representatives vote by state for President. Would these non-state representatives be able to vote? Would they get one vote per territory? And would their vote be legitimate, since those territories

---

[304]   United States Constitution, Article I, Section 2, Clause 1.

did not sign on to the U.S. Constitution? By blurring the distinction between states and federal districts, we open a Pandora's box of trouble, including not just how this would work, but whether this calls into question the very foundation of this nation being a union of free, independent, and sovereign states.

Is there a solution that would allow the residents of the district representation without fundamentally changing the relationship with the states? Possibly. Consider how members of the military are treated. They may reside on a military base, fort, or arsenal which, like Washington, D.C. is federal land and under the control of Congress, yet they are considered citizens of the state that base resides in. Could we treat the residents of Washington, D.C., the same way? Since all of D.C. exists in land that used to belong to Maryland, could its residents be citizens of Maryland and counted toward their representation? It would require repealing the 23rd Amendment, but I think it might be a better, more effective, and less disturbing solution than trying to treat the residents of the district as if they were citizens of a state.

Section 2 – Congress Can Do What it Can Do.

The Congress shall have power to enforce
this article by appropriate legislation.

Sometimes, you just have to look at lawyers and shake your head. Congress already has the power to create legislation to execute the powers granted it in the Constitution, but apparently lawyers can't resist adding language to anything.

To make all Laws which shall be necessary and
proper for carrying into Execution the foregoing
Powers, and all other Powers vested by this
Constitution in the Government of the United
States, or in any Department or Officer thereof.[305]

---

[305]   United States Constitution, Article I, Section 8, Clause 18.

Conclusion

It seems like human nature looks at a situation and has an insatiable need to come up with a solution for the symptom rather than for the problem. Instead of looking at the big picture (the fact that people living in a federal district don't have all the privileges of state citizenship), they ask only how can we give them the right to vote for President or, technically, electors for President. That, however, is not the argument that should be made. If we knew our Constitution better, knew the reasons for amending it, and if we understood the structure of our nation, then maybe we could come up with better solutions than throwing a band-aid on a boo boo and fix the real injury instead.

Amendment XXIV – Poll Taxes

Voting is an alienable right, meaning the right to vote is granted by government, so the state can take it away. Like squeezing on a balloon, every time the Constitution was amended to protect the rights of former slaves and their families, some state and local governments would find a way for this discrimination to pop up again.

Section 1 – Pay to Play

> *The right of citizens of the United States to vote in any primary or other election for President or Vice President, for electors for President or Vice President, or for Senator or Representative in Congress, shall not be denied or abridged by the United States or any state by reason of failure to pay any poll tax or other tax.*

> *POLL TAX: a tax of a fixed amount per person levied on adults and often linked to the right to vote*[306]

While poll taxes were most often associated with the Jim Crow south of the late 19th century, the collection of taxes to be allowed to vote not only existed before then, but was used as a source of government revenue and treated the same as the fees we pay today for drivers', hunting, and fishing licenses.

After the 15th Amendment was ratified, protecting the right to vote for all races, several states enacted poll taxes as a method of restricting

---

[306] Merriam-Webster Dictionary https://merriam-webster.com

access to this right. While poll taxes aren't necessarily race biased, many of these new taxes included "grandfather" clauses, allowing those who had voted before the 15ᵗʰ Amendment to be exempt from the tax. Then, in 1964, the ratification of the 24ᵗʰ Amendment meant the right to vote could not be abridged for the failure to pay taxes. That does not mean that poll taxes are illegal, only that you cannot be denied the opportunity to vote for not paying them. Since their purpose is to control who can vote, this amendment makes them pretty much useless. Since the amendment states "by reason of failure to pay any poll tax or other tax" you cannot be prevented from polling because you didn't pay your property or income tax either.

It is human nature not only to find ways to get around the rules, but to try to use the rules to your advantage. We see this in the debate over voter ID laws. Whenever the idea of requiring a photo ID in order to vote is raised, there are some that scream "Poll Tax." Let's forget the fact that the purpose of voter ID laws is not to deny any group the right to vote, but to protect the rights of citizens to not have their elections corrupted by malicious actors. Let's also remember that every voter ID law I have seen not only includes IDs commonly in use, but access to free IDs for those who don't already have one. The idea that requiring you prove who you are (at no additional cost to yourself) is somehow a poll tax is ludicrous. I'm not saying people who rely on such ridiculous language should be shut up, because I'm more than willing to let them show the world their foolishness. I only wish more people would see how absurd an argument it is.

Section 2 – Lawyer's Boilerplate

> *The Congress shall have power to enforce*
> *this article by appropriate legislation.*

If there is one thing about the Constitution that I find boring, it's the repetitive, redundant language that's included in these later amendments. Congress already has the power to create legislation to execute the powers granted it in the Constitution, but apparently lawyers can't resist adding language to anything.

Conclusion

As I have said, it is human nature not only to find ways around rules we don't like, but to misuse them to achieve our own aims. Just as poll tax laws were used to deny the right to vote, this amendment is being used in a similar fashion by some not to deny the right to vote, but to deny the rights of millions of Americans to have their votes protected. What is sad is that this does not surprise me; instead, this shows that we need to learn to restrain our instincts and to use the system not only to protect our rights, but the rights of others. Because only when all Americans have all their rights protected will we truly be the land of the free and the home of the brave.

Amendment XXV – Presidential Succession

As the pace of life and history has increased over the years, the need for Presidential powers to always be available has become more urgent. While most of what Washington, D.C. does is not really that time critical, as Commander-in-Chief, the President may be called on to act quickly to a military or security threat. In 1788, if something had happened to George Washington, it would have taken weeks, even months, for that information to propagate around the world. In contrast, when an attempt to assassinate President Reagan (on March 30, 1981) left him wounded and in surgery, the whole world knew in a matter of minutes.

The need for a plan for the succession of powers should something happen to the President isn't something new; it was included in the original Constitution ratified in 1787. However, while that plan was simple, leave it to politicians to confuse things. When William Harrison became the first President to die in office in 1841, his cabinet gave his Vice President, John Tyler, the title of "Vice President Acting President". The Constitution says that, in the event of the death of the President, the powers and duties "shall devolve to the Vice President", so doesn't that include his title?[307] Eventually Congress agreed that the newly sworn in President Tyler not only had the duties and powers, but in the case of the death of the President, the office itself devolved to the Vice President.

---

[307] United States Constitution, Article II, Section 1, Clause 6.

Then in 1919, after several debilitating strokes, Woodrow Wilson's cabinet suggested his Vice President, Thomas Marshall, should take over. Wilson's wife and doctor kept the President's condition secret from Congress and the public, leaving the powers of the President in question. Later, and unlike his predecessor, when President Eisenhower suffered heart problems and a mild stroke, he wrote a letter to then Vice President Nixon identifying him as the person who would determine if and when the President was incapacitated and giving instructions for what to do in that situation. While not legally binding, and since there was no constitutional method to determine the capacity of a President to fulfill his duty, it was an attempt to establish some procedure should Eisenhower's condition require it. While Nixon did serve as acting President twice because of the President's health issues, Eisenhower never needed to step down.

When President Kennedy was assassinated in 1963, there was a brief time of confusion because of reports that Vice President Johnson was also wounded. Even though Congress had passed legislation dealing with this situation, it was not the first time such disorder reigned. These events led to the adoption of the 25th Amendment, not so much to establish a line of Presidential succession, but what to do if the Vice President is unable to serve or if the President is incapable of fulfilling his office but does not step down.

Section 1 – Presidential Succession

> *In case of the removal of the President from*
> *office or of his death or resignation, the Vice*
> *President shall become President.*

Article I, Section 1, Clause 6 states that, if the President died, the powers and duties devolve to the Vice President. The question that arose in 1841 was: Do only the powers devolve or does the Vice President become President? Section 1 clarifies the question by simply stating the if the President is no longer in office, then the Vice President becomes President.

Section 2 – Vice Presidential Vacancies

> *Whenever there is a vacancy in the office of the*
> *Vice President, the President shall nominate a Vice*
> *President who shall take office upon confirmation*
> *by a majority vote of both Houses of Congress.*

In 1973, when then Vice President Spiro Agnew resigned, President Nixon nominated Gerald Ford as his new Vice President. Then, in 1974, when President Nixon resigned, Vice President Gerald Ford assumed the Presidency and nominated Nelson Rockefeller to be his Vice President. A pretty busy couple of years for the 25th Amendment, but what we witnessed was an orderly transfer of power in a very tumultuous time.

A couple of things should be noted here. First, the nominated Vice President must be confirmed by both houses. This is different from the situation where the Vice President does not receive a majority of votes in an election, in which case it is the Senate which chooses the winner. Second, it only takes a simple majority of each house for the nomination to be confirmed and the new Vice President to take office. This could become quite a spectacle in today's hyper-partisan environment should we have a divided government where the party of the President does not have a majority of both houses.

Section 3 – Temporary Transfer of Power

> *Whenever the President transmits to the President pro*
> *tempore of the Senate and the Speaker of the House*
> *of Representatives his written declaration that he is*
> *unable to discharge the powers and duties of his office,*
> *and until he transmits to them a written declaration*
> *to the contrary, such powers and duties shall be*
> *discharged by the Vice President as Acting President.*

There are situations when the President may be temporarily unable to perform his duties. In the 19th century, if the President was unavailable for a day or two the bureaucracy could deal with that, but starting in the 20th century that was no longer the case. In the time it took to get stitches, America could be attacked and military action needed. If the President was unable to discharge his duties, the Vice President needed to step up. However, unlike the situation of death or resignation, this was a temporary condition, so rather than assuming the office, the powers and duties of the President would devolve to the Vice President until the President was able to assume them again. The process is simple; the President sends a letter to the leaders of the two houses of Congress, the President pro tempore of the Senate, and the Speaker of the House, when he is or will be incapacitated, and another when he can resume his duties. Ronald Reagan used this process in 1985 when he needed surgery that required he be anesthetized.

Section 4 – Suspension of Presidential Powers

Now we get to the interesting part. Remember the Woodrow Wilson story? What do we do if the President isn't capable of performing his duties, but can't or won't step down?

Clause 1 – Suspending Presidential Powers

> *Whenever the Vice President and a majority of either*
> *the principal officers of the executive department or*
> *of such other body as Congress may by law provide,*
> *transmit to the President pro tempore of the Senate*
> *and the Speaker of the House of Representatives*
> *their written declaration that the President is unable*
> *to discharge the powers and duties of his office,*
> *the Vice President shall immediately assume the*
> *powers and duties of the office as Acting President.*

The Vice President assumes the powers of Acting President if he or she along with a majority of the President's cabinet (that's who the "principal officers of the executive department" are) determine that the President is unable to discharge his duties,.

It seems that shortly after Donald Trump took the oath of office, there were those calling on Vice President Pence to "invoke the 25th Amendment", which was yet another example of politicians and pundits showing just how ignorant of the Constitution they are.

First, not only does the President's running mate, the person he chose to run with him, have to agree that he is incapable of doing his duty, but at least half of his cabinet has to as well. That means eight of the fifteen cabinet officers, all chosen by the President, must agree that he cannot do his job. Do people really think that nine of the people a President has chosen to help him run the executive branch are going to betray him because some politicians and pundits say so?

Second, contrary to much of what I read and heard about this attempted coup against the duly elected President Trump, this would not "remove the President from office", but only temporarily have Vice President Pence be Acting President. Also, as we are about to see, it's not just the Vice President and the cabinet who have to agree the President is incapable, both houses of Congress must agree as well.

Clause 2 – Resuming Presidential Powers

> *Thereafter, when the President transmits to the President pro tempore of the Senate and the Speaker of the House of Representatives his written declaration that no inability exists, he shall resume the powers and duties of his office unless the Vice President and a majority of either the principal officers of the executive department or of such other body as Congress may by law provide, transmit within four days to the President pro tempore of the Senate and the Speaker of the House of Representatives their written declaration that the*

President is unable to discharge the powers and duties
of his office. Thereupon Congress shall decide the issue,
assembling within forty-eight hours for that purpose
if not in session. If the Congress, within twenty-one
days after receipt of the latter written declaration, or,
if Congress is not in session, within twenty-one days
after Congress is required to assemble, determines
by two-thirds vote of both Houses that the President
is unable to discharge the powers and duties of his
office, the Vice President shall continue to discharge
the same as Acting President; otherwise, the President
shall resume the powers and duties of his office.

This is where things start to sound more like an action movie than real life, maybe because Section 4 of the 25th Amendment has never been invoked in American history. After the Vice President and the cabinet tell Congress that the President is not fit, all the President has to do is send another letter to Congress saying he is. This is basically the same process as Section 3 only with the Vice President and Congress sending the first letter rather than the President.

Now, what happens if the Vice President and the cabinet do not agree that the President is capable of performing his duties? Basically, Congress has three weeks to vote on whether the President is incapable of performing his duties. If a two-thirds majority of both houses state the President is incapable of performing his duties, then the Vice President continues as Acting President; otherwise the President resumes his duties.

Conclusion

The 25th Amendment is a logical addition to the Constitution, a tool to help ensure the peaceful transition of power in potential times of chaos. Foreseeing the need for both a temporary transfer of powers and for a permanent change in office, this amendment also recognizes the human condition and our habit of manipulating facts and situations to get the outcome we desire. It is unfortunate that many with the ability to reach a large number of Americans would rather stoke the flames of controversy by mischaracterizing what this amendment says than educate the electorate on the actual words of the Constitution and how to use them to better govern our nation.

Amendment XXVI – Voting Age

H ere we see the very first time the right to vote is protected based on someone's age. Some people say the 14th Amendment did so, but as we will see, that is not true.

Section 1 – Voting Age

> *The right of citizens of the United States,*
> *who are 18 years of age or older, to vote,*
> *shall not be denied or abridged by the United*
> *States or any State on account of age.*

Some people say the 14th Amendment created a national voting age of 21. However, what it did was include age with a list of traits that would determine if voting rights were being infringed. If a group of citizens over the age of 21 were denied the right to vote, except as criminal punishment, that state's representation and apportionment would be decreased by the number of those citizens. The 26th Amendment not only changes that age to 18, but rather than using it as a justification to deny representation, it did establish a national voting age.

This change seems to have been driven primarily by the military draft for the Vietnam war. The slogan "old enough to fight, old enough to vote" made the point that if someone could be drafted into military service, they should be allowed representation in the form of the right to vote. In my research, I found no mention of the fact there was nothing preventing states from lowering the voting age. In 1970, four states, Alaska, Georgia, Hawaii, and Kentucky, all had voting ages lower than

21. That same year, President Nixon signed an extension to the Voting Rights Act of 1965 that included language requiring the voting age be set to 18 for all state, local, and federal elections. Oregon and Texas challenged this in the supreme Court case *Oregon v. Mitchell*. In a somewhat schizophrenic decision, the court held that while Congress could set the age for federal elections, they struck down the provision for state and local ones.

I call it schizophrenic because there is no language in the Constitution that delegates any authority to Congress to regulate elections, whether for state, local, or federal office. In fact, there are no federal elections, only state elections for federal offices. In an attempt to "split the baby," they claimed Congress had a power not delegated to it, something that has become all too common nowadays. The need to maintain two voting registries would not only have been costly, but nearly impossible to maintain. This quickly led to passage in Congress and ratification by the states of the 26th Amendment setting the national voting age to 18. In what can only be called a record setting event, the bill that became the 26th Amendment passed the Senate on March 10, 1971, the House on March 23rd, and was ratified by enough states on July 1st.

Section 2 – Redundant Language

> *The Congress shall have the power to enforce*
> *this article by appropriate legislation.*

Thankfully, this is the last time I'll have to repeat myself: Congress already has the power to create legislation to execute the powers granted it in the Constitution.

> *To make all Laws which shall be necessary and*
> *proper for carrying into Execution the foregoing*
> *Powers, and all other Powers vested by this*

*Constitution in the Government of the United
States, or in any Department or Officer thereof.*[308]

Conclusion

It is a truism that bad facts make bad law. The desire to accommodate those who thought the voting age should be lowered, even though it was not yet set nationally, led to a bad law followed by a bad opinion of the supreme Court. In one of the few cases of doing the right thing after making a mess, Congress proposed a constitutional amendment to fix what it saw as a problem, and enough states ratified it in a matter of months. Now, if only Congress and the American people would learn to test and verify their facts before jumping into proposing laws and amendments.

---

[308]   United States Constitution, Article I, Section 8, Clause 18.

Amendment XXVII

*No law, varying the compensation for the services of
the Senators and Representatives, shall take effect, until
an election of Representatives shall have intervened.*

This was one of the first 12 amendments proposed for the Bill of Rights. More than two centuries after it was proposed by Congress, this was ratified and became the 27th Amendment. This is not only a simple amendment, but the fact that it was proposed so long ago is probably why it doesn't include the boilerplate lawyer language that was in the previous few amendments.

The idea is simple: If you are in Congress and vote on legislation to change your pay, it cannot take effect until after the next Congress is elected and seated. A simple amendment to fix a simple problem.

Afterword

What do we do now?

So now you've read the entire Constitution. You've not only read every article, section, and clause that makes up the supreme law of our country, but hopefully you've done so diligently. What's next? I started this book with a quote from John Jay, and that is where I think we go from here.

> *Every member of the State ought diligently to read and to study the constitution of his country, and teach the rising generation to be free. By knowing their rights, they will sooner perceive when they are violated, and be the better prepared to defend and assert them.*[309]

You've read the Constitution of this country, so now it's time to study it and to teach the rising generation to be free. I have shared the insights I gleaned from my study of the Constitution; now it's time for you to develop your own. Please do not simply take what I have written here and repeat it to others. Spend time looking into the inheritance you have as an American citizen. Verify what you have read here and learn to describe what you have studied in your own words. Develop your own

---

[309] John Jay's Charge to the Grand Jury of Ulster County (1777) and Charge to the Grand Juries (1790).

stories and ways of describing what the Constitution says and how our governments are supposed to work. Then you'll be able to teach others.

John Jay said we should teach the rising generation to be free. Today I think that means more than just teaching our children. The American people are so generally ignorant about the Constitution that we should be prepared to teach everyone we can, not only about this document, but about the rights and liberties it was designed to protect. Not everyone will listen and many will argue that we're wrong. That's OK, because our goal should not be to force people to adopt our position, but to be prepared to share it with others accurately and graciously. Our goal should be to help others perceive when their rights are being violated and help them to be prepared to defend not only their rights, but the rights of others. If our positions are true and our methods winsome, then our message of liberty and the protecting of rights for everyone will spread.

While we are teaching others to defend and assert their rights, we must learn to do so as well. And not just our own rights, but the rights of everyone. As I said in the Introduction, if you want to eat an elephant, you do so one bite at a time. While we need to begin holding accountable all those whom we elect to represent us, we should focus on finding state and local candidates who will uphold their oaths of office to support the Constitution of both their state and the United States.

We need to learn to look beyond what programs those candidates oppose or support, what goodies they promise to deliver, and focus on what really matters: What they do to protect our rights. That means we need to get to know these people long before election day, even before the primary. Build a relationship with those who want the job, and make sure they understand what you expect of them if they wish to keep it.

We have inherited a great prize, a nation "conceived in Liberty, and dedicated to the proposition that all men are created equal."[310] It's up to us in what condition we leave this prize to our children and grandchildren. At the beginning, I asked you to join me on a journey to learn what the Constitution says and how our government was designed to work.

---

[310]   Abraham Lincoln, Gettysburg Address.

Now I ask you not only to put what you have learned into practice, but to share your knowledge with others.

> *I must study politics and war, that our sons may have*
> *liberty to study mathematics and philosophy.*[311]

We have studied the Constitution, hopefully so our children will have the liberty to study mathematics and philosophy and live in the freest nation in the world.

---

[311] John Adams, Letters of John Adams, Addressed to His Wife.

Made in the USA
Coppell, TX
16 November 2020